WHY NOT PARTIES?

Why Not Parties?

PARTY EFFECTS IN THE
UNITED STATES SENATE

Edited by NATHAN W. MONROE,
JASON M. ROBERTS, and DAVID W. ROHDE

The University of Chicago Press ⋆ *Chicago and London*

NATHAN W. MONROE is Assistant Professor of Political Science at the
University of California, Merced.

JASON M. ROBERTS is Assistant Professor of Political Science at the
University of North Carolina at Chapel Hill.

DAVID W. ROHDE is the Ernestine Friedl Professor of Political Science at
Duke University.

The University of Chicago Press, Chicago 60637
The University of Chicago Press, Ltd., London
© 2008 by The University of Chicago
All rights reserved. Published 2008
Printed in the United States of America

17 16 15 14 13 12 11 10 09 08   1 2 3 4 5

ISBN-13: 978-0-226-53487-9 (cloth)
ISBN-13: 978-0-226-53489-3 (paper)
ISBN-10: 0-226-53487-1 (cloth)
ISBN-10: 0-226-53489-8 (paper)

Library of Congress Cataloging-in-Publication Data

Why not parties? : party effects in the United States Senate /edited by Nathan W. Monroe,
Jason M. Roberts, and David W. Rohde.
    p. cm.
    Includes bibliographical references and index.
        ISBN-13: 978-0-226-53487-9 (cloth : alk. paper)
        ISBN-10: 0-226-53487-1 (cloth : alk. paper)
        ISBN-13: 978-0-226-53489-3 (pbk. : alk. paper)
        ISBN-10: 0-226-53489-8 (pbk. : alk. paper) 1. United States. Congress.
Senate—Congresses. 2. Political parties—United States—Congresses. I. Monroe,
Nathan W. II. Roberts, Jason M. III. Rohde, David W.
    JK1161.W54 2008
    328.73′0769—dc22

                                                      2008007422

♾ The paper used in this publication meets the minimum requirements of the
American National Standard for Information Sciences—Permanence of Paper for
Printed Library Materials, ANSI Z39.48-1992.

Contents

Acknowledgments · vii

1   Introduction: Assessing the Impact of Parties in the U.S. Senate
    Nathan W. Monroe, Jason M. Roberts, and David W. Rohde · 1

PART I

2   Electoral Accountability, Party Loyalty, and Roll-Call Voting in the
    U.S. Senate
    Jamie L. Carson · 23

3   Party and Constituency in the U.S. Senate, 1933–2004
    John Aldrich, Michael Brady, Scott de Marchi, Ian McDonald,
    Brendan Nyhan, David W. Rohde, and Michael Tofias · 39

4   Scoring the Senate: Scorecards, Parties, and Roll-Call Votes
    Jason M. Roberts and Lauren Cohen Bell · 52

PART II

5   The Senate Whip System: An Exploration
    Erin M. Bradbury, Ryan A. Davidson, and C. Lawrence Evans · 73

6   Party Loyalty and Discipline in the Individualistic Senate
    Kathryn Pearson · 100

7   Make Way for the Party: The Rise and Fall of the Senate National
    Security Committees, 1947–2006
    Linda L. Fowler and R. Brian Law · 121

8   Agenda Influence and Tabling Motions in the U.S. Senate
    Chris Den Hartog and Nathan W. Monroe · 142

9   Filibustering and Majority Rule in the Senate: The Contest over
    Judicial Nominations, 2003–2005
    Gregory Koger · 159

PART III

10 Minority-Party Power in the Senate and House of Representatives
    Sean Gailmard and Jeffery A. Jenkins · 181

11 Catch-22: Cloture, Energy Policy, and the Limits of Conditional
    Party Government
    Bruce I. Oppenheimer and Marc J. Hetherington · 198

12 Distributive and Partisan Politics in the U.S. Senate:
    An Exploration of Earmarks
    Michael H. Crespin and Charles J. Finocchiaro · 229

References · 253
Contributors · 271
Index · 275

Acknowledgments

This volume is the product of two conferences held in 2006—in April at Duke University and in September at the University of Minnesota—on party effects in the U.S. Senate. Each of the chapters that follow (with the exception of our introduction) was first presented at one of these two conferences. Thus, the debt of gratitude we owe begins with those who helped us make those conferences possible and successful.

Funding for the Duke conference was generously provided by the Duke University–University of North Carolina American Politics Research Group and the Duke Political Institutions and Public Choice (PIPC) Program. We also wish to express our appreciation to Susan Emery of the Duke Political Science Department for making many of the arrangements, and we thank Michael Brady, Dan Lee, Ian McDonald, Brendan Nyhan, and other PIPC Program students for their help in organizing the conference.

For the Minnesota conference, funding and space were provided by the Department of Political Science, the Benjamin Evans Lippincott endowment, and the Center for the Study of Politics and Governance. We thank John Freeman and Larry Jacobs for helping secure funding, and Justin Wedeking for helping to organize the conference.

Beyond the authors in the volume, a number of scholars offered comments and feedback during the conferences, undoubtedly raising the quality of the chapters that follow. For playing that role, we thank Erik Engstrom, Tim Johnson, Frances Lee, Mat McCubbins, Greg Robinson, David Samuels, Wendy Schiller, Barbara Sinclair, Steve Smith, Charles Stewart, and Shawn Treier.

During the Duke conference, we were treated to a group conversation with Congressman Dan Lipinski (D-IL). We thank him for his insights on the "reality" of party effects in Congress, which will influence our scholarship well beyond this volume.

At the back end of this project, as we approached publication, John Tryneski at the University of Chicago Press provided us with tremendous support and guidance (and a very clever title!), and Rodney Powell supplied exceptional editorial assistance. We also benefited greatly from the comments provided by two anonymous reviewers. Any mistakes that remain are ours alone, and are undoubtedly the result of our failure to fully take advantage of the excellent advice and guidance of those mentioned above.

1

Introduction: Assessing the Impact of Parties in the U.S. Senate

NATHAN W. MONROE, JASON M. ROBERTS,
AND DAVID W. ROHDE

According to the conventional view of legislative organization and decision making in the U.S. Senate, the subtitle of this volume (party effects in the Senate) is something of an oxymoron. While research on the House has been both abundant and party-focused in recent years, the more sparse literature on the Senate still largely treats parties as secondary considerations in a chamber dominated by individual senators leveraging a decentralized procedural environment. This essay and this volume begin to reconsider this view. Motivated by the disparate theoretical explanations of the House and Senate, the naked-eye partisanship of the contemporary Senate, and the need for more research on the Senate in general, we ask: to what degree (if any) should we expect party effects in the U.S. Senate, and what is the evidence to support the expectations?

In the remainder of the essay, we first discuss briefly the recent political science literature on party effects in Congress generally and in the House in particular, to set the context for the consideration of the Senate.[1] Next we consider some of the challenges that parties face in trying to work their will in the Senate, and the challenges that scholars face in studying the Senate more generally. We then offer some observations about the partisan climate in the Senate of the past several years, and we conclude with a discussion of the limited work on parties in the Senate and then highlight some of the contributions made by the rest of the essays in this volume.

Parties in Congress and the Search for Consequences

Historically, the role and influence of parties in Congress had been of substantial interest to political scientists, but by the 1970s and 1980s that interest had waned significantly.[2] The decline of attention to parties was due to a combination of a consensus that they no longer had a consequential impact on legislative behavior and outcomes, and (more importantly) a parallel consensus that there were solid theoretical reasons that explained the lack of impact. Weak parties were not a historical constant. From 1890 to 1910, the House was dominated by powerful Speakers (particularly Thomas Reed and Joseph Cannon), who led unified majorities and controlled the House's agenda and operations. In 1910, however, there was a revolt against Republican Speaker Cannon by Democrats and a small group of GOP progressives. The Speaker lost many of his formal powers, and over the next few decades the seniority system solidified the power and relative independence of committee leaders (Cooper and Brady 1981). Party leaders had few powers within the House that could reward or punish individual members, and the majority party could not penalize disloyalty on the part of committee and subcommittee chairs.

In addition, political parties had little impact on the electoral fortunes of members. The link between party identification and voting had weakened substantially. Nominations were allocated through primaries rather than the choices of party bosses or conventions populated by activists, as had once been the case. Moreover, candidates received little campaign money from their parties, and not much in the way of in-kind assistance either. The candidates raised nearly all of the money they spent, and were therefore more likely to be responsive to the political action committees and individual donors that were the source of these funds, rather than to their parties.

Thus the consensus argument could be summarized as follows: because parties were neither electorally nor legislatively important to members, those members had little reason to be responsive to the wishes of party leaders or to champion the party's platform. The most influential statement of these views was by David Mayhew in *Congress: The Electoral Connection* (1974). Mayhew's conclusion (27) was that "no theoretical treatment of the United States Congress that posits parties as analytic units will go very far. So we are left with individual congressmen, with 535 men and women rather than two parties, as units to be examined." Mayhew went on to discuss the things members needed in order to foster their electoral and legislative interests, and argued (99–100) that "in regard to these member needs the best service a party can supply to its congressmen is a negative one; it can leave them alone." The consequences, analysts believed, were the patterns we observed within the House: low levels of interparty conflict and of intraparty loyalty, coupled with the frequent incidence of cross-party coalitions.

The Renewed Attention to Parties in the House

So legislative scholars saw regularities of behavior and thought they had a set of theoretical arguments that accounted for those regularities. This scholarly consensus was undermined, however, by changes in the observed patterns precisely during the years the consensus formed. Interparty conflict increased substantially, reflected both in quantitative measures of party voting on roll calls and in qualitative accounts of legislative battles. In addition, during the 1970s the Democratic majority adopted changes in their internal rules that were difficult to explain within the context of the accounts of Mayhew and others (Rohde 1991). For example, they adopted seniority reforms that permitted the removal of disloyal committee and subcommittee chairs, thus depriving themselves of the independence from party influence that Mayhew saw as so important. They also adopted rules that restricted the powers of committee chairs (many of whom were conservative Southerners) and enhanced those of subcommittee leaders, who tended to be stronger supporters of party positions. Furthermore, the Democrats increased the influence of party leaders over committee assignments with the expressed intent of enhancing the leaders' ability to influence individual members' legislative choices. In perhaps the most consequential change, the party gave the Speaker the right to appoint and remove the chair and Democratic members of the Rules Committee, which controlled legislative access to the House floor and the terms of debate for bills.

These developments stimulated much research that was published from the mid-1980s through the mid-1990s. This work sought to explain these developments in the House and to assess their consequences. Rohde (1991) argued that the main source of the Democratic reforms was a change in the ideological homogeneity of the Democrats produced by shifts in the electoral landscape. Because Democrats became more similar in their policy views, they were more intent on pushing for new liberal legislation, and they became more willing to strengthen leaders' powers to facilitate that effort and to undermine the committee chairs they perceived as roadblocks. As a result, the increased Democratic cohesiveness was further reinforced by the party's enhanced influence, and the leaders could better exploit their new procedural advantages and produce more attractive legislative results.[3]

Sinclair (1992, 1995) also analyzed the source and impact of the Democratic reforms. Her account emphasized the more complex legislative environment that the reforms produced, with increased ability to amend legislation on the floor and decreased influence for committees, making proposed bills more vulnerable to attack and change. As a result, members were not only willing to accept a greater leadership role in passing the legislation the members wanted; they demanded it.

Cox and McCubbins (1993) offered a somewhat different point of view about party influence. They contended that the consensus about weakened parties in the House was substantially overstated, and that we had a version of party government during the postwar period. They emphasized that party members had a common electoral fate due to partisan electoral tides and thus had an incentive to create and maintain partisan institutions in the legislature. Such institutions, they claimed, also enhanced the ability to conclude and enforce legislative bargains. Changes in the homogeneity of the majority party influenced the size of the party's positive agenda and the locus of proposal power, but the majority had the ability to block bills it didn't like both before and after such changes.

A Dissenting View

Of course, not everyone was convinced by these arguments about party influence. In particular, Keith Krehbiel launched a vigorous and sustained counterattack in response to the new party theorists. In an early thrust, Krehbiel (1993b) sought conceptual clarification of what constituted significant party behavior. He argued that the tendency in the literature to attribute causal influence to party in situations where it was just correlated with a variable of interest (e.g., roll-call voting) was insufficient. The failure to recognize this rendered much purported evidence of party influence at least suspect. To demonstrate party effects, he argued, it is necessary to show consequences over and above the impact of just the actors' preferences. In this analysis, Krehbiel considered the composition of House standing committees and of conference committees, and in each case he argued that there was no demonstrable party effect by the standard he proposed.

Krehbiel followed the same line of argument in other work and addressed other issues of measurement and evidence. One theoretical point he emphasized (1991) was the matter of the majoritarian nature of the House. If a majority of the membership controls decisions in the House, then they should refuse to endorse a result different from what the majority would want based on their preferences. Thus, we should not expect the majority party to be able to secure outcomes that are tilted in favor of the median position of the majority party rather than the median position of the House as a whole. Moreover, this should not only be true of the outcomes on specific roll calls or individual bills, but it should also be the case when the chamber decides on its basic rules or on the allocation of positions and powers. That is, the chamber would not permit the Speaker to be granted powers that could achieve nonmajoritarian policy outcomes, nor would it permit committee memberships to be allocated in a way that would lead to such results (Krehbiel called this issue "remote majoritarianism"). In his 1991 book, Krehbiel also presented empirical analysis related to possible party effects on committee composition and the use of the House Rules Committee's powers to shape floor debate.[4] In each of these instances, he contended that the evidence did not reflect significant party effects.[5]

More recently, Krehbiel considered party effects at some length in his prizewinning book, *Pivotal Politics* (1998). In the process, he made clear that he was not arguing that the use of various powers and capabilities by parties did not have effects on legislation and behavior. He said (171), "The point is not that majority-party organizations and their deployment of resources are inconsequential. Rather, it is to suggest that competing party organizations bidding for pivotal votes may roughly counterbalance one another, so final outcomes are not much different from what a simpler but completely specified nonpartisan theory predicts." Thus the point of contention is not whether the majority party is effective, but rather whether the two parties are about equally effective.

The "Republican Revolution" Provides Additional Evidence

Nearly all of the work considered to this point dealt with the period of the Democratic majority. After the 1994 midterm elections, however, the GOP controlled both chambers of Congress for the first time in forty years, and the events in the House under Republican rule offered much new evidence that analysts saw as relevant to the discussion of party effects. For example, Aldrich and Rohde (1998), pursuing the analysis of conditional party government, considered how the House Republicans adjusted the rules of the House after they took over. Despite their complaints about the Democratic leadership's dominance over committees and members while Democrats were in the majority, the GOP further strengthened their own leadership's powers over committee assignments and the floor agenda, and they undermined the independence of committees and their leaders even more than the Democrats had. Because the 1994 elections made the parties even more homogeneous and polarized, Aldrich and Rohde argued that this delegation and centralization reflected the theory's expectations. In subsequent work (Aldrich and Rohde 2000a), they articulated in detail the argument that there was a substantial asymmetry in the powers of the majority and minority parties in the House, rendering the contention of balanced effects between the parties implausible in theory and incorrect empirically. They also contended (2005) that the relationship between committees and the majority leadership continued to tilt further in favor of the latter, with additional grants of power and more examples of leadership influence.

Sinclair (2000) employed systematic analysis coupled with instructive case studies to demonstrate that the patterns of lawmaking in Congress had become increasingly orthodox, and that the majority-party leadership in the House had substantial consequences in this regard. She also addressed the central importance of the House Rules Committee in controlling the agenda (Sinclair 2002a) and argued that the evidence showed that the majority party used procedural devices to structure outcomes and to achieve policies that were, at least sometimes, tilted toward the median position of the majority party.

Cox and McCubbins (2005) extended their analysis of the majority party's ability to "usurp" the House's authority to control the legislative process, employing data from 120 years of legislative decisions. They argued that the majority party seizes agenda control at virtually all stages of the process in order to block bills the party does not favor from coming to the floor. Moreover, they contended that this "negative agenda power" was theoretically expected to be constant and invariant, and that their empirical evidence bore out this expectation. On the other hand, they argued that "positive agenda power" (the ability to secure passage of favored bills) would ebb and flow with changes in the homogeneity of the majority party.

In addition to these three long-term research agendas dealing with party effects in the House, many other scholars pursued the issue. We offer here only a few salient examples to show the variety of analyses in a large and continually growing literature. Ansolabehere, Snyder, and Stewart (2001a) analyzed party influences on roll-call votes by comparing candidates' responses to surveys to their voting behavior in three Congresses. They found independent party effects in about 40 percent of roll calls, with the incidence of effects being highest on the types of votes expected by party theorists. Cox and Poole (2002) addressed the same subject with a statistical estimator based on the spatial model and applied it to voting in every House from 1877 on. Their analysis found significant party effects in every Congress but one, and again the effects were most pronounced on the expected types of votes, such as procedural matters and "label-defining" votes.

Exploring a potential electoral linkage for party effects, Brady, Han, and Pope (2007) studied the relationship between primary elections and candidate ideology. Primary electorates prefer more extreme candidates than general-election voters, and candidates respond by taking positions that are closer to the primary electorate. The authors view this pattern as supporting the idea that primary constituencies pull members away from the district's median preference. Lawrence, Maltzman, and Smith (2006) took their analysis to the end of the legislative process in the House, searching for evidence of party effects on final-passage votes. They juxtaposed the predictions of a partyless majoritarian model with three other models. On the basis of their empirical analysis, they concluded (33) that "the partyless theory receives little support, but a model based on majority party agenda control works well. Legislative outcomes are routinely on the majority party's side of the chamber median." A very specific analysis of party agenda control is presented by Young and Wilkins (2007), again relative to a partyless model. They compare members' votes on final passage of legislation to their votes on closed rules (blocking amendments on those bills) for all bills with closed rules over five Congresses. Their results yield patterns of vote switching that they contend could not be explained absent significant party effects.

The work discussed here and considerable parallel research provide a great deal of evidence supporting the existence of party effects in the House. Indeed, on the basis of these findings, we think it is a fair assessment that the overwhelming majority of congressional scholars have accepted this conclusion, despite Krehbiel's determined efforts. Yet Krehbiel has had a profound impact on the course of legislative research via his penetrating critiques of what he regarded as unclear theory, inadequate measurement, and unpersuasive or inconclusive evidence. These are matters we will have to keep in mind as we turn to the search for party effects in the Senate, on which there is little scholarly consensus.

If the Senate, Why and How?

A core aspect of the theories that support party effects in the House is the majoritarian character of that chamber. Majorities can alter the House's rules; they can allocate influence to committees; they can set the agenda via scheduling and special rules (blocking the capability to amend bills, if they wish); and they can terminate debate and force a legislative showdown. Given the theoretical centrality of this feature, it is probably not surprising that (as the discussions in the subsequent chapters in this volume demonstrate) many analysts have concluded that the lack of majority control of these processes in the Senate negates the possibility of significant party effects in that body. The visible weapon of the filibuster can prevent the termination of debate on most matters unless at least 60 percent of the membership is willing to support the move. With regard to efforts to change Senate rules, the filibuster is even more formidable, requiring two-thirds support to end debate (chapters 9 through 11 of this volume consider the filibuster at length, from different perspectives, reaching somewhat disparate conclusions). Parties are less able to employ committees to structure legislation because floor amendments usually cannot be prohibited except with the support of all members. Moreover, the lack of a general germaneness rule in the Senate permits amendments on any subject to be added to virtually any bill (though see chapter 8 for a counterargument).

While these aspects of the Senate context are all indeed important, we want to argue (and the other chapters will demonstrate) that to draw from them the conclusion that parties do not exert important independent effects is a precipitous judgment. While we believe that it is unquestionably true that the differences between the institutional contexts of the House and Senate make it impossible for party effects to be as strong in the latter as in the former, it is still possible for them to be important and worth taking into account in our analyses of congressional politics. Indeed, we think the failure to do so risks missing essential features of the process. Yet in light of the kinds of issues raised by Keith Krehbiel in his critiques of partisan analyses, it is incumbent on us to explain the motivations for members to be responsive to parties in the Senate context, and the mechanisms by which parties can affect behavior and outcomes. To that effort we now turn.

Some Preliminary Considerations

Before getting into the details of motives and mechanisms, we think it is worth recognizing that many people in or close to the Senate's operations clearly believe that parties are consequential within the chamber. Thus we want to take a moment to consider some evidence on this score that may help us to see aspects of the process we might not otherwise notice. Specifically, we want to cite examples that indicate that presidents, senators, and the electorate all demonstrate that they, at least in some instances, care about party control beyond its just being a reflection of the configuration of preferences.

With regard to presidents and senators, the best example relates to the party switch by Republican senator James Jeffords of Vermont in the spring of 2001. The 2000 congressional elections had left the Senate evenly divided between the parties, but the tiebreaking vote of Vice President Dick Cheney granted control of the Senate to the GOP. This situation lasted until May, when Jeffords—a moderate who found himself progressively more out of sync with his party's positions—announced that he intended to become an independent and to vote with the Democrats on organizing the Senate.

The key theoretical point here related to partyless legislative models is that regardless of what party Jeffords belonged to, the one hundred members of the Senate and the distribution of preferences within the chamber would remain the same. Thus from that theoretical point of view, there should have been no reason for the various actors to care about a Jeffords shift, because it should not have had an effect on Senate operations and legislative outcomes. Yet it was clear that many people did care intensely. Thinking about who and why can help us to see aspects of party influence.[6]

First, the other Republican senators cared. A switch would move them from majority status to the minority, costing virtually everyone one or more committee or subcommittee chairmanships. It is clear that members value such positions highly, both because they can provide political benefits such as fundraising opportunities and because members think they can use the positions to influence policy (see chapter 12 on this point). Therefore, the party's ability to allocate or deny those posts is a potential avenue for party influence over members' behavior, as when Arlen Specter's succession to the chairmanship of the Judiciary Committee in 2003 was called into question by conservatives because they didn't trust his loyalty to party interests. It was only after Specter gave assurances about how he would behave as chair that his position was confirmed.

The Democrats also cared, for much the same reasons as the Republicans. They worked hard to persuade Jeffords to switch because they thought it would make a difference in their individual political fortunes, in their party's electoral prospects, and in policy. Collectively, the Democrats gained an additional seat on every committee, giving them the ability to outvote the GOP members in shaping bills. Finally, President Bush cared. Indeed, one of the best indications of the evaluations of actors regarding party effects is that when Jeffords went to tell the president of his decision, he gave a promise that he would not make the actual switch until Bush's tax proposal was enacted. Again, if party does not matter in shaping outcomes, why bother? Clearly, Bush and Jeffords believed that his change of status could have affected the legislative result.[7]

An example relating to the electorate is perhaps even more striking. It involves the defeat of Senator Lincoln Chafee of Rhode Island in 2006. Evidence on patterns of roll-call voting demonstrates that Chafee was the most moderate GOP senator. He was the only Republican senator to vote against the authorization of the use of force in Iraq, and he had publicly stated that he had not voted for President Bush in 2004. Partly because of his political independence of Bush, Chafee was well liked by his constituents. Exit-poll data from the 2006 election showed that 63 percent of voters approved of the job he was doing.[8] On the other hand, Bush was decidedly unpopular with Rhode Island voters, 75 percent of whom disapproved of the president's performance. Chafee's Democratic opponent, Sheldon Whitehouse, argued that while Chafee might vote on specific bills the way voters wanted, he would also vote to put the Republican leadership in control of the Senate. Whitehouse urged voters to send someone to Washington who would vote the Republicans out of power. The exit-poll data indicate that this argument resonated with the electorate, as 63 percent of respondents indicated they wanted the Democrats to control the Senate; and of those wanting Democratic control, 78 percent voted for Whitehouse. In fact, 34 percent of those voters who *approved* of the job Chafee was doing actually voted against him and for the Democrat! These patterns reveal an electorate that saw the election in terms of party control of the Senate and voted out a senator that they liked and approved of in order to affect which party was in the majority. Clearly, the voters thought that party control could make a difference in what happened.

These examples are, of course, not conclusive evidence. But we think that they should at least give one pause before one rejects the possibility of party effects in the Senate, and that they justify the kind of in-depth analysis carried out by the authors in this volume. We will now carry on with the discussion of motives and mechanisms.

Motivations for Party Effects

To justify a theoretical expectation of party effects, we must first be able to explain why members would let them occur. That is, in the spirit of the partyless models, why wouldn't senators just reflect the preferences of the electorates that chose them? It is on this score that the research on party effects in the House is of the greatest potential relevance, because while the institutional environments of the House and Senate may be very different, there is little reason to expect that members' motives are substantially different.

Following the lead of Fenno (1973), many party theorists have adopted a multiple-motives assumption regarding members. Specifically, in addition to members' desire for election and reelection, theorists posit that at least some are also motivated by policy goals, power within their institution, and the possibility of political advancement. In addition, some analysts have assumed that the desire for majority status is equally important as a motive. Finally, one should note that even the reelection motive does not automatically mean that members will respond directly and only to the median preference of their constituency. The electoral context is more complex than that, and members could be at least as much influenced by primary electorates, financial donors, and organized interests (consider, for example, the discussion in chapter 4 of interest group "scorecards"). We would argue that each of these motivations has the potential to foster party effects.

The potential influence of power motives is obvious. Senators who are interested in attaining leadership positions within the party or on committees will recognize that those other members who control their chances of success may evaluate them partly in terms of their efforts on behalf of party interests. This was the case with regard to Arlen Specter and the Judiciary Committee chairmanship, mentioned above.

Similarly, a senator's own electoral fortunes or ability to shape policy can be affected by the evaluations and actions of other party members. An example of this is the change of Republican committee-assignment procedures in 2005. Until that time, GOP assignments were done by permitting each senator to choose among vacancies in order of seniority. Recognizing, however, how important to members achievement of a desired committee post could be, and that Republican leaders now had no influence over assignments, conservatives proposed an alternative. That was to permit the party's leader to appoint members to half of the vacancies on the top twelve Senate committees and thus enhance the party's influence over members' choices. There was, moreover, no doubt among moderate GOP senators about the purpose of the proposed rule. As Olympia Snowe of Maine said (*Roll Call,* November 18, 2004, 17), "There is only one reason for that change, and it is to punish people. . . . It is a punitive instrument to suppress diverse views." The proposal was adopted *by secret ballot* by a one-vote margin. From the point of view of partyless theories, it seems quite impossible to explain the motivations for this choice. It seems clear that a majority of Republicans had a sincere preference for granting to their leaders the ability to influence members, and that they believed it would be effective.[9] Shared policy views in this era of polarization (Poole and Rosenthal 2007) help to explain this behavior.

Returning to the electoral arena, we see that the relatively extreme policy views of party activists in primaries will influence their evaluations of the performance of incumbents, and failure to visibly support party positions on salient issues could undermine a senator in a primary contest (e.g., Joseph Lieberman of Connecticut in 2006). The same kinds of factors could influence a candidate's ability to raise campaign funds. Thus even individual electoral interests can foster party effects (as demonstrated empirically in chapter 2).

Finally, there is the matter of majority control. Control of the Senate can enhance the achievement of all of the other goals; it brings more influence over policy, more individual power, and more access to electoral resources. For decades, from the 1950s through 1980, there was little or no doubt a priori who was likely to control the Senate after an election: the Democrats were the expected victors throughout that period. Since the unexpected GOP victory in 1980, however, control has been in the balance and in doubt in most elections. Cox and McCubbins (1993) have discussed how party reputations can affect partisan electoral tides and thus influence majority control. Uncertainty about majority control can increase the incentives among senators for collaborative action within the Senate in order to influence public perceptions of their party and, in turn, its electoral fortunes.

Thus the wide range of goals of individual senators can explain their potential motivation to act on behalf of party effects in the Senate. We now turn to consider the means to realize those motivations.

The Mechanisms of Party Effects

As we noted above, there are good reasons for believing that party effects should be minimal in the Senate. Unlike in the House, Senate rules allocate substantial power to individual senators, making them better able to resist pressure from their parties and to retaliate against efforts to impose punishments on them for deviance on policy. A single senator can slow down the legislative process within the chamber by herself (by objecting to unanimous consent requests, for example) and can block it entirely with enough support from others. This grants to each member significant bargaining power. Moreover, members of the minority usually cannot be prevented from proposing undesired or politically embarrassing policy initiatives on the floor.

For these reasons, one clearly would not expect party effects in the Senate to be as strong as in the House. Yet this does not automatically mean that such effects should be nonexistent. There may be mechanisms in the Senate that are different from, but analogous to, those features of the House that support party powers. Some of these are very similar between the chambers, and we have mentioned them already. Committee chairs in both chambers want to hold on to their positions. If their party has the ability to take away chairmanships from disloyal members, those members will have an incentive to be responsive to the party's wishes. Similarly, members want assignment to desirable committees. If the party can influence the allocation of seats, responsiveness is again encouraged. These effects may not be as potent in the Senate as in the House, but they can be important (as argued more extensively in chapter 6).

Similarly, there are parallels between the House and Senate in terms of the impact of electoral forces. Analysis by Poole and Rosenthal (2007) demonstrates that both chambers have evidenced similar polarization in voting in the last few decades. While, as Krehbiel would note, these voting patterns can be seen as merely reflecting changing member preferences, it is important to note that party could be one factor shaping the changes in preferences, and thus this could be an avenue for independent and significant party effects. For example, we noted that senators and representatives can have their own policy preferences; those preferences may be more extreme and more partisan than those that would be induced only by constituency influences. Members with such preferences have an incentive to take actions not readily visible to the public that would produce more-partisan policy outcomes than would result if members merely followed constituents' desires (Rohde 1991). Research by Van Houweling (2007) indicates that such behavior characterizes aspects of the Senate's operation. A related avenue for such party effects is recruitment. Above, we discussed findings that show that primaries have made members more extreme than their general-election constituencies. This process can also increase the likelihood of selecting members with intense and extreme personal preferences. Theriault's research (2007) indicates that much of the polarization in Senate voting is the result of the move to Senate service by Republicans who had served in the House in the 1990s and later. It could well be that recruitment to the House garnered extreme members, who were in turn recruited for Senate candidacies.

While the Senate and House situations are similar in the preceding respects, we have seen that they are quite different in terms of institutional arrangements. In the House, the ability of the majority party to exert disproportionate influence has largely revolved around altering the balance of power between parties and committees (Aldrich and Rohde 2005). In the House reforms of the 1970s, Democratic members affected this balance of power by simultaneously undermining the independent power of committees and their leaders and strengthening the majority leadership's capabilities. Then the Republican Revolution extended and expanded those efforts. The Senate situation was very different. Because of the Senate's rules, its committees and their chairs had less independent power than their House counterparts, and they were less capable of making their policy preferences stick in final outcomes. They were, in Fenno's words (1973), "more permeable."

This, paradoxically, made it easier for parties to be influential in the Senate. The problematic balance of power from that point of view is between the parties and the power of individual members. So if the majority party proposes a bill, it does not have a Rules Committee that can, like the one in the House, block amendments and thus protect the party's proposal. The majority party does, however, have access to analogous devices, including tabling proposed amendments in order to avoid a direct vote on them (see chapter 8 for more on this) and the majority leader's ability to fill the amendment tree to prevent amendments from being offered (Gold 2004, 100–101). Again, we do not claim that these devices give the Senate majority party power equivalent to its House counterpart. But we do claim that these abilities can be the source of consequential party effects.

To be sure, we and the other scholars writing in this volume are not the only ones who have noted that parties can and do have discernible effects in the Senate. Mann and Ornstein (2006a) do not spare the Senate from their harsh critique of the institutional failures of Congress. Citing examples ranging from the confrontation over judicial nominees to bankruptcy-reform legislation to general oversight, Mann and Ornstein indict leaders of both the House and the Senate for letting partisan politics interfere with the institutional prerogatives of Congress. They write (155), "Members of the majority party, including the leaders of Congress, see themselves as field lieutenants in the president's [George W. Bush's] army far more than they do as members of a separate and independent branch of government." Their analysis of the lack of meaningful congressional oversight is echoed in chapter 7 in this volume, which points to the declining power of Senate committee chairs.

In an exhaustive analysis of the issue content of roll-call votes over the past two decades, Frances Lee (2008) finds that party leaders in the Senate deliberately manipulate the content of bills that come to the floor in order to highlight partisan differences in the chamber. She links agenda manipulation and the increasing institutional strength of the Senate's party leaders to the growth of party polarization in the Senate.

Smith (2005) points out that the nature of the Senate forces party leaders to be more accommodating of members' needs and requests if they are to be successful at managing the chamber. He notes the growth in the amount of appropriations for Senate legislative parties and ties it to the creation of party institutions to serve members' electoral and policy needs. These new institutions help coordinate the party's message to the media and the electorate, while at the same time facilitating coordination within each party.

Some scholars have claimed that Senate rules are not as much of a roadblock to party influence as they appear to be. For example, in their consideration of the majority party's negative agenda-control powers, Campbell, Cox, and McCubbins (2002) find that modern Senate majority parties are quite adept at negative agenda control. In fact, they find a large and consistent difference in the roll rate for minority and majority parties in the Senate across several decades. They conclude that despite vast rule differences between the House and the Senate, "the Senate majority party *does* have the ability to affect the floor agenda" (164).

We think this growing body of research, which continues to "notice" the imprint of Senate partisanship in one form or another, along with the arguments and examples we have presented, constitutes sufficient grounds to consider the prospect of party effects in the Senate at least a plausible claim. We leave it to the authors in the rest of the volume to explore further, develop theories, and test the supposed implications of a partisan Senate.

The Chapters That Follow

The chapters in this volume are organized chronologically, in a sense. Part 1 (chapters 2 through 4) considers how the roots of senatorial action—namely, links to constituents—interact with partisan considerations. In chapter 2, Jamie L. Carson asks whether (and to what extent) party loyalty in voting behavior is a liability for incumbent legislators. Building upon and extending prior work examining the electoral consequences of roll-call voting in the House of Representatives, this chapter looks at senatorial elections from 1974 to 2004 and finds that while ideological extremity may hurt senators' chances of reelection, party loyalty is often rewarded by constituents when they go to the polls. Chapter 3 continues the constituent-party theme, with John Aldrich and colleagues considering how constituent and party interests may vary across issue dimensions. Using comprehensive data from 1933 to 2004, they show that the second dimension of conflict in the Senate, which captures the primary crosscutting issue(s) on the agenda, is more closely related to state demographics, while the first dimension is more closely related to party and presidential voting. Rounding out this discussion in chapter 4, Jason M. Roberts and Lauren Cohen Bell consider constituents of a different sort: interest groups. Combining interest group scorecard and Senate roll-call data, they find that when casting votes, individual senators do not defect from their party's preferred position substantially more frequently than do their counterparts in the House of Representatives. In many cases, however, the ability of the Senate majority party to pursue its policy goals is constrained as a consequence of decisions by interest groups to score certain key votes.

Part 2 (chapters 5 through 9) moves into the thick of the Senate's process and procedural battles. It begins in chapter 5 with Erin M. Bradbury, Ryan A. Davidson, and C. Lawrence Evans offering the first scholarly description of the Senate whip system in action. The authors use novel data, gathered from the personal papers of former Senate leaders, to answer several questions about the effectiveness of Senate party leaders' power: How many and what kinds of issues are singled out for leadership pressure? What is the size of the leadership's base of support as major floor decisions near? How successful are Senate leaders at retaining the support of potential defectors? They conclude that the tactical impact of the whip system reflects and reinforces the tactical nature of majority leadership in the U.S. Senate more generally. In chapter 6, Kathryn Pearson takes a broader look at the disciplinary tools available to Senate leaders. Drawing comparisons with the House, she argues that although Senate leaders' options are limited, Senate norms are slowly changing, and senators have shown increasing willingness to cede power to their leaders. Although norms of individualism, fused with several institutional features particular to the Senate, largely protect senators from party discipline, even "individualistic" senators have increasing incentives to toe the party line when the stakes for the party are high. According to Linda L. Fowler and R. Brian Law, in chapter 7, some of this move toward more party control, via the committee system, was an accidental by-product of the parties' responses to members' desires to expand their committee portfolios. These authors present data on overall trends in the Senate committee hierarchy and then examine the implications of these changes for the Senate Armed Services and Foreign Relations committees from 1947 to 2006, using a new measure of committee attractiveness. The results of their analysis suggest that party leaders have the opportunity to gain influence when senators are less invested in committee careers.

The final two chapters of this section on process and procedure take a turn toward obstructionism and agenda setting. In chapter 8, Chris Den Hartog and Nathan W. Monroe challenge the conventional-wisdom assumption that majority-party influence is rendered difficult or impossible because of the Senate's open amendment process. They lay out a cost-based framework for thinking about legislative agenda influence and argue that motions to table serve as a mechanism by which the majority party can protect its agenda against amendment threats. Looking at data from the 103rd and 104th Congresses, they show that minority-party amendments are frequently shot down by motions to table offered by the majority-party leadership. Gregory Koger, in chapter 9, considers the other major procedural hurdle for majority-party success in the Senate: the filibuster. Focusing on the fight over President Bush's judicial nominations, he argues that although a majority of the chamber can suppress filibustering if it is sufficiently determined and ruthless, senators are reluctant to convert the chamber into a majority-rule legislature.

The final part of the book (chapters 10 through 12) considers the endgame: parties and policy outcomes. The first two chapters continue on the topic of the filibuster but come to different conclusions about how this procedural device ultimately affects Senate outcomes. In chapter 10, Sean Gailmard and Jeffery A. Jenkins find some evidence that the Senate minority party possesses greater negative agenda control than the House minority party. However, contrary to conventional wisdom, they conclude that the clearest formal source of the Senate minority's negative agenda control—the filibuster—appears *not* to be a significant instrument of power across a range of legislative vehicles. In a more case-specific investigation in chapter 11, however, Bruce I. Oppenheimer and Marc J. Hetherington find stronger evidence of the filibuster's effects. Looking at Senate efforts to pass major energy legislation in the 1970s and in the 2001–5 period, they conclude that Senate majority-party leaders face a catch-22. If they pursue median party positions, they stimulate minority-party filibusters and lack the sixty votes to invoke cloture. But to avoid a filibuster, the leaders must move toward median chamber positions. They are thus caught between the defeat of the legislation they prefer and the passage of legislation they do not truly want. To close the volume, in chapter 12 Michael H. Crespin and Charles J. Finocchiaro examine whether and to what degree the distribution of pork-barrel project dollars across states is biased toward the majority party. Using a data set that reports the source of each project, the authors are able to determine for each appropriations subcommittee whether the Senate delivers pork in a universal fashion or whether the majority party maintains an advantage across committees in the upper chamber. They find that the majority party does maintain an advantage when it comes to earmark dollars, though the advantage is not present on all of the appropriations bills.

Final Thoughts

Taken as a whole, the chapters in this volume present a strong case for party effects in the U.S. Senate. While most conventional views of the Senate emphasize how the chamber differs from the House, this book highlights the chambers' analogues, especially as they contribute to party effects. Much as with the House, we see that the electoral connection can both constrain and enhance the ability of Senate parties to pursue policy goals. Similarly, just as in the House, we see that control of key procedural devices is the primary means through which the majority party in the Senate can exert its will on outcomes. Finally, as chapter 12 details, being a member of the Senate majority has clear benefits in terms of securing particularistic policies (i.e., pork).

That said, we don't see this volume as the last word on party effects in the Senate. Indeed, we hope the opposite is true: that this work might serve as a catalyst for increased scrutiny of Senate policymaking. Though we think the chapters that follow clearly advance our understanding of how Senate parties affect outcomes, important questions remain. First and foremost, the filibuster—as the disagreements in this book highlight—continues to confound efforts to measure and enforce party effects. Most scholars and observers agree that the filibuster *can* render parties impotent to affect outcomes, but it is also clear that the filibuster is not universally applied. Understanding and specifying the conditions under which the filibuster will rear its head as an effective tool to subvert the majority will is clearly important if one is interested in predicting when parties will be strong.

Second, we continue to want for a general understanding of the conditions necessary and sufficient for strong parties. As Rohde (1991) and other authors have shown in the House context, important aspects of party influence are conditional on inter- and intraparty (dis)agreement. Is Senate party influence conditional? If so, what is it conditional upon? And do changes in these conditions translate to party power (or loss thereof) in the same manner as in the House? A fully translated and specified theory is needed for the Senate.

Finally, though this book highlights many of the previously unappreciated similarities between House and Senate, it is clear that the tools and tactics of Senate party leaders differ in important ways from those of their House counterparts. Much of the Senate literature to date has focused more on the personal skills of various Senate leaders than on a general understanding of party leadership in the chamber. The job ahead will require scholars to draw the lessons from these personality-specific analyses into a more comprehensive, abstract theoretical framework of Senate party leadership.

We look forward to following the literature that we hope will come.

Notes

1. Note that we are not pretending to offer here a complete account of what has become a rich and complex literature, but rather to offer the reader a sense of the debates and findings.

2. See Rohde (1991); and Collie (1986).

3. This theoretical argument was dubbed "conditional party government": the granting of strong powers to a party was conditional on substantial internal homogeneity of preferences and on substantial disagreement with the views of the other party.

4. Krehbiel (1997) further addressed the partisan use of the Rules Committee in response to work by Dion and Huber (1996).

5. For responses to these arguments, see Rohde (1994).

6. We offer here only a few details. More information and references to sources can be found in Abramson, Aldrich, and Rohde (2003, 226–27).

7. Note also that in an "event study" of the Jeffords switch, Den Hartog and Monroe (forthcoming) show that market investors thought the switch was important. They find that on the days surrounding Jeffords's announcement, Republican constituent firms in the energy sector (i.e., oil and gas companies) saw stock prices fall, while Democratic constituent firms (i.e., renewable-energy companies) experienced a rise in stock values.

8. More details on the race and sources of the data cited can be found in Abramson, Aldrich, and Rohde (2007, 281).

9. On this point, see the discussion in chapter 7 regarding the evolution of party control over committee assignments.

PART I

2

Electoral Accountability, Party Loyalty, and Roll-Call Voting in the U.S. Senate

JAMIE L. CARSON

Vote your conscience first, then your constituency, and your party comes third.

REP. WALTER JONES (R-NC), on how he responds to party pressure from Republican leaders

In a democratic system of government, few issues are more important than representation and electoral accountability. This is why, when studying the factors influencing voting patterns in the U.S. Congress, it is necessary to identify the effects that constituency, ideology, and party affiliation have on legislative behavior. Party leaders increasingly rely on rank-and-file members for their support on roll-call votes in closely divided chambers, but such support may come with a price. Every time a legislator votes in support of his or her party on an important roll call, there is the chance that the "wrong" position on one or a series of votes may put the legislator at risk in the next election. In fact, as Mayhew (1974, 65–66) asserts, "It is on roll calls that the crunch comes; there is no way for a member to avoid making a record on hundreds of issues, some of which are controversial in the home constituencies."

The preceding discussion raises an important question for students of representation and congressional politics. To what extent can party loyalty be a liability for incumbent legislators? Despite varying degrees of attention to the issue of electoral accountability in the literature (see, e.g., Stokes and Miller 1962; Erikson 1971; Wright 1978; Mann and Wolfinger 1980; Kingdon 1989; Jacobson 1993; and Canes-Wrone, Brady, and Cogan 2002), this remains a largely unanswered question for students of legislative behavior. While it is clear that legislators behave strategically when expressing public positions on roll-call votes (Mayhew 1974), it is uncertain what effects such voting behavior has on legislators' electoral fortunes. Until recently, it was fairly common for scholars to conclude that roll-call voting has little or no observable electoral consequences for legislators—especially since we rarely see incumbents in the contemporary era get defeated—or to simply assume that party leaders allow legislators to defer to their constituents when a tough roll-call choice occurs.

When the issue of electoral accountability and legislative voting has been examined more systematically in prior work, analyses share one common factor: each focuses exclusively on the House of Representatives. Therefore, we know considerably less about the electoral consequences of voting behavior for senators. This is unfortunate, because the Senate provides a useful venue to examine the electoral effects of voting behavior and partisan loyalty, given the relatively greater heterogeneity associated with statewide constituencies.[1] In this article, I move beyond the House-centric nature of previous scholarship to systematically examine the representational connection between roll-call behavior and electoral accountability in the context of Senate elections. More specifically, I examine the effects of both ideological extremity and party loyalty on senators' electoral fortunes in the context of all Senate elections from 1974 to 2004. From this, I hope to offer new insights regarding the electoral effects of roll-call voting patterns in the Senate and present a comparative assessment of the differences between House and Senate elections.

The organization of the chapter is as follows. I briefly review research on electoral accountability in the U.S. House before turning to a more general discussion of prior research on U.S. Senate elections. From there, I examine relevant theoretical issues underlying the analysis and then discuss the data and methodology I employ here. Next, I present results detailing the electoral consequences of ideological extremity and party loyalty in the U.S. Senate. I conclude by discussing the implications of the results and exploring possible avenues for future research.

Electoral Accountability and U.S. House Elections

The literature on electoral accountability in Congress is replete with studies examining the effects of ideological extremity on likelihood of reelection success. For instance, Erikson (1971) was among the first to systematically explore the relationship between roll-call voting in the House and election returns. Using electoral and survey data from 1952 to 1968, Erikson found that conservatism among Republican legislators had a pronounced, negative effect on their vote margins. In an analysis of the 1974 U.S. House elections, Burnham (1975) demonstrated that electoral losses among Republicans were greatest among the more conservative members of the party. Kingdon (1989) concluded that members act strategically when casting roll-call votes and are careful to avoid expressing positions that may be viewed as too extreme by constituents. More recently, Ansolabehere, Snyder, and Stewart (2001a) and Erikson and Wright (2001) have each found evidence that candidates' vote share is inversely related to support for the party's ideological extreme.

In one of the most comprehensive and related analyses to date, Canes-Wrone, Brady, and Cogan (2002) examine the relationship between House members' electoral margins and their overall support for their party as reflected by Americans for Democratic Action (ADA) scores to demonstrate that legislators are held accountable for their roll-call behavior. Using elections data from 1956 to 1996, they find that incumbents receive smaller electoral margins on average the more they vote in support of their party across aggregate roll calls. Moreover, they illustrate that this effect is comparable to other determinants of electoral margins, including challenger quality and campaign spending. Finally, they argue that the distinction between "safe" and "marginal" representatives is tenuous at best, since this phenomenon affects all members equally, regardless of their previous electoral performance.[2]

In moving away from an exclusive emphasis on ideological extremity, recent work has begun to examine the relationship between electoral outcomes and party loyalty to determine if partisan cooperation can actually be a liability for individual legislators. Indeed, Carson (2005) examines the voting patterns of legislators on key votes taken in Congress since the early 1970s and finds that experienced candidates are more likely to run as an incumbent's party unity score increases on these votes. In proposing a model of "strategic party government," Lebo, McGlynn, and Koger (2007) investigate the relationship between aggregate party behavior in Congress and electoral outcomes over time. They test their model on macro-level data from 1789 to 2000 and find that an increase in partisan unity on legislative voting has adverse electoral costs for both parties. This chapter seeks to build upon this latter work by testing similar claims on micro-level data for members of the U.S. Senate during the contemporary era.[3]

Research on U.S. Senate Elections

From a purely comparative perspective, Senate elections have received far less scholarly attention than elections to the U.S. House of Representatives. With the exception of work by Mann (1978), Mann and Wolfinger (1980), Hinckley (1980), and Jacobson (1980), most early analyses of congressional elections focused almost exclusively on the House. While this emphasis helped illuminate a number of important findings in the context of House elections, it did little to identify significant patterns or trends in association with Senate elections or allow comparisons to be drawn between House and Senate elections.

Over time, and especially in recent years, Senate elections have begun to receive slightly more attention by students of congressional elections. Of particular relevance to this analysis, Wright and Berkman (1986) examined the 1982 U.S. Senate elections to determine the extent to which policy issues played a role in the selection of senators. Using data from the CBS News/New York Times 1982 congressional poll and from twenty-three statewide exit polls, they found both that Senate candidates behave as though policy issues matter to their constituents and that voters are systematically responsive to the policy positions of U.S. senators. This finding challenged much of the previous research, which had suggested that policy considerations were of relatively minor importance in congressional elections.

In the early 1990s, further emphasis on the Senate helped illuminate a number of relevant findings in the context of Senate elections. Most notably, students of congressional elections began to recognize that Senate elections are considerably more competitive than House elections, largely because of the greater number of experienced candidates challenging Senate incumbents (see, e.g., Westlye 1991; Abramowitz and Segal 1992; and Krasno 1994). Unlike most House incumbents, who generally run against lawyers or other candidates lacking electoral experience, incumbent senators typically face experienced challengers or well-known amateurs (Krasno 1994; Jacobson 2004), which tends to increase the challengers' visibility and makes for a harder-fought and more intense electoral campaign.[4]

In addition to campaign intensity, the influence of money in Senate elections has received attention in the context of congressional-elections research. In discussing the impact of campaign spending on Senate elections, for instance, Gerber (1998) challenges the prevailing notion in the congressional-elections literature that spending by the incumbent legislator has little or no discernible effect on the outcome (see, e.g., Jacobson 1980, 1985; Abramowitz 1988; and Grier 1989). Arguing that the previous findings concerning the impact of incumbent spending are in large part biased, Gerber adopts an instrumental variables approach in his analysis of Senate elections. On the basis of his results, he asserts that the marginal effects of incumbent and challenger spending are approximately the same. Accordingly, Gerber concludes that balancing the spending levels of Senate candidates could fundamentally alter the electoral environment for both incumbents and challengers.[5]

Additionally, recent work by Kahn and Kenney (1999) has helped to further illustrate the implications of the greater competitiveness of Senate elections. In focusing on U.S. Senate races between 1988 and 1992, Kahn and Kenney examine the extent to which the intensity of Senate campaigns influences the behavior of the voting populace. Since the news media tends to place more emphasis on Senate races (because of their greater competitiveness) than on House contests, Kahn and Kenney find that the central themes of both Senate candidates come to the forefront of the political campaign. Consequently, voters become more aware of the positions advanced by competing candidates and more knowledgeable when heading to the voting booth. Thus, knowledgeable citizens make informed decisions when selecting between competing candidates, which increases the relative degree of electoral accountability in Senate races.

Theoretical Issues

The preceding discussion provides a useful basis for thinking about issues of electoral accountability and roll-call voting in the U.S. Senate from a purely theoretical viewpoint. In view of similarities between the House and the Senate in terms of roll-call voting, the earlier findings concerning House elections give us related expectations regarding electoral accountability in the context of Senate elections. While the issues taken up in the Senate may be somewhat different than those considered in the House, they should still deal with a diverse array of issues, many of which will garner sufficient interest from "attentive publics" (Arnold 1990). Additionally, those persons most capable of using legislators' behavior as a political device—namely, party activists, challengers for Senate seats, and political elites—have ample opportunities to become aware of controversial roll calls and, in turn, to transform them into electorally salient political issues.

Given the notable variation in House and Senate elections, we should also expect some differences in terms of the electoral implications of roll-call voting behavior in the Senate. To begin with, the greater competitiveness of Senate races may result in an increased proportion of electorally consequential roll calls for senators. With more experienced candidates vying for a limited number of Senate seats, the election campaign may focus more heavily upon specific policy issues or positions (see, e.g., Wright and Berkman 1986; and Kahn and Kenney 1999). In particular, the positions that Senate incumbents express on prominent roll calls may become salient issues in an upcoming election campaign, especially if they diverge from the overriding interests of a legislator's constituency.

We might also expect variation in the electoral effects of roll-call voting in the Senate due to certain inherent differences between the House and Senate. As Mayhew (1974, 66) maintains, controversial positions taken on one or even a few isolated roll calls should not normally have an enormous impact on an incumbent's chances of getting reelected. However, he also asserts (67) that "on rare occasions single roll calls achieve a rather high salience among the public generally. This seems especially true of the Senate, which every now and then winds up for what might be called a 'showdown vote,' with pressures on all sides, presidential involvement, media attention given to individual senators' positions, and suspense about the outcome." Furthermore, as Arnold (1990, 61–62) emphasizes, "The question facing a legislator is seldom whether a specific roll-call vote might cost him the next election . . . Each issue may have only a slight impact on a legislator's electoral margin; yet small effects can quickly add up to become large effects when summed over the many issues that Congress considers each year."

The nature of the legislative agenda in the Senate may also play a role in determining the extent to which roll-call votes yield observable electoral consequences. Unlike the House, the Senate routinely deals with treaty ratifications and presidential nominations (e.g., judicial and executive-branch posts). Given the highly visible and potentially contentious nature of such roll-call decisions, expressing a controversial position on even one salient vote of this nature could jeopardize a senator's chances of getting reelected.[6] Indeed, an incumbent senator with a track record of controversial positions could attract an experienced and well-financed challenger in the next election, making it extremely difficult for the incumbent to retain his or her seat.

Additionally, the principal differences in senators' constituencies may influence the relationship between voting behavior and electoral performance in the Senate. Since members of the House represent roughly the same number of persons per district, within a specific geographic region, their constituencies tend to be relatively homogeneous. As a result, the positions House members express on roll calls may be less likely to stimulate conflict among their constituents, because of greater similarities in voter preferences. Senators, on the other hand, often represent large and more heterogeneous constituencies, making it more difficult to avoid alienating segments of the population with their roll-call voting behavior. For this reason, we should expect positions expressed by senators on roll calls that are out of touch with their constituents to be of greater electoral consequence than those recorded by their colleagues in the House.

The discussion above raises an important question. To what extent are senators routinely pulled in competing directions by their party and their constituency? When senators are elected from a state in which the citizens' preferences largely overlap with the underlying preferences of the senator's political party, there is little need to worry that supporting their party on highly visible or closely contested votes will adversely affect their chances of reelection. When the preferences of their constituency and their political party do not overlap, however, their electoral status becomes more tenuous. These *cross-pressured* legislators may be called upon to make tough choices on votes in the Senate. If they vote with the party too often on controversial or highly salient issues or are viewed as being too extreme relative to their state, they risk alienating their political base in the subsequent election. But if they vote in line with their statewide constituency and against the party, they may lose favor with the party leadership. Regardless of the choice made under these circumstances, they put themselves at increased risk of isolating one of their two core bases of support.

Much of the extant literature on party loyalty in Congress assumes that the party leadership gives cross-pressured members the benefit of the doubt when they face a tough roll-call choice. Indeed, some argue that when legislators encounter this type of choice, it is preferable to "vote the district" than to be constrained by party discipline (Cox and McCubbins 1993, 2007; Desposato and Petrocik 2003; Mayhew 1974).[7] Unfortunately, this characterization fails to consider that the political stakes on certain legislative issues may be too high to allow cross-pressured members to defect, especially if the margin of majority-party control in the chamber is slim. Additionally, party leaders may be more reluctant to allow a member to defect if it is on a procedural issue, as this is where we should expect to see parties attempting to structure the legislative agenda (Bell and Roberts 2005; Cox and McCubbins 2005; Jenkins, Crespin, and Carson 2005).

Of course, as Kathryn Pearson demonstrates in this volume, party leaders in the Senate have far fewer opportunities to discipline recalcitrant senators than do their counterparts in the House, because of obvious procedural differences between the chambers. At the same time, Pearson observes that despite the relative weakness of norms in the Senate regarding the ceding of powers to party leaders, these norms have gradually been changing. Indeed, she documents a fairly clear trend of increasing party loyalty among "individualistic" senators over time, especially as the parties seek electoral advantage by creating a unified message to convey to their constituents. Thus, Pearson shows that party leaders have become more willing to use party discipline in certain circumstances in order to achieve party objectives, especially when it means the difference between success and failure in the policy realm.

This chapter seeks to provide a measure of balance to this body of knowledge by exploring the extent to which incumbent senators are held accountable for loyalty to their political party. If the political stakes are high, if the vote is expected to be close, or if the party leadership has a great deal riding on the final outcome of a particular piece of legislation, party leaders may place increased pressure on legislators to support the party's position. In other words, there is reason to suspect that party pressure may be *conditional* upon the circumstances associated with the legislation under consideration. Moving beyond the House-centric approach adopted in previous research, I examine the issue of electoral accountability and roll-call voting in Senate elections to determine whether senators are rewarded or punished for party loyalty and ideological extremity in terms of their voting behavior.

Data and Methods

Drawing upon legislative voting behavior since the 1970s, this analysis examines whether patterns of legislative voting in the Senate directly affect incumbent success in individual races. To address this question, I utilize a pooled regression model comparable to those in the elections literature (see Jacobson 1993; and Canes-Wrone, Brady, and Cogan 2002). The statistical model incorporates the usual predictors of congressional-election outcomes while including two additional explanatory variables—ideological extremity of senators and each senator's party unity score in the year that he or she seeks reelection. The dependent variable is the incumbent's vote share in legislator i's state during year t. To isolate the effects of senators' roll-call behavior on electoral fortunes, I control for a variety of factors that have previously been shown to affect incumbents' electoral performance, including electoral security, the partisanship of the state, incumbent and challenger spending, level of seniority, party leadership status, state population, and challenger quality.

In sum, I posit the following model of incumbent senators' electoral vote margins:

$$\text{INCUMBENT VOTE SHARE}_{it} = \beta_0 + \beta_1 \text{Ideological Extremity}_{it} + \beta_2 \text{Party Unity Score}_{it}$$
$$+ \beta_3 \text{Electoral Security}_{it-1} + \beta_4 \text{Partisanship of the State}_{it}$$
$$+ \beta_5 \text{Challenger Quality} + \beta_6 (\ln(\text{Challenger Spending})$$
$$- \ln(\text{Incumbent Spending}))_{it} + \beta_7 \text{Freshman}_{it}$$
$$+ \beta_8 \text{Party Leadership Status}_{it} + \beta_9 \text{State Population}_{it} + \varepsilon$$

Ideological extremity is measured as the absolute value of each senator's first-dimension DW-NOMINATE score (Poole and Rosenthal 1997) to assess legislators' overall voting tendencies on the traditional liberal-conservative economic dimension. Relevant information concerning party unity scores for individual senators was taken from Congressional Quarterly's annual series, *Congressional Roll Call*, for each election year from 1974 to 2004. Electoral security reflects the percentage of the two-party vote the incumbent received in the previous congressional election. Partisanship of the state is measured as the proportion of the two-party vote received by the presidential candidate of the incumbent's party in the most recent election in his or her state.

The variable for challenger quality is dichotomously coded 1 if the candidate previously held elected office, 0 otherwise. This coding follows Jacobson's classic study that views having run a successful elective campaign as a proxy for candidate quality (1980, 106–7).[8] To control for the effects of incumbent spending and challenger spending, following Jacobson's work on money in elections, I include the difference in the natural logarithm of both dollar amounts in the model (Jacobson 1980, 40).[9] The analysis begins with the 1974 Senate elections because this is the first year that comprehensive campaign finance data for individual Senate races were available. Additionally, I control for freshman status among incumbent senators, whether legislators were serving as a party leader in the most recent Congress, and the population of the state (Lee and Oppenheimer 1999). I also include election-specific fixed effects to account for any macro-level changes from one election year to the next.

Results

Before turning to the systematic results, I report average party unity scores across time for senators seeking reelection (fig. 2.1) and for those not running for reelection in a given year (fig. 2.2). Not surprisingly, we see a general increase in average party unity among both groups of senators during this thirty-year period. This pattern reflects the increasing polarization of the Senate documented by others, especially on the subset of votes where more than 50 percent of one party is voting against the other on individual roll calls. Interestingly, we do not observe any consistent patterns in figures 2.1 and 2.2 pertaining to majority and minority parties (i.e., the party in the majority does not routinely have higher average party unity scores than the minority party across the different subsets of legislators).

When comparing average party unity scores across the subsets of members in figures 2.1 and 2.2, we observe another noticeable pattern—incumbent senators not seeking reelection in a given year generally have higher

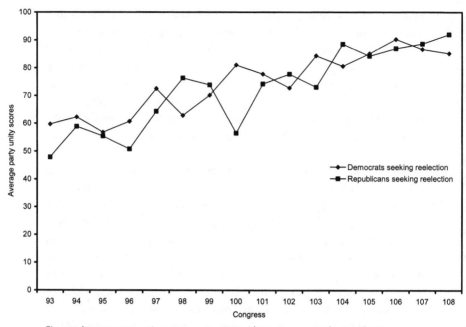

Fig. 2.1: Average party unity scores among incumbent senators seeking reelection

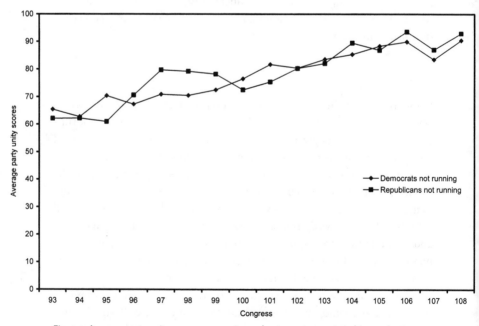

Fig. 2.2: Average party unity scores among incumbent senators not seeking reelection

average party unity scores than their colleagues who are seeking election to another term. Although this pattern is not as pronounced for Democrats (e.g., it occurs in 11 of the 16 Congresses), it is almost always the case for Republicans (in 15 out of 16 Congresses). This pattern is striking in that it supports the conventional view that senators seeking reelection may feel pressure to moderate their voting behavior in an attempt to avoid alienating voters, especially if they represent a fairly heterogeneous constituency.

Shifting to the more systematic analysis, I present in table 2.1 estimates from a series of models. The results for model 1 are a streamlined version of the full model similar to results reported by Canes-Wrone, Brady, and Cogan (2002) for the U.S. House, but they include fixed effects to account for any election-specific differences that may occur. Although the estimates for model 1 are comparable to those reported by Canes-Wrone, Brady, and Cogan for nearly all of the control variables (the variable tapping freshman status is not significant in the Senate), the variable measuring ideological extremity does not appear to be statistically significant in this context. In other words, holding constant the usual factors shown to affect congressional-election outcomes, the effect of incumbent senators' ideology is not a significant predictor of their two-party vote share, unlike for their colleagues serving in the House.[10]

In the next column of the table, I estimate the same variables from the previous model but also include covariates tapping senators' party unity score, their status as a party leader, and state population. For the estimates included in model 2, I observe that ideological extremity and party unity are both statistically significant. However, ideological extremity is negatively signed, whereas the party unity score for individual senators is positive. In other words, senators who are viewed as being too extreme relative to their state are more likely to see a decline in their vote share when other factors that affect election outcomes are controlled for. At the same time, senators who regularly vote with their party on roll calls are likely to be rewarded when voters go the polls. That being said, it should be noted that the substantive effect of a senator's party unity score is relatively small in comparison to factors such as challenger quality and candidate spending, which exert a larger overall effect on incumbent vote share.

In model 3, I estimate the same model just reported but also include a variable tapping an incumbent senator's previous vote share as a measure of electoral security. While Canes-Wrone, Brady, and Cogan (2002) do not include a similar variable in their analysis of House elections, I believe that it is nevertheless important to include this variable, since it provides a baseline for comparison with respect to incumbent safety. Indeed, while the

TABLE 2.1. Senators' legislative voting and electoral vote share, 1974–2004

Variables	Model 1	Model 2	Model 3	Model 4	Model 5
Ideological Extremity	−2.78	−7.90**	−4.55	−4.31	−31.61**
	(2.35)	(3.56)	(3.30)	(3.31)	(12.69)
Party Unity Score		0.08**	0.06**	0.07**	0.08**
		(0.04)	(0.03)	(0.03)	(0.03)
Electoral Security			0.30**	0.25**	0.29**
			(0.06)	(0.06)	(0.06)
Partisanship of the State	−0.003	−0.01	0.03		−0.13
	(0.05)	(0.05)	(0.04)		(0.09)
Ideological Extremity ×					0.49**
Partisanship of the State					(0.22)
Challenger Quality	−4.88**	−4.78**	−3.58**	−3.57**	−3.37**
	(0.85)	(0.86)	(0.82)	(0.86)	(0.81)
ln(Challenger Spending) −	−3.56**	−3.51**	−3.20**	−3.07**	−3.14**
ln(Incumbent Spending)	(0.39)	(0.40)	(0.37)	(0.36)	(0.37)
Freshman	−1.07	−1.31	0.12	−0.08	0.15
	(0.87)	(0.88)	(0.84)	(0.90)	(0.83)
Party Leadership Status		−2.74*	−3.47**	−3.18**	−3.26**
		(1.48)	(1.27)	(1.31)	(1.28)
State Population		−0.001	−0.0001	−0.001	−0.0001
		(0.001)	(0.001)	(0.001)	(0.0001)
Constant	62.40**	60.37**	37.16**	38.95**	45.30**
	(3.86)	(4.32)	(4.47)	(4.41)	(5.68)
1976 Election	−2.73	−3.26	−1.02	2.07	−1.16
	(3.23)	(3.13)	(2.49)	(2.57)	(2.43)
1978 Election	−5.73**	−6.02**	−3.27	−0.79	−3.11
	(2.83)	(2.90)	(2.43)	(2.53)	(2.40)
1980 Election	−4.86*	−4.82*	−3.26	0.03	−3.20
	(2.88)	(2.88)	(2.24)	(2.46)	(2.14)
1982 Election	−0.18	−1.36	0.14	2.69	−0.66
	(2.64)	(2.72)	(2.14)	(2.20)	(2.10)
1984 Election	1.53	0.45	1.66	5.25**	1.12
	(2.82)	(2.90)	(2.30)	(2.52)	(2.33)
1986 Election	−3.27	−4.26	−2.19	−0.16	−2.69
	(2.57)	(2.63)	(2.13)	(2.21)	(2.08)
1988 Election	−1.23	−2.24	0.47	3.29	0.03
	(2.57)	(2.62)	(2.04)	(2.13)	(2.03)
1990 Election	−3.65	−5.03*	−3.43	−0.84	−3.81
	(2.91)	(2.96)	(2.45)	(2.47)	(2.39)
1992 Election	−1.08	−2.41	−0.14	2.43	−0.77
	(2.68)	(2.79)	(2.29)	(2.41)	(2.28)
1994 Election	−2.64	−4.29	−1.76	0.65	−2.39
	(2.60)	(2.74)	(2.30)	(2.46)	(2.27)
1996 Election	−4.88**	−6.70**	−5.28**	−2.69	−5.75**
	(2.46)	(2.62)	(2.27)	(2.33)	(2.23)

TABLE 2.1. *continued*

Variables	Model 1	Model 2	Model 3	Model 4	Model 5
1998 Election	−2.34	−3.83	−0.88	2.05	−1.42
	(2.55)	(2.59)	(2.08)	(2.16)	(2.06)
2000 Election	−0.79	−1.49	−0.27	2.36	−0.88
	(2.88)	(2.89)	(2.45)	(2.54)	(2.44)
2002 Election	−1.46	−3.30	−0.86	1.80	−1.49
	(2.57)	(2.65)	(2.22)	(2.34)	(2.21)
2004 Election	−2.58	−4.48	−3.11	−0.34	−3.61
	(2.78)	(2.89)	(2.37)	(2.51)	(2.33)
Sample size (N)	401	401	399	356	399
R^2	0.506	0.515	0.577	0.548	0.583

Note: Robust standard errors are given in parentheses below OLS coefficients.

$*p \leq .10; **p \leq .05$

results are very similar across models 2 and 3, it is interesting to note that ideological extremity is no longer significant. When I include in model 3 prior vote share to account for the degree of incumbent safety, the significant effect for ideological extremity disappears. This set of estimates offers support for the earlier finding (model 1), which indicates that ideological extremity may not be a strong predictor of two-party vote share in the Senate. In contrast, we see that the variable tapping senators' party unity is once again positive and statistically significant in this model (although the substantive effect is again very small relative to other variables in the model).[11]

In the fourth column of table 2.1, I estimate nearly all the variables included in model 3, but this time I break out the results in terms of degree of safeness within the state (thus excluding the partisanship-of-the-state variable from the model). In Model 4, I include only those Senate races where a legislator represented a state considered to be safe, as measured by percentage of the two-party vote received by the presidential candidate of the incumbent's party in the most recent election. By doing this, I seek to demonstrate that voting patterns may actually be conditioned upon the underlying nature of the constituency, which may be missed when including this variable in the regression model. Indeed, I find that senators' party unity scores exert a positive and statistically significant influence on incumbent vote share, suggesting that senators whose constituencies are more supportive of party support are actually rewarded when voters go to the polls. The variable tapping ideological extremity is not statistically significant in model 4, which implies that senators are not necessarily punished for their extreme behavior relative to the state constituency that they represent.

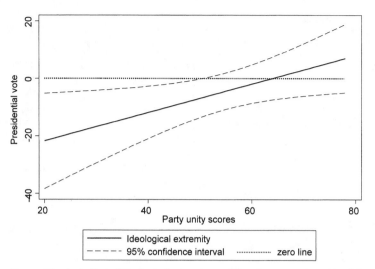

Fig. 2.3: Marginal effect of ideological extremity conditional upon partisanship of the Senate. "Presidential vote," reflecting partisanship of the state, is the proportion of the two-party vote received by the presidential candidate of the incumbent's party in the most recent election.

In the final column of the table, I estimate all the covariates included in model 3 but also include an additional variable tapping the interactive effect between ideological extremity and state partisanship as reflected by presidential vote. This specification mirrors a slightly different way of evaluating whether senators' voting patterns are conditioned upon the underlying nature of the constituency they represent. We observe that the interaction effect is statistically significant in model 5, yet only one of the baseline components (ideological extremity) is as well. Following the advice of Brambor, Clark, and Golder (2006) with respect to interpreting multiplicative interaction terms, I plot the effect graphically. As the results in figure 2.3 demonstrate, the marginal effect of ideological extremity as reflected by the absolute value of senators' DW-NOMINATE score is conditional upon the underlying partisanship of the state. In other words, incumbent senators are only punished for ideologically extreme behavior when they represent a statewide constituency that is more moderate.

Conclusion

While students of congressional politics have examined the representational connection between voting behavior and electoral outcomes in the context of House elections, virtually no systematic attention has been given to the same relationship in the context of Senate elections. This chapter takes a first step in filling that void, by examining the electoral effects of ideological extremity and party loyalty in all Senate elections held from 1974 to 2004. From the estimates reported in table 2.1, I find only modest support for the notion that ideological extremity affects the proportion of the two-party vote that incumbent senators receive. More interesting, however, is the recognition that this effect tends to be conditioned upon the senator's underlying constituency. Senators who represent more polarized states are not regularly punished for extreme behavior, since they are simply voting in line with their constituency. This result is of further interest given that it is different than what has previously been uncovered in the context of the U.S. House (on this point, see Canes-Wrone, Brady, and Cogan 2002).

Furthermore, the results from four of the models strongly support the idea that party unity is directly related to incumbent electoral performance in the Senate. This finding is of particular interest because it challenges the prevailing notion in the literature that voting with one's party on a regular basis jeopardizes a legislator's chances of reelection. Indeed, it would appear that the relationship between party loyalty and electoral performance is conditional upon the nature of the constituency represented. If senators represent statewide constituencies that are becoming more "red" or "blue," as the conventional wisdom would have us believe, then voting with one's party more often should not have a detrimental effect on one's electoral fortunes if the aggregate patterns of voting reflect the beliefs of one's constituents. Even though the substantive effect of this variable is not as large as other covariates included in each model, it is nonetheless instructive that we are *not* observing a negative relationship between party loyalty and electoral performance.

In seeking to build upon the results reported here, it would be useful to consider whether the saliency of roll-call behavior affects incumbent electoral performance. For instance, are senators more likely to be rewarded or punished for their voting behavior on a more narrow range of highly visible and controversial votes? Is it possible that electoral effects become more pronounced on final passage as opposed to procedural votes that are less likely to be noticed by attentive publics (i.e., political elites, interest groups, and prospective challengers)? Also, should we expect to see voting behavior change in anticipation of an upcoming Senate election, when other factors are controlled for? Although the preliminary results reported in this vein are suggestive, it would be instructive to systematically examine whether senators are more likely to moderate their behavior in the months preceding an election. Examination of these and related questions should help us further recognize important linkages between constituents, parties, and the ideology of individual senators in connection with observed patterns of voting behavior.

Notes

Previous versions of this chapter were presented at the Conference on Party Effects in the United States Senate, sponsored by Duke University, April 7–8, 2006; and at the Conference on Party Effects in the United States Senate II, sponsored by the Department of Political Science and the Center for the Study of Politics and Government at the University of Minnesota, September 29–30, 2006. I am especially thankful to Erik Engstrom, Jeff Jenkins, Jason Roberts, David Rohde, Wendy Schiller, and Steve Smith for helpful comments on previous versions of this chapter.

1. As noted by John Aldrich et al. in this volume, the Senate provides a useful venue for examining party effects relative to the House, given the greater heterogeneity of constituencies and competitiveness in Senate elections.

2. See Bovitz and Carson (2006) for related evidence of electoral accountability in conjunction with legislative voting on individual roll calls in the U.S. House.

3. For a related discussion concerning the electoral consequences of partisan loyalty in the U.S. House, see Carson, Koger, and Lebo (2006).

4. This is especially true given the greater amount of media coverage afforded Senate races, since there are fewer of them in a given electoral cycle (on this point, see Abramowitz 1988; and Kuklinski and Sigelman 1992). With more media attention devoted to the challenger (who thus has more campaign visibility), incumbent senators have to work substantially harder to get reelected.

5. On the subject of campaign war chests and their lack of deterrent effects on candidate entry decisions in Senate races, see Goodliffe (2007).

6. See Overby et al. (1992) for evidence of constituency influence on the confirmation vote in the Senate for Justice Clarence Thomas.

7. In the context of House races, Griffin (2006) finds that elected officials who represent competitive districts tend to be more responsive to their constituents' preferences.

8. For an alternative view on how to measure challenger quality, see Green and Krasno (1988).

9. As Jacobson (1980) argues, the advantage of using the natural logarithm of campaign expenditures for empirical analysis of elections is that doing so avoids the assumption of a linear relationship between money and votes, thereby accounting for diminishing marginal returns from campaign spending.

10. Interestingly, even when fixed effects are not included for the results reported in model 1, ideological extremity is not statistically significant ($p < .14$).

11. To be certain that the null results for ideological extremity are not a function of inflated standard errors stemming from multicollinearity in the third model, I calculated the variance-inflation factors (VIFs) after fitting the regression model. At no point did the VIFs approach levels that would suggest the null findings are a function of multicollinearity.

3

Party and Constituency in the U.S. Senate, 1933–2004

JOHN ALDRICH, MICHAEL BRADY, SCOTT DE MARCHI,
IAN MCDONALD, BRENDAN NYHAN, DAVID W. ROHDE,
AND MICHAEL TOFIAS

Rational choice models of internal legislative rules have dominated the study of Congress over the last quarter century. While this research agenda has been extremely productive, congressional scholars have not devoted sufficient attention to the connections among elections, parties, and legislative behavior. That complex tripartite relationship deserves greater attention, particularly in the study of the Senate, where the formal powers of party are weaker than in the House of Representatives.

One important question in this area is the extent to which members of the Senate are responsive to the characteristics of their constituencies when they vote on the floor, particularly when those characteristics conflict with party membership. Research in this area is surprisingly thin. In particular, while it is clear that party is closely linked to the liberal-conservative dimension of legislative conflict, the influence of constituent characteristics on Senate voting is not well understood, particularly as it differs by issue type.

Our theoretical expectations are straightforward. It is almost tautological that party membership should be more closely associated with voting on liberal-conservative issues than it is for crosscutting ones. Conversely, we expect that the effect of constituency will be greater for issues that are orthogonal to ideology, particularly when those issues are highly salient.

Using comprehensive data from the period 1933–2004, we measure the association between constituency (via state demographics) and Senate voting behavior (via ideal point estimates derived from roll-call voting). As expected, we find that the second dimension of conflict in the Senate, which captures the primary crosscutting issue(s) on the agenda, is more closely related to demographics, while the first is more closely related to party and presidential voting. In addition, we show that there was a massive upswing in the association between demographics and second-dimension voting during the period in which race was a highly salient issue that split the Democratic Party. However, as the parties polarized after the issue of race was incorporated into the partisan divide, the relationship between demographics and Senate voting declined to a similarly low level for both dimensions.

Previous Research

Our research fits within the larger body of work on representation and its relationship to the preferences and composition of members' constituencies (e.g., Turner 1951; Miller and Stokes 1963; Fenno 1973; Fiorina 1974; Bailey and Brady 1998; Uslaner 1999). In particular, the most closely related previous studies have used demographics to predict Americans for Democratic Action (ADA) scores and have defined legislative shirking as the residuals from those regressions (see, for instance, Kalt and Zupan 1984). A related literature examines constituency heterogeneity as a key predictor of the extent to which legislators may deviate from constituency preferences (Fiorina 1974; Bond 1983; Bishin 2000; Gronke 2000; Bishin, Dow, and Adams 2006).

But as Goff and Grier (1993) point out, it is impossible to define "shirking," because Condorcet-winning platforms rarely exist in multidimensional policy spaces. Instead, they argue, politicians construct idiosyncratic coalitions.[1] Other authors reach a similar conclusion. For instance, Krehbiel (1993a) notes that same-state senators vote together only slightly more often than we would predict from chance alone, while Schiller (2002, 110) shows that same-state senators "target distinct sets of geographic areas and related demographic groups to increase electoral support" (see also Schiller 2000a).

Rather than trying to measure individual "shirking," we instead seek to measure the strength of the association between legislative behavior and constituency demographics and to determine how it has varied over time. Given the extent to which parties structure legislative behavior, we expect that historical patterns will change in tandem with the evolution of the party system. From Poole and Rosenthal (1991, 1997, 2007), we know that there are two major dimensions of legislative conflict. The first and more important dimension represents the locus of conflict between the two major parties, primarily reflecting disagreement over economic policy. It accounts for most of the variance in congressional voting, correctly classifying more than 90 percent of roll-call votes in recent years. The second dimension, by contrast, represents a variety of issues that do not map cleanly onto the first dimension. As a result, it varies in importance over time and typically explains much less variance than does the first dimension (Poole and Rosenthal 2007).

The most salient second-dimension issue in recent decades was race, which cut across party lines in the mid-twentieth century. Poole and Rosenthal, who define the relevant period as "roughly" 1940 to 1966, document how the first dimension of DW-NOMINATE explains almost no variance in House voting on civil rights in these years (the Senate held fewer civil rights votes). During this period, Southern Democrats comprised a virtual third party. The race issue was subsequently mapped onto the first dimension in what Carmines and Stimson (1989) call an "issue evolution," a dynamic process in which highly salient new issues disrupt the alignment of the established party system. In this case, the Republican Party became known for racial conservatism, particularly with the presidential nomination of Barry Goldwater in 1964, and the Democratic Party became identified with racial liberalism. Over time, that shift among elites translated into long-term changes in mass partisanship, especially among Southern whites.

Estimation and Theory

Before defining our theoretical expectations, it is useful to be clear about the assumptions underlying our analysis. Let $C_{i,j,k,t}$ denote the preferences of individual i in constituency j for candidate k at time t. We assume that the primary determinant of voter preferences over candidates is a series of exogenous variables $X_{i,j,k,t}$ and historical context $H_{j,t}$ (Fenno 1973). This formulation yields:

$$C_{i,j,k,t} = f(X_{i,j,k,t}, H_{j,t}) \qquad (1)$$

Since we do not have comprehensive individual-level data for all fifty states, we shift to the constituency level. We assume that voter characteristics can be adequately characterized using measures of aggregate state demographics. We also assume that the past presidential vote in the constituency $V_{j,t-1}$ captures historical partisan allegiances not captured by demographics. These changes alter equation 1 to:

$$C_{j,t} = f(X_{j,t}, V_{j,t-1}) \qquad (2)$$

Finally, we assume that legislators reveal an ideological position through their voting records and that this behavior is a function of constituent preferences. If we use DW-NOMINATE scores **DW** in dimensions $d \in \{1,2\}$ to approximate these positions, then the scores of each member of Congress i who represents constituency j in a given period t will be:

$$\mathbf{DW}_{d,i,t} = g(f(\mathbf{X}_{j,t})) \tag{3}$$

However, we also wish to allow for the influence of party affiliation and historical partisan allegiances on voting and therefore include the legislator's party $\mathbf{P}_i$ and the constituency's past presidential vote $\mathbf{V}_{j,t-1}$ in the equation. Consequently, we represent estimated ideal points as follows:

$$\mathbf{DW}_{d,i,t} = g(f(\mathbf{X}_{j,t}, \mathbf{V}_{j,t-1}), \mathbf{P}_i) \tag{4}$$

Thus $g()$ is some function mapping constituent characteristics, past presidential vote, and legislator party affiliation into an ideological position. Assuming $g()$ is linear, we can estimate equations 3 and 4 via ordinary least squares (OLS).

We can now define our theoretical expectations about these statistical models. Since the first dimension captures the primary liberal-conservative divide in politics, it should be closely associated with party affiliation. Consequently, we expect that demographic predictors will contribute relatively little to first-dimension ideal point estimates. By contrast, since the second dimension captures issues that are orthogonal to the liberal-conservative divide, ideology should be less relevant. Thus, model 3, which only includes demographic predictors, should fit estimated second-dimension ideal points better than the first. We expect this relationship to be strongest when the second dimension is highly salient. By contrast, the combined model in equation 4 should fit the first dimension more closely because of its association with party.

Data

Our data set of senators, including the DW-NOMINATE first- and second-dimension estimates that we use as our dependent variables, comes from Keith Poole's Voteview Web site.[2] We examine all 3,621 full or partial Senate terms served by individual members from the 73rd to the 108th Congress (1933–2004).

We use a number of measures to capture the demographic characteristics of each state over the period in question:

· Seniors age sixty-five and over
· African Americans

- Farmers and farmworkers
- Finance workers
- Population born outside the United States
- Government workers
- Manufacturing-sector workers
- Logarithm of total population[3]
- Urban population
- Population density
- Logarithm of per capita personal income (adjusted for inflation)

Except for per capita income, all our data come from the 1930–2000 U.S. Census.[4] Personal-income data are collected from the Bureau of Economic Analysis.[5] The 1960–90 census data were found in Adler n.d., data from the 1930–50 censuses were collected directly from source texts, and the 2000 census data were downloaded online.[6] All of the age, race, and workforce measures are constructed as proportions of state population.

We account for mid-decade population and demographic changes by interpolating demographic variables between decennial censuses. Current practice in congressional demographic analyses has been to carry forward original census data from the beginning of a decade without modification (Adler 2002). Applied to the Senate, this practice effectively assigns static demographic characteristics to each state for a ten-year period, thereby truncating a key source of variance outside the legislature. We therefore estimate mid-decade values based on a linear interpolation of data between censuses.[7]

As stated above, we also use past presidential vote as a measure of historical partisan allegiances when we estimate equation 4. This variable uses the Democratic percentage of the two-party presidential vote from the election that is concurrent to, or immediately preceding, the election of a given Congress (for example, we associate the presidential election of 1996 with the 105th and 106th Congresses of 1997–2000).[8]

Results

To compare model fit between the two primary dimensions of DW-NOMINATE, we estimate OLS models for the pooled 1933–2004 data set. Table 3.1 contrasts a demographics-only model with a model including demographics, presidential vote, and party for each dimension.

The first and third columns report the demographics-only models for the first and second dimensions of DW-NOMINATE, respectively. We find

TABLE 3.1. Models of DW-NOMINATE, 73rd–108th Senates

Coefficient	DW-NOMINATE, 1st dimension		DW-NOMINATE, 2nd dimension	
	Demographics only (SE)	Demographics, presidential vote, and party(SE)	Demographics only (SE)	Demographics, presidential vote, and party (SE)
Proportion 65 or older	0.044 (0.75)	−0.77 (0.44)	2.59 (1.19)	2.32 (0.85)
Proportion African American	0.11 (0.17)	0.88 (0.099)	2.06 (0.28)	1.70 (0.21)
Proportion in farming	1.40 (0.69)	−0.85 (0.38)	−2.09 (1.02)	−0.28 (0.88)
Proportion in finance	−0.37 (2.61)	1.06 (1.52)	−7.73 (3.36)	−5.53 (2.39)
Proportion foreign-born	0.34 (0.42)	−0.098 (0.21)	−0.26 (0.54)	0.40 (0.44)
Proportion govt. workers	0.71 (1.04)	−2.15 (0.59)	0.38 (1.49)	0.74 (1.15)
Proportion in manufacturing	1.48 (0.54)	−0.93 (0.28)	−4.72 (0.71)	−3.22 (0.58)
Total population (log)	−0.027 (0.021)	−0.025 (0.012)	−0.021 (0.026)	−0.015 (0.019)
Proportion in urban area	0.075 (0.16)	−0.0062 (0.082)	−0.17 (0.20)	−0.32 (0.16)
Population density	−0.00054 (0.000090)	−0.00020 (0.000061)	−0.00034 (0.00013)	−0.00047 (0.000093)
Per capita income (log)	0.056 (0.050)	0.0084 (0.024)	−0.12 (0.043)	−0.094 (0.042)
Democratic presidential vote		−0.36 (0.062)		−0.86 (0.13)
Republican Party member		0.60 (0.019)		−0.56 (0.033)
Constant	−0.36 (0.53)	0.39 (0.26)	1.76 (0.50)	2.00 (0.44)
Observations	3621	3621	3621	3621
R^2	0.07	0.71	0.33	0.54

Note: Standard errors are clustered by senator.

that the demographics model of the second dimension explains a larger proportion of the variance than the comparable first-dimension model; the R^2 is 0.33, compared with 0.07.[9] By contrast, the first dimension of DW-NOMINATE is much more closely associated with party and presidential vote than is the second dimension. Models of the two dimensions using only party and presidential vote (not presented but available upon request) show that the R^2 for the first dimension is 0.62, compared with 0.28 for the second. Given that the first dimension captures the liberal-conservative divide during this period (Poole and Rosenthal 1991, 1997, 2007), these findings are not surprising; we expect that issues that do align with the first dimension will be less closely related to demographics than those that do not.

In addition, the increased variance explained by demographics on the second dimension appears to be related to a larger set of constituency variables than race alone. When we examine coefficients from the pooled model, we find that the coefficients of the proportions of senior citizens and of African Americans are positive and statistically significant, while mean income, population density, and the proportion of farming, finance, and manufacturing workers are all negative and statistically significant. By contrast, we find that only three predictors are statistically significant for the first dimension (the proportion of farming and manufacturing workers, both positive; and population density, which is negative).

The second and fourth columns of table 3.1 represent fully specified models that include demographics, past (Democratic) presidential vote, and membership in the Republican Party. Unsurprisingly, the addition of these variables reverses the pattern of model fit. The R^2 for the first dimension, which is closely associated with party, soars to 0.71, while the equivalent second-dimension model has an R^2 of 0.54.[10] However, demographics still remain important. The addition of demographics to a model with only the senator's party and Democratic presidential vote share improves model fit, particularly on the second dimension. We find that root mean squared error falls from .22 to .19 for the first dimension and from .47 to .38 for the second dimension (results available upon request).

The pooled analysis above suggests that the second dimension of DW-NOMINATE has been more closely associated with our demographic variables than has the first dimension. We next examine how these relationships have changed over time. Figure 3.1 presents the adjusted R^2 scores from the demographics-only models estimated for each Congress.[11] Strikingly, the second dimension is more closely related to demographics than the first for every Congress but one in our sample. The difference was largest from the 78th to 91st Congresses (1943–70), a period that overlaps closely with the 1940–66 peak of the second dimension identified by Poole and Rosenthal.[12] As mentioned earlier, this was the period in which the issue of race became sufficiently salient to split the Democratic Party by region. The gap in

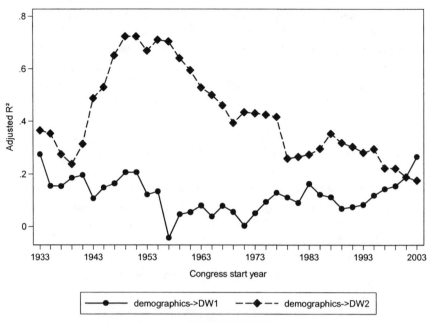

Fig. 3.1: Demographics-only models of DW-NOMINATE by Congress

model fit between dimensions subsequently narrowed, however. Figure 3.1 indicates that by the 108th Congress, second-dimension model fits were actually slightly *worse* than those for the first dimension.

Does this finding also hold once party and the state presidential vote are taken into account? Figure 3.2 compares the performance of the fully specified model presented earlier in explaining the first and second dimensions of DW-NOMINATE. As expected, model fit is generally higher for the first dimension when party and presidential voting are included as predictors. However, during the 80th to 92nd Congresses (1947–72), model fits are again better for the second dimension. In short, both sets of models show unexpectedly large increases in model performance for the second dimension in approximately the same period that the second dimension was most salient. We view these findings as further evidence of a strengthened linkage between constituency and the second dimension during the pre–civil rights era.

Given the results above, we examine whether our fully specified model is consistent with the issue-evolution account. If so, we would expect the relationship of party to the second dimension to become more pronounced as the issues on this dimension are conscripted by the major parties. To test this expectation, we plot the coefficient for the GOP party variable during each Congress for both dimensions of DW-NOMINATE while also controlling for the demographic variables and presidential vote presented earlier. Figure 3.3 presents these coefficients and their 95 percent confidence intervals for 1933–2004. As expected, the figure illustrates the increased partisanship on the first dimension and the divergence of the parties on the second dimension. Indeed, the coefficient for the second dimension starts to move in a negative direction quite early. By the 79th Congress of 1945–46, its 95 percent confidence interval does not include zero, and the coefficient trends down until the 91st Congress of 1969–70, when it stabilizes.

Taken together, these results have two implications. First, the second dimension appears to have been more closely rooted in demographics than the first over the last seventy years. The first dimension, which is essentially partisan, is not strongly associated with demographics, but the second dimension, which includes a number of crosscutting issues, seems to have deeper demographic roots. Second, the issue of race—which dominated the second dimension during the mid-twentieth century—appears to have made members of the Senate *more* responsive to the aggregate characteristics

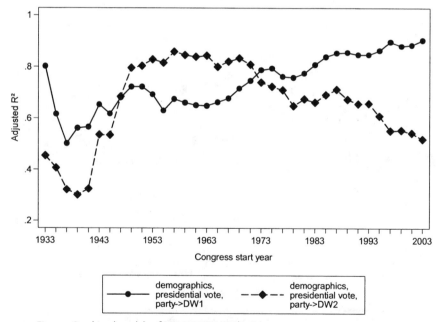

Fig. 3.2: Combined models of DW-NOMINATE by Congress

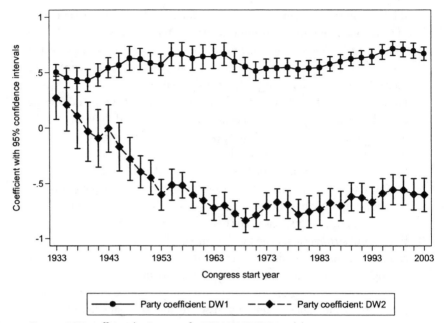

Fig. 3.3: GOP coefficient by Congress for DW-NOMINATE models

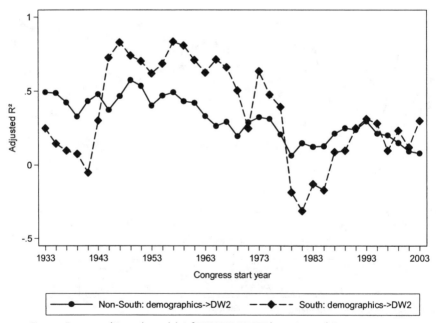

Fig. 3.4: Demographics-only models of DW-NOMINATE by region and Congress

of their constituencies than in any comparable period in the last seventy years.

Since our results are consistent with the issue-evolution story, it is important to consider whether our models pool across regions. Our finding that the second dimension of DW-NOMINATE was closely linked to demographics during the pre–civil rights era may be driven by an especially strong relationship in the South, where the issue of race was especially salient. Figure 3.4 tests this conjecture with demographic models of the second dimension that are disaggregated by region and estimated on each Congress in the data.[13] The resulting pattern of model fit over time suggests that the South drove the demographic predictability of the second dimension of DW-NOMINATE in the pre–civil rights era. When we disaggregate by region, we see that adjusted R^2 is relatively stable for non-Southern states, whereas it spikes dramatically in the South starting in the 79th Congress and remains consistently high until the 90th Congress (1945–68).[14] This period again corresponds closely with the years in which the second dimension was especially salient. Adjusted R^2 then plunged in the South before regaining parity with non-Southern states in the early 1990s.

Conclusion

We have offered evidence for several new conjectures about the relationship between constituency characteristics, party, and legislative behavior. Specifically, we have demonstrated that first-dimension DW-NOMINATE scores bear little relationship to state demographics, while second-dimension scores are more strongly related to them. In addition, we show that the relationship between demographics and the second dimension of DW-NOMINATE strengthened dramatically in the pre–civil rights South before waning in subsequent years. In other words, the association between demographics and voting increased on the second dimension during a period in which the salience of parties was suppressed. However, as the alignment of parties in the South came to more closely resemble the two-party politics found in the rest of the nation, this increased association came to an end.

In effect, the disruption of the normal issue alignment allows us to observe the relationship between constituency and legislative voting when it is less structured by party. When Southern Democrats were divided from the rest of their caucus, the explanatory power of demographics increased dramatically on the second dimension. This finding has important implications for understanding how parties affect the relationship between constituency and legislative voting. Possible extensions might include conducting a parallel analysis for the House of Representatives, which we have only been able to study for the 1983–2004 period because of data limitations (Aldrich et al. 2006), or considering whether hypothesized issue evolutions on abortion and women's rights affected the relationship between constituency and legislative behavior (Stimson 2004). In general, however, it seems clear that legislative behavior in the Senate cannot be fully understood without considering both party *and* constituency.

Notes

1. They also argue that the effect of demographics may vary by party, but previous work on the House found that such interaction effects only improve model fit slightly (Aldrich et al.), so we do not include them.
2. See http://www.voteview.org.
3. Total population was logged because it displayed high variance. It was not normalized to another variable. By contrast, urban population and population born outside the United States were normalized to total state population, and population density was normalized to land area, so these variables were not logged.
4. Where possible, we followed the coding in Adler n.d. For 1930–40, coding decisions were made by the authors to maximize comparability to recent data, though some slippage was unavoidable.
5. Since census data on median income do not extend back to the 1930s, we collect state-level aggregate personal-income data from the Bureau of Economic Analysis and divide by interpolated state population.
6. Specifically, we sum non-statewide district data from our House analysis (Aldrich et al. 2006).
7. Geometric interpolation was also tested and did not perform better (results available upon request).
8. While we use the Democratic percentage of the two-party vote in our models, our results hold if the measure is a percentage of the total vote or deviation from the national vote.
9. Despite their well-known limitations, we use R^2 and adjusted R^2 as crude model fit statistics in this chapter.
10. Contrary to our expectations, the coefficient for Democratic presidential vote is negative for the second dimension in the fully specified model, which controls for demographics and party. When we examine bivariate correlations, we discover an apparent example of what is known as Simpson's paradox (Simpson 1951). As we expect, presidential vote is positively correlated with second-dimension scores for the sample as a whole ($r = 0.11$), but the correlations are negative when we disaggregate by party ($r = -0.08$ for Democrats and $r = -0.06$ for Republicans). When we control for party in the model above, the presidential-vote coefficient therefore becomes negative. A similar relationship holds for the first and second dimension of DW-

NOMINATE, which are negatively correlated between parties but positively correlated within them.

11. Since it is not necessary to cluster by senator in these models, we use adjusted R^2 to measure model fit.

12. Root mean square error also declined on the second dimension during this period (results available upon request).

13. We define the South as Alabama, Arkansas, Florida, Georgia, Kentucky, Louisiana, Mississippi, Missouri, North Carolina, South Carolina, Tennessee, Texas, and Virginia.

14. To test whether the increased relationship between demographics and the second dimension is simply an artifact of the issue of race, we construct two nested models. The first predicts the second dimension of DW-NOMINATE for each Congress using black, South, South*black, and our other demographic variables. The second uses only black, South, and South*black. Using a series of F-tests, we reject the hypothesis that the effect of the other demographic variables is jointly zero for every Congress in our data except for the 76th and the 105th–108th (for all others, $p < .01$; results available upon request).

4

Scoring the Senate: Scorecards, Parties, and Roll-Call Votes

JASON M. ROBERTS AND LAUREN COHEN BELL

On December 21, 2005, in the closing moments of the first session of the 109th Congress, the Senate passed S. Con. Res. 74, a concurrent resolution correcting the enrollment of H.R. 2863, the Department of Defense Appropriations Act of 2006. Forty-five Republican senators voted against the measure, which struck the provision of the act that would have permitted drilling in the Arctic National Wildlife Refuge (ANWR). Despite the fact that the majority of the Republican members of the chamber opposed the concurrent resolution, it passed by a vote of 48–45.

Majority-party losses such as these[1] are not uncommon in the Senate; between the 102nd and 107th Congresses (1991–2002), the majority party was beaten more than five hundred times—a number that represents more than 13 percent of all recorded votes held in the chamber during that period.[2] Oddly, however, just nine months before the Republicans' loss on the ANWR vote, the party had scored a victory on the very same issue. On March 15, 2005, the Senate narrowly rejected, by a vote of 51–49, an amendment to S. Con. Res. 18, the Concurrent Budget Resolution for Fiscal Year 2006, that would have prohibited drilling. Both votes were taken on amendments to budget bills, both amendments were offered by Senator Maria Cantwell (D-WA), and both simply required that the provision permitting drilling be struck from the main measure. Nevertheless, between March and December, seven Republican senators changed their votes: four abstained, and three senators that previously had voted to allow drilling in ANWR voted to prohibit it.[3] One difference between the two votes, however, is that the March 15 vote was identified by the National Association of Manufacturers (NAM) as being one of the organization's probable "key votes" for 2005; no such designation was made by any organization for the December vote.

These ANWR votes demonstrate the limited ability and/or willingness of Senate party leaders to enforce party unity. They also raise questions about how senators' voting decisions are affected by competing pressures from parties, constituents, and interest groups. In this chapter, we compare the relative success of the majority party and interest groups on "scored" votes across both chambers of Congress. We compare House and Senate majority-party losses and interest group scoring activities in order to gain a better understanding of the extent to which interest groups offer members of Congress inducements to defect from the party's preferred position when casting salient roll-call votes, as well as the relative success of parties and interest groups across the two chambers. As Hurley (1989, 129) notes, an analysis that considers senators' decisions in light of the votes that interest groups consider most salient may be "a viable way to discover the critical determinants of congressional voting." Although we cast a wider net than she suggests by looking at all roll-call votes cast in the House and Senate between the 102nd and 107th Congresses (1991–2002), we combine interest group scorecard and roll-call data in order to gain empirical leverage on the questions of how members and parties balance their electoral and policy goals and the extent to which parties and interest groups can affect the votes of individual members. In keeping with the other essays in this volume, our analysis allows us to compare the relative success of the majority party in the House and the Senate.

After first discussing the theoretical underpinnings of our study, we turn to an analysis of the effects of legislative parties, electoral considerations, and interest groups on roll-call voting behaviors. The results indicate that party leaders in the Senate generally are able to secure their preferred outcomes on roll-call votes, but that some senators are willing to defect from their parties' preferred positions when particular interest groups announce their intention to include the votes on their end-of-year or end-of-Congress scorecards.

Members' Voting Decisions

Conventional wisdom on the U.S. Congress typically treats the House of Representatives as having strong legislative parties and leaders while it treats the Senate as atomistic and lacking strong party leadership. House leaders are said to have centralized decision making and top-down control of rank-and-file party members during the 1990s (Smith and Gamm 2005), while the Senate has decentralized, individualistic leadership and a weak presiding officer (Gamm and Smith 2000). Moreover, the Senate's Rules Committee does not have the power to act as a gatekeeper to the chamber floor, there is no general germaneness rule, the chamber does not have a strict calendar system, and there are few debate-limiting mechanisms (Oleszek 2007). As Sinclair (1989) notes, myriad external incentives—including presidential ambition—provide inducements for individual senators to act in their personal self-interest rather than in the collective interest of their legislative parties. This further reduces their reliance on the party for cues about the "correct" way to vote.

With six years between elections, senators are freed from the constraints of strict party and constituency discipline. In addition, senators are subject far more to norms than to formal rules of procedure. Therefore, it is reasonable to assume that when it comes to voting, senators have less incentive to vote with their party than do their colleagues in the House of Representatives. If we operate under that assumption, the majority-party loss rate we report above would come as no surprise, since, as the two ANWR votes suggest, party leaders possess limited power to enforce party discipline in the U.S. Senate.

Despite the perceived differences in the two chambers' leadership and agenda-control mechanisms, many of the seminal studies of members of Congress's voting decisions do not distinguish between House and Senate members. For example, Kingdon (1977, 1989) and Fenno (1978) note that in general, members of Congress balance three important considerations: maintaining constituency support, gaining power within Washington, and crafting good public policy. When a member's goals in each of these areas do not align, he or she may find it difficult to cast a vote that satisfies his or her constituents, party leaders, or interest groups with which the member has a close relationship (Kingdon 1989). Additional evidence suggests that senators' votes are both constrained and motivated by the same factors that affect the votes of members of the House of Representatives. Bailey and Brady (1998), for example, note that constituency pressures, party influences, and interest group ratings motivated senators' votes on international trade issues in the early 1990s. Other previous studies extend these conclusions.

When senators cast roll-call votes, they—like their House counterparts—seek to strike a balance between the often conflicting demands of congressional parties, constituents, and interest groups. Each of these influences on senators' votes, and the ways in which senators attempt to balance them, is discussed below.

Parties in the Senate

Party leadership in the Senate often appears to be a contradiction in terms, as floor leaders frequently find themselves frustrated by senators of their own party who refuse to acquiesce to the leadership's preferences (Evans and Oleszek 2000). In addition, Senate leaders lack many of the formal party tools that their House counterparts possess. Each senator—including the leader of each party—is a formal equal, so party identification is often less significant in the Senate than it is in the House, where the majority-minority distinction is profound. Moreover, unlike in the House of Representatives, party discipline in the Senate generally has been more a function of the personalities of the chamber's leaders than a function of formal, institutionalized mechanisms of party control (Sinclair 2001a; Caro 2002). Thus, senators and Senate parties attempt to be attentive to the varied demands from citizens and interest groups in a chamber that offers few formal rules to constrain their choices.

Regardless of the differences in the two chambers' formal rules of procedure, however, recent scholarship has begun to recognize that party leaders in the Senate generally are able to take advantage of the chamber's norms and traditions to exercise limited control over rank-and-file party members (Snyder and Groseclose 2000; Forgette and Sala 1999; Sinclair 2001a; Campbell, Cox, and McCubbins 2002; Overby and Bell 2004). For example, Forgette and Sala (1999) use historical evidence to demonstrate that on salient roll-call votes, Senate party leaders have long been able to obtain some degree of party discipline even in the absence of formal mechanisms of control, while Snyder and Groseclose (2000) find that party effects are evident especially when leaders expect votes to be close or when the votes are on particularly salient issues. Likewise, Campbell, Cox, and McCubbins (2002) contend that the presence of negative agenda control in the Senate prevents the majority party from being regularly rolled on final-passage votes. In this volume, Sean Gailmard and Jeffery A. Jenkins contend that *minority-party* strength in the Senate seriously hinders the majority party's ability to win its preferred policies.

There are several reasons to believe that Senate parties may possess some control over vote outcomes, even though the mechanisms of control in the Senate are somewhat different from those in the House of Representatives. For example, Senate party leaders exert some control over committee assignments, leadership positions, and a large proportion of the floor agenda. Individual senators who wish to accomplish representational or legislative goals through such means as having their proposals debated on the floor, serving on a particular committee, or using dilatory tactics to forestall legislation they consider harmful must enjoy at least a somewhat positive relationship with their party leaders. Being a member of the majority party correlates strongly with individual senators' ability to achieve legislative success (Moore and Thomas 1991), which further demonstrates that majority-party status in the Senate may provide benefits to members similar to those provided by majority-party status in the House of Representatives.

Constituents

In addition to their parties, senators are influenced by their constituents' preferences. While the combination of six years between elections and heterogeneous constituencies means that senators need not see every vote as linked to their next reelection campaign, senators cannot ignore their constituents. For example, Stratmann (2000) finds that senators balance the demands of their political parties with the demands of their constituents. He notes that "legislators alter their party line voting in response to changing constituency preferences" (672) and suggests that when confronted with a choice between pleasing constituents and pleasing their parties, senators put reelection considerations ahead of their parties' wishes and do what their constituents want.

The extent to which constituents and parties vie for senators' attention during legislative decision making may be a function of the extent to which senators perceive their constituents to be informed about their activities in Washington. As Schmidt, Kenny, and Morton (1996) explain in their study of whether voters act to punish senators who depart from their constituents' preferences, "retrospective voting is more successful when voters are more informed" (547). The authors conclude that "voter information improves the efficiency with which the electoral mechanism works" to discipline senators who vote against the wishes of their constituents (564). One way that voters acquire information about the votes cast by members of the Senate is through the annual Senate scorecards produced by dozens of interest groups.

Senators, Interest Groups, and Scorecards

Interest groups are instrumental in facilitating the exchange of information between and among the actors in the legislative decision-making process. Not only do interest groups provide information to senators' constituents, but senators, constituents, and party leaders also rely on interest groups and the scorecards they produce in order to identify publicly salient and/or electorally exploitable votes. The premise of a congressional scorecard is simple: an interest group identifies a list of "key votes" in the House and the Senate, formally takes a position on the issues involved, and then rates each member of the appropriate chamber positively (if the member's vote supported the group's preferred position) or negatively (if the member's vote did not support the group's preferred position). Then the interest group makes its ratings public, theoretically to provide voters with a quick guide to understanding where their members of Congress stand on key issues (Arnold 1990).

Many recipients of the annual ratings scorecards do not realize that interest groups frequently notify members of Congress in advance that they will be including a particular vote on their next ratings list (Keller 1981; Bell 2002; Cochran 2003). Because the groups cannot always be certain what votes will actually occur, they also let members of Congress know which issues they intend to score if a vote occurs. In this way, groups sacrifice their ability to provide an exogenous measure of member behavior in order to increase their ability to influence the outcomes of particular votes. The rewards for voting with a powerful interest group may include forestalling a reelection challenge as well as more substantial electoral support (Arnold 1990), since interest group salience may also increase the probability that senators' roll-call records will be closely scrutinized by powerful political interests and lead to the emergence of a quality electoral challenge (Carson 2005).

While the need to prevent the emergence of quality challengers may be less immediate in the Senate than in the House, senators ignore interest group scorecards at their own peril. Not only do interest groups use their scorecards to make decisions about which candidates to endorse during congressional elections (Veron 1992), but some groups also provide financial support to candidates who score well. For example, some members of Congress have sought to inflate their ratings on the scorecard of the National Federation of Independent Business (NFIB) because the group's political action committee guarantees a campaign contribution to any member receiving at least a 70 percent rating.[4]

As this brief discussion suggests, congressional scorecards are not exogenous measures of members' compatibility with a particular group's favored position, but instead are frequently used to encourage members of Congress to vote in the way the organization prefers. Thus, the scorecards become another of the myriad competing influences that senators must balance as they make their voting decisions. As Schmidt, Kenny, and Morton

(1996) have noted, better-informed voters will be more likely to punish senators for voting wrongly; as a result, interest group scorecards may also create tension for senators when deciding what priority to give to constituents' views that conflict with interest group and/or party preferences.

Data and Methods

The consensus in the literature is that similar sets of factors motivate the voting decisions of senators and House members, even if there is not agreement about the relative weight to assign each factor within senators' decision calculi. Understanding how parties and members balance these conflicting sources of pressure requires us to isolate and analyze situations in which senators' and parties' electoral goals and policy goals are in conflict. We do this by focusing on the interaction between interest groups' scoring decisions and members' roll-call voting behaviors across the two chambers. We are most interested in those instances in which key interest groups and the party want a member to vote in opposite directions, since when the party and the interest groups encourage the member in the same direction, we would expect to see most members comply.

We examine the interaction between interest groups and parties by collecting roll-call voting matrices for the House and Senate for the 102nd–107th Congresses (1991–2002).[5] For each vote, we coded the position taken by the majority of each legislative party and then determined whether the party was rolled on that particular vote. This allowed us to examine the effect of the scorecards on party rolls in the aggregate. To gain additional insights into what factors motivate individual senators to defect from their party's preferred position, we also coded each legislator's votes as either supporting or opposing the position taken by a majority of his or her party.

In addition to these extensive roll-call data, we compiled the roll-call votes and the groups' preferred positions on them that were included on the scorecards of five well-known interest groups: Americans for Democratic Action (ADA), the American Conservative Union (ACU), AFL-CIO, the National Federation of Independent Business (NFIB), and the League of Conservation Voters (LCV). Each of these groups has previously been identified (among others) by *CQ Weekly* as influential congressional vote raters (Cochran 2003; Veron 1992; Keller 1981).[6]

After compiling the scorecard data, we used it to identify those votes that were scored by one or more interest groups during the period of study, as well as each group's preferred outcome on the votes it scored. These data were merged with our roll-call data for the analyses presented below.

Finally, we merged the election-returns history of each of the senators included in our analysis for each of the six congressional elections encompassed by the period of our study. We included these elections data in order to directly test the extent to which electoral considerations affect senators' willingness to defect from their party's preferred voting behavior and to determine the extent to which interest group pressure may interact with electoral vulnerability to accomplish the same.

After generating descriptive statistics to characterize majority-party loss rates under a variety of interest group scoring conditions, we turn to a member-level test of the extent to which interest group scores and electoral vulnerability affect members' voting behaviors and contribute to party rolls in the Senate. To do this, we fit a series of logit models predicting whether a senator voted with the majority of his or her party. We pool the data across majority regimes (the 102nd, 103rd, and most of the 107th Congress for Democrats; the 104th through 106th and part of the 107th Congress for Republicans)[7] and present the results of separate models for majority- and minority-party members.[8] Our key independent variables are a series of indicators for whether the interest groups that are included in the analysis scored the vote and urged a position opposite to that of the majority of the member's party. We also interact these interest group scoring variables with a variable indicating whether the senator was seeking reelection at the end of the current Congress (Brambor, Clark, and Golder 2006). We expect members who are running for reelection to be less likely to want to draw the ire of key interest groups. The models also included a variable to control for the member's revealed preferences using first-dimension DW-NOMINATE coordinates, which range from −1 (liberal) to 1 (conservative) (McCarty, Poole, and Rosenthal 1997). To account for circumstances in which we might expect senators' voting behaviors to be different from their usual patterns, each model includes a dummy variable for final-passage votes and one for cloture votes. Finally, each model includes Congress-specific fixed effects.

Empirical Results

Although we are primarily interested in understanding the individual-level manifestations of cross-pressuring, we turn first to a discussion of the relationship between majority-party losses and the votes that interest groups choose to score across both chambers. As table 4.1 demonstrates, the loss rate for the majority party in the Senate averages 13.9 percent across the entirety of our period of study (1991–2002).[9] This exceeds the loss rate in the House of Representatives during the same period by almost exactly 50 percent—table 4.2 reveals that the House average loss rate is 9.2 percent between the 102nd and 107th Congresses. Nevertheless, despite fewer tools to exert pressure on wayward senators, the majority-party leadership in the Senate is able to secure its preferred outcome more than 85 percent of the time. However, a look at tables 4.1 and 4.2 reveals that when even a single interest group scored a vote, the majority party's loss rate increases to 24.6 percent in the Senate, as compared to 22.6 in the House. When two or more groups scored a vote, the majority party's loss rate increases to more than one time in every three (37.6 percent) in the Senate and 25.8 in the House.

The results reported in tables 4.1 and 4.2 also point out the differences in defeat rates across the two parties. The baseline loss rates for the Democrats and Republicans are similar, but across both chambers we see that Democratic majorities are more likely to lose on scored votes. The loss rate for Senate majority-party Democrats is more than one in four when one interest group was scoring that vote, and it triples, to more than 40 percent, when two or more groups scored a vote. We see similar results for Republican majorities, albeit starting at a lower baseline defeat rate.

The right side of tables 4.1 and 4.2 also breaks down the number and rate of majority-party losses by each group we included in our study. The results demonstrate that regardless of which group was scoring, the majority-party leadership was defeated far more frequently when any of the groups in the study scored a vote than when none did. This suggests that at least for some senators and House members, interest group pressures are associated with defections from the party's preferred position. The aggregate results also demonstrate that party majorities get defeated more frequently when certain groups score votes than when others do. For example, Republican majorities rarely lost on votes scored by the NFIB, which is not surprising given the policy congruence between Republicans and pro-business groups. In contrast, the Senate Democratic Party lost on more than half of the votes scored by the LCV, suggesting that the members of the Democratic caucus are cognizant of the effect of this group on voter preferences. This finding provides provisional support for the notion that cross-pressured members will defect from their party's preferred position. Taken as a whole, the results in tables 4.1 and 4.2 provide some support for our hypothesis that interest group scoring activities can be instrumental in majority-party losses in both chambers.

While the results presented in these two tables are instructive and demonstrate a macro-level association between roll-call outcomes and interest group scoring decisions, we are more interested in determining the effect

TABLE 4.1. Senate majority-party losses and interest group scorecard activities, 102nd–107th Congresses (1991–2002)

Majority party	Congress	Majority-party losses (rate), by number of groups scoring a vote					Majority-party losses (rate) on scored votes by interest group				
		Congress average	0	1	2	3+	ADA	ACU	AFL-CIO	LCV	NFIB
Democrat	**102nd–103rd, 107th**	**273/1738 (15.71)**	**184/1444 (12.74)**	**60/219 (27.40)**	**22/53 (41.51)**	**7/22 (31.82)**	**35/107 (32.71)**	**31/124 (25.00)**	**18/66 (27.27)**	**32/62 (51.61)**	**11/36 (30.56)**
	102nd (1991–92)	100/550 (18.18)	65/452 (14.38)	25/67 (37.31)	7/21 (33.33)	3/10 (30.00)	15/40 (37.50)	12/43 (27.91)	7/25 (28.00)	12/19 (63.16)	2/14 (14.29)
	103rd (1993–94)	93/724 (12.85)	66/607 (10.87)	20/99 (20.20)	5/12 (41.67)	2/6 (33.33)	11/40 (27.50)	5/48 (10.42)	5/18 (27.78)	8/21 (38.10)	7/16 (43.75)
	107th (Fall 2001–2002)	80/464 (17.24)	53/385 (13.77)	15/53 (28.30)	10/20 (50.00)	2/6 (33.33)	9/27 (33.33)	14/33 (42.42)	6/23 (26.09)	12/22 (54.55)	2/6 (33.33)
Republican	**104th–107th**	**299/2372 (12.61)**	**260/2028 (12.82)**	**58/260 (22.31)**	**22/64 (34.38)**	**2/18 (11.11)**	**31/133 (23.31)**	**39/132 (29.55)**	**11/57 (19.30)**	**9/59 (15.25)**	**7/49 (14.29)**
	104th (1995–96)	100/919 (10.88)	77/809 (9.52)	16/90 (17.78)	6/14 (42.86)	1/6 (16.67)	10/40 (25.00)	7/27 (25.93)	6/19 (31.58)	5/27 (18.52)	4/26 (15.38)
	105th (1997–98)	94/612 (15.36)	66/512 (12.89)	21/68 (30.88)	7/25 (28.00)	0/5	9/40 (22.50)	17/48 (35.42)	2/15 (13.33)	2/14 (14.29)	1/9 (11.11)
	106th (1999–2000)	67/672 (9.97)	48/564 (8.51)	12/82 (14.63)	7/22 (31.82)	0/4	7/40 (17.50)	11/46 (23.91)	2/17 (11.76)	1/16 (6.25)	0/12
	107th (2001)	38/169 (22.49)	29/143 (20.28)	7/20 (35.00)	1/3 (33.33)	1/3 (33.33)	5/13 (38.46)	4/11 (36.36)	1/6 (16.67)	1/2 (50.00)	2/2 (100.00)
102nd–107th Congresses		**572/4110 (13.92)**	**444/3472 (12.79)**	**118/479 (24.63)**	**44/117 (37.61)**	**9/40 (22.50)**	**66/240 (27.50)**	**70/256 (27.34)**	**29/123 (23.58)**	**41/121 (33.88)**	**18/85 (21.18)**

Note: ADA = Americans for Democratic Action; ACU = American Conservative Union; LCV = League of Conservation Voters; NFIB = National Federation of Independent Business.

TABLE 4.2. House majority-party losses and interest group scorecard activities, 102nd–107th Congresses (1991–2002)

| Majority party | Congress | Congress average | Majority-party losses (rate), by number of groups scoring a vote | | | | Majority-party losses (rate) on scored votes, by interest group | | | | |
			0	1	2	3	ADA	AFL-CIO	LCV	NFIB	NRLC
Democrat	102nd–103rd	189/1,995 (9.47)	145/1846 (7.85)	38/123 (30.89)	6/17 (35.29)	0/9 —	29/80 (36.25)	5/53 (9.43)	12/40 (30.00)	4/21 (19.05)	—
	102nd (1991–92)	83/901 (9.21)	64/830 (7.71)	15/57 (26.32)	4/10 (40.00)	0/4 —	13/40 (32.50)	3/23 (13.04)	4/15 (26.67)	3/11 (27.27)	—
	103rd (1993–94)	106/1,094 (9.69)	81/1016 (7.97)	23/66 (34.85)	2/7 (28.57)	0/5 —	16/40 (40.00)	2/20 (10.00)	8/25 (32.00)	1/10 (10.00)	—
Republican	104th–107th	427/4,686 (9.11)	354/4317 (8.20)	54/285 (18.95)	17/72 (23.61)	2/12 (16.67)	32/160 (20.00)	22/73 (30.14)	26/93 (27.96)	7/85 (8.24)	7/49 (14.29)
	104th (1995–96)	110 (8.33)	92/1219 (7.55)	15/82 (18.29)	3/18 (16.67)	0/2 —	5/40 (12.50)	5/24 (20.83)	8/24 (33.33)	3/36 (8.33)	—
	105th (1997–98)	123 (10.55)	100/1071 (9.34)	17/73 (23.29)	6/20 (30.00)	0/2 —	11/40 (27.50)	9/18 (50.0)	6/27 (22.22)	0/14 (0.00)	3/20 (15.00)
	106th (1999–2000)	133 (11.00)	114/1112 (10.25)	10/71 (14.08)	7/21 (33.33)	2/5 (40.00)	11/40 (27.50)	6/19 (31.58)	7/28 (25.00)	3/21 (14.29)	3/20 (15.00)
	107th (2001–2)	61 (6.16)	48/915 (5.25)	12/59 (20.34)	1/13 (7.69)	0/3 —	5/40 (12.50)	2/12 (16.67)	5/14 (35.71)	1/14 (7.14)	1/14 (7.14)
	102nd–107th Congresses	616 (9.22)	499/6163 (8.10)	92/408 (22.55)	23/89 (25.84)	2/21 (9.52)	61/240 (25.42)	27/126 (21.43)	38/133 (28.56)	11/106 (10.38)	7/49 (14.29)

Note: ADA = Americans for Democratic Action; LCV = League of Conservation Voters; NFIB = National Federation of Independent Business; NRLC = National Right to Life Committee.

of interest group scoring decisions on senators' voting behaviors at the individual level. Thus, we turn now to a discussion of our logit models, the results of which are presented in table 4.3. As we would expect, a member's ideological orientation is a significant predictor of party defections across majority-control regimes. Liberal Democrats are less likely to defect from the party position than are their more moderate counterparts; likewise, moderate Republicans defect more often than do conservative Republicans. However, we do find that the effect of ideological predisposition on party defections is more pronounced for minority-party members. This result is not surprising, as it comports with the finding of Lawrence, Maltzman, and Smith (2006) that the "win rate" for majority-party members is relatively constant, while minority-party win rates closely track with member ideology. This suggests that the majority party's agenda-control mechanisms do manifest themselves in vote outcomes.

Upon examination of the estimates of the effect of interest group scoring decisions, it is clear that all five groups included in our study do appear to have an independent impact on senators' roll-call voting behavior.[10] A contrary signal by any of the liberal-leaning interest groups in our study is associated with an increased probability of defection from the party position for Senate Democrats, while pressure from the ACU or NFIB is associated with an increased probability of support for the party position for these senators. These effects are consistent across groups and occur regardless of whether the Democrats hold majority status in the chamber. We see a similar effect of interest group scoring decisions on Senate Republicans. The ACU stands out in this regard as being strongly associated with defeats of the Republican Party leadership, while the Republican Party is more united on votes scored by the ADA and AFL-CIO. Since the ADA and ACU do not regularly provide advance notice of which votes they will score, we believe this is likely an artifact of their vote-selection processes.[11]

The results in table 4.3 reveal little support for the idea that senators running for reelection are more susceptible to interest group scoring decisions. With Democratic majorities, we find a statistically significant inverse effect only for scoring decisions by the ACU. This means that Democrats seeking reelection were less likely to defect from Democratic majority-party leaders on votes that the ACU included on its scorecards. However, this may be the result of the group's choosing to include votes on its scorecards that it believed would make Democrats standing for reelection appear to be very closely aligned with the party leadership. Thus, we find little evidence that interest group scoring decisions interact with senators' reelection considerations as senators decide whether or not to defect from their parties'

TABLE 4.3. Interest group scoring and party defection in the Senate, 1991–2002

	Democratic majority		Republican majority	
	Democrats	Republicans	Democrats	Republicans
DW-NOMINATE	−2.03*	1.37*	−2.88*	2.03*
(1st dimension)	(0.06)	(0.05)	(0.06)	(0.04)
ADA	−0.95*	0.03	−0.83*	0.38*
	(0.11)	(0.05)	(0.14)	(0.05)
ACU	0.26*	−0.63*	0.41*	−0.87*
	(0.04)	(0.12)	(0.05)	(0.07)
AFL-CIO	−0.14	0.18*	−0.46*	0.18*
	(0.17)	(0.06)	(0.13)	(0.07)
LCV	−1.23*	0.09	−1.47*	−0.09
	(0.13)	(0.06)	(0.24)	(0.06)
NFIB	0.21*	0.40	−0.11	—
	(0.08)	(0.27)	(0.08)	
Running for reelection	0.10*	0.17*	−0.06*	0.39*
	(0.03)	(0.02)	(0.03)	(0.03)
ADA × Reelection	0.16	−0.14	0.17	0.05
	(0.23)	(0.09)	(0.31)	(0.11)
ACU × Reelection	−0.19*	0.37	0.05	−0.03
	(0.09)	(0.27)	(0.11)	(0.15)
AFL-CIO × Reelection	−0.18	−0.19	0.005	−0.005
	(0.35)	(0.12)	(0.29)	(0.16)
LCV × Reelection	−0.03	0.002	−1.03*	0.09
	(0.26)	(0.12)	(0.54)	(0.13)
NFIB × Reelection	−0.23	0.47	0.25	—
	(0.16)	(0.67)	(0.20)	
Vote Margin	0.02*	0.007*	0.004*	0.006*
	(0.003)	(0.003)	(0.002)	(0.0002)
Final Passage	0.32*	−0.14*	0.14	0.12*
	(0.03)	(0.02)	(0.03)	(0.03)
Cloture	0.55*	0.13*	0.35*	0.40*
	(0.04)	(0.04)	(0.04)	(0.04)
103rd Congress	0.37*	−0.15*	—	—
	(0.03)	(0.03)		
105th Congress	—	—	0.07	−0.40*
			(0.04)	(0.04)
106th Congress	—	—	0.30*	−0.23*
			(0.04)	(0.03)
107th Congress	0.40*	0.19*	0.45*	0.40*
	(0.02)	(0.02)	(0.04)	(0.04)
Constant	0.19*	0.71*	0.43*	0.86*
	(0.03)	(0.02)	(0.03)	(0.02)
Pseudo-R^2	0.06	0.03	0.03	0.04
Log likelihood	−40048.99	−36040.02	−45475.9	−49042.8
Number of cases	95904	78792	110845	130287

Note: ADA = Americans for Democratic Action; ACU = American Conservative Union; LCV = League of Conservation Voters; NFIB = National Federation of Independent Business.

*$p \leq .05$

preferred position. This skepticism is bolstered by our finding no evidence that Republicans seeking reelection were more likely to defect from the party position than other Republicans. These results conflict with our previous findings for members of the House of Representatives (Bell and Roberts 2005). However, the length of senators' terms and the heterogeneous nature of their constituencies may mitigate the effectiveness of any single interest group in providing senators incentives to defect from their parties' preferred positions during their reelection bids. Moreover, with statewide constituencies, senators may actually prefer to seek the protection of their parties when casting salient roll-call votes, since they may be less likely to be known to a large number of their constituents beyond the "brand name" that their party label provides (Cox and McCubbins 2005). Additional analysis on this point might help to explain the differences between House and Senate members with regard to the effect of reelection, but such additional analysis exceeds the scope of the present study.

While the results in table 4.3 demonstrate a consistent statistical relationship between interest group scoring decisions and members' roll-call behavior, they do not demonstrate that these effects are substantively significant. Given the large number of votes included in each model and the difficulty of directly interpreting logit coefficients, we present our results in probabilistic form in table 4.4. Cell entries represent the probability that a scoring decision would lead to a member's defecting from his or her party for all groups and parties in our sample.[12]

The first row of table 4.4 reports baseline defection rates on votes that are not scored by any groups for a member who is not seeking reelection and who has a DW-NOMINATE coordinate at his or her party's average. Looking at the column for Democrats serving under a Democratic majority, we see that interest group scoring decisions have a large substantive impact on their defection rate. On votes scored by the ADA, the average defection rate increases to 34.4 percent from the baseline of 16.7 percent. However, this increase in defection is likely the result of the controversial nature of the votes the ADA typically selects for inclusion on its scorecard and not a result of members' defecting in order to appease the group. When we consider situations in which the groups do provide prior notification that a vote is important to them, we find that members' defection rates increase considerably. For example, LCV scoring decisions almost triple the baseline defection rate, to 40.6 percent. The results in the first column of table 4.4 strongly suggest that the LCV was quite effective at getting majority-party members to vote in its preferred direction, even in the face of opposition by the party leadership.

TABLE 4.4. Effect of interest group scoring on party defection in the Senate, 1991–2002

	Democratic majority		Republican majority	
	Democrats	Republicans	Democrats	Republicans
Baseline	.167	.183	.149	.130
	(.164–.170)	(.179–.187)	(.147–.152)	(.128–.132)
ADA	.344	.178	.289	.092
	(.298–.394)	(.166–.191)	(.232–.351)	(.085–.099)
ACU	.135	.296	.104	.262
	(.126–.145)	(.248–.349)	(.095–.114)	(.237–.288)
AFL-CIO	.190	.158	.217	.110
	(.139–.252)	(.143–.175)	(.173–.265)	(.097–.124)
LCV	.406	.171	.436	.140
	(.348–.467)	(.155–.188)	(.335–.553)	(.128–.154)
NFIB	.141	.133	.164	—
	(.122–.160)	(.080–.202)	(.144–.185)	
Running for reelection	.154	.159	.158	.092
	(.148–.161)	(.153–.166)	(.151–.165)	(.087–.096)
ADA × Reelection	.287	.173	.272	.062
	(.210–.372)	(.151–.197)	(.177–.389)	(.052–.074)
ACU × Reelection	.147	.201	.105	.200
	(.130–.165)	(.134–.281)	(.087–.123)	(.161–.246)
AFL-CIO × Reelection	.203	.162	.230	.078
	(.117–.309)	(.136–.192)	(.150–.330)	(.059–.103)
LCV × Reelection	.395	.148	.684	.093
	(.293–.503)	(.124–.177)	(.478–.853)	(.074–.113)
NFIB × Reelection	.158	.086	.141	—
	(.124–.196)	(.024–.220)	(.102–.186)	

Note: ADA = Americans for Democratic Action; ACU = American Conservative Union; LCV = League of Conservation Voters; NFIB = National Federation of Independent Business.

Turning to the era of Republican majorities, we still see that interest group scoring decisions can induce party defection, but the effect is much less pronounced for Republicans serving in the majority. The only group that has a substantive effect on the voting behavior of Senate Republicans during the period of study is the ACU. On votes that the ACU scores in opposition to the Republican Party's position, the defection rate for majority-party members doubles, from 13 percent to just over 26 percent. Given the narrow size of Republican majorities, even modest increases in defection rates can lead to party defeats, as was demonstrated in table 4.1. In addition, Republicans seeking reelection appear to be particularly responsive to ACU influence, as their defection rate doubles when the group scores a vote, from less than 10 percent on average to 20 percent. As we noted above, the ACU rarely announces the votes it will score in advance, so this finding is likely an artifact of the vote-selection process. Overall, the data in table 4.3 demonstrate that the Republican Party leadership has been more successful at preventing defections than were their Democratic predecessors. This is consistent with recent popular and scholarly accounts of the Republican Party as expecting and enforcing greater levels of party discipline (see, e.g., Evans and Oleszek 1997; and Fleisher and Bond 2004).

As the preceding results demonstrate, interest group scorecard activities affect both aggregate party success rates and individual members' decisions about whether to support the positions that their parties prefer. Although these effects vary somewhat by party, with Democratic majorities seemingly more susceptible to the influences of the groups' scorecards at both the party and individual levels, our results demonstrate that both the Republican and Democratic parties lose more frequently on votes that are scored by one or more of the groups included in this study.

Conclusion

In this chapter, we have attempted to integrate disparate bodies of literature on legislative decision making, on the role of political parties in Congress, and on the activities of interest groups in order to provide a unified analysis of how senators balance policy and electoral goals when making voting decisions. Although congressional scholars have long known that members of Congress have conflicting goals and are frequently cross-pressured, few previous studies have offered the kind of test of the relative weight senators attribute to these competing influences that we conduct in this analysis. Moreover, most previous studies of the voting behaviors of members of Congress have focused exclusively on the House of Representatives, as senators are thought to be less susceptible to cross pressures from their party leaders, constituents, and interest groups.

This analysis has demonstrated, first, that extant theories of partisanship and voting behavior that previously have been applied to the House can be applied to the Senate as well. Our aggregate results demonstrate that Senate party leaders lose less than 14 percent of the time, only slightly more frequently in substantive terms than the loss rate for party leaders in the House of Representatives, even though House leaders appear to possess far stronger tools of party discipline than do their Senate counterparts. This finding suggests that, contrary to the conventional wisdom about the Senate—but consistent with the themes of this volume—it is a chamber within which party leaders are able to secure their preferred results in the vast majority of cases (Campbell, Cox, and McCubbins 2002). Relatedly, our failure to demonstrate that senators facing reelection are more likely to defect from the party's preferred position when the groups in our study are scoring the vote indicates that senators may be less susceptible to—or less likely to succumb to—cross pressures than are their counterparts in the House of Representatives.

Our results indicate some support for the notion that when senators find themselves at odds with either their congressional party leaders or powerful interest groups, they may be willing to defect from their party in favor of the groups' preferences. The magnitude of the changes we identify in the predicted probabilities of voting with the party on votes that are scored by some interest groups—particularly the League of Conservation Voters—demonstrates the potential for cross-pressured senators, whether Republican or Democrat, to sacrifice party loyalty when they perceive constituency or policy benefits from doing so.

This finding has implications for theories of how parties influence individual members. As we have noted, interest group scorecards are not truly exogenous measures of the voting behavior of members of Congress. Instead, they are carefully constructed tools of political influence designed to promote the groups' agendas beyond the goals of the political parties or individual members. To the extent that senators, like their counterparts in the House of Representatives (Bell and Roberts 2005), are willing to abandon their parties for the sake of promoting groups' preferred outcomes, congressional majority parties will be unable to use the powers associated with their status in the chamber to enforce party discipline or to foster more responsible party governance.

Notes

1. For our purposes, a loss is a vote in which a majority of the majority party votes on the losing side. One could use the positions of the majority leader and majority whip to determine the party's position; however, we use the majority of the majority in order to conform with the extant literature (Cox and McCubbins 2005) and because there are instances in which the two party leaders do not vote in the same direction.

2. Note that we use all non-unanimous votes in making this determination, while some scholars use only votes on final passage. See Krehbiel and Woon (2005) for a discussion of vote types and inferential error.

3. Although the December 21, 2005, vote came as a result of a series of compromises designed to end a Democratic filibuster of the must-pass Department of Defense appropriations bill, and retaliatory tactics by Senate president pro tempore Ted Stevens

(R-AK), if the vote had been carefully orchestrated by the Republican leadership for the sole purpose of ending the dilatory tactics, we would not have expected to see seven Republican senators shift their positions on the question, since the provision could have been removed from the defense-appropriations measure had three Republican "no" voters simply abstained from the December vote.

4. See the 2004 fundraising solicitation of the NFIB's Leadership Trust PAC, at http://www.nfib.com/PDFs/politics/NFIB_LT.pdf. For discussions of how members of Congress seek campaign contributions from the groups that rate them, see Arnold (1990); and Keller (1981).

5. Roll-call data are available at http://www.pooleandrosenthal.com. We extend our thanks to Keith T. Poole for providing and maintaining this resource.

6. In addition to these organizations, we attempted to collect data from other groups previously identified as influential by *CQ Weekly*, including the National Rifle Association, the Christian Coalition, and the United States Chamber of Commerce. However, these groups refused to make their scorecard data available to us, or would not provide historical data, expressing concern about making such information available for academic research purposes. It is also worth noting that the ADA and ACU are broad ideological groups and not focused on a single interest. Excluding them from our analysis does not change any of our substantive findings.

7. The Republican Party was considered the majority party for the first 169 votes of the 107th Senate. As part of the power-sharing agreement worked out between the two party leaders, the Republican Party held the post of majority leader, and one of its members chaired each standing committee despite the 50–50 party division in the chamber. Following the switch of James Jeffords (VT) from the Republican Party to independent status, the Democratic Party assumed the mantle of majority party. Given that Jeffords caucused with the Democratic Party after departing the Republican Party, we treat him as a Democrat for the remainder of the 107th Congress.

8. The results are substantively the same if we fit separate models for each Congress, so the results are pooled for parsimony. Congress-by-Congress results are available upon request.

9. If we exclude votes that were not scored by groups in our study, the roll rate drops to 12.79 percent.

10. A joint F-test reveals that they are jointly different than zero.

11. As Cox and McCubbins (1993) point out, the effect of the ADA's scoring mechanism during Democratic regimes was to downplay divisions within the Republican Party. ADA uses its scorecards to promote its friends and punish its enemies, and it did this during the 102nd and 103rd Congresses by selecting votes that allowed Democrats to receive the lion's share of the group's high scores (Cox and McCubbins 1993, 62–67). We find it unlikely that the ADA and the new Republican leadership, after the Republicans gained control of both chambers of Congress in 1995, found many areas of policy agreement. This fact, coupled with the highly cohesive nature of the Republican majority since 1995, likely led the ADA to select votes that promoted its Democrat friends' records while keeping the scores for Republicans low. The

statistical effect of this is to give the impression that party voting increases among Republicans as a result of a vote's appearing on the ADA scorecard, which would be anachronistic, given that the ADA selects the votes for inclusion only at the end of each session.

12. Predicted probabilities were generated using CLARIFY for Stata (King, Tomz, and Wittenberg 2000).

PART II

5

The Senate Whip System:
An Exploration

ERIN M. BRADBURY, RYAN A. DAVIDSON,
AND C. LAWRENCE EVANS

This chapter explores an understudied feature of decision making in the U.S. Senate with novel data gathered from the personal papers of former Senate leaders. Our goal is to shed new light on the role played by party leaders in the Senate legislative process and to contribute to ongoing scholarly controversies about the nature and extent of party influence on Capitol Hill. As part of a broader research program, we have gathered extensive archival records pertaining to the internal workings of the Democratic and Republican whip operations in the Senate. Included are records of more than two dozen "whip counts" conducted by the Senate Democratic majority during 1989, the first session of the 101st Congress.

A whip count is a private poll conducted by congressional party leaders prior to major floor votes in which rank-and-file members of the relevant party are asked about their views on the pending matter. Typically, member positions are categorized as "yes," "leaning yes," "undecided," "leaning no," "no," or nonresponsive on the item being polled. In conjunction with other archival materials, media accounts, and the roll-call record, these data enable us to address a number of significant questions about party leadership in the Senate. How many and what kinds of issues are singled out for leadership pressure? What is the size of the leadership's base of support as major floor decisions near? How successful are Senate leaders at retaining the support of potential defectors?

The analysis that follows is structured around six sections. The first provides background about scholarly perspectives on party power, with an emphasis on the Senate. In the second section, we summarize the evolving role of party whips in the chamber and make the case that evidence from the late 1980s, although somewhat "time-bound," is still useful for examining leadership strategies and party influence. Next, we explore the kinds of measures that draw majority whip activity in the Senate. We then proceed to analyze how members respond to whip counts, and the relationship between whip-count positions and roll-call behavior. The impact of leadership strategies on the fate of legislation is then considered. We conclude by summarizing our findings and possible directions for future research.

Background

By all accounts, there has been a substantial increase in partisan behavior in Congress since the 1970s. In the majority-rule-oriented House, the incidence of party unity votes has increased from just 28.9 percent in 1969–70 to 53.2 percent in 1989–90 to almost 70 percent during the 104th Congress (1995–96).[1] Although the Senate traditionally has been viewed as less partisan than the House, partisan behavior has also increased markedly in that chamber. During 1969–70, 34.5 percent of Senate roll calls were party unity votes. By 1989–90, the percentage had grown to 44.8, and during the mid-1990s almost two-thirds of Senate roll calls divided Republicans from Democrats. This heightened partisanship has been interpreted by many observers as evidence of a more active and influential party leadership in Congress. Rohde (1991), Aldrich (1995b), Sinclair (1995), and Cox and McCubbins (1993, 2005) have produced landmark studies arguing that party leaders in the House exert a significant and pervasive impact on decision making.

But what about the Senate? Can theories and generalizations about the congressional parties be extended to that chamber? Research about party influence in the House tends to emphasize the procedural powers of formal leaders. The Speaker exercises effective control over the Rules Committee and through it manages access to the floor agenda. The standing rules of the chamber generally require that all amendments be germane to the underlying measure, restricting the ability of the minority party to "change the subject" and secure floor action on its priorities. The "motion on the previous question" provides the House leadership with the procedural leverage necessary to bring debates to a close. In the Senate, however, the leaders of the majority party lack all of these procedural advantages. Since the 1930s, the Senate majority leader has had the privilege of first recognition on the floor, but preferential recognition rights are no substitute for the impressive agenda prerogatives granted to House majorities (Evans and Oleszek 2000).

Still, a number of studies suggest that, under the right conditions, Senate leaders may have the procedural, informational, and public relations resources necessary to make a difference in the legislative process. In her chapter in this volume, for example, Kathryn Pearson marshals considerable evidence that the ability of Senate leaders to use internal resources to promote party discipline has increased in recent decades. Snyder and Groseclose (2000) use lopsided votes to develop a measure of member preferences free of leadership influence (leaders are unlikely to exert pressure when outcomes are not in doubt, they argue) and find that party influence is significant in both chambers over the 1871–1998 period. Campbell, Cox, and McCubbins (2002) show that Senate majority parties are seldom "rolled" on the floor, while partisan minorities in the chamber often find themselves on the losing end of floor votes. The implication is that majority-party leaders in the Senate may have enough procedural leverage to keep issues that would divide their caucus off the floor. Along those lines, in their chapter in this volume, Chris Den Hartog and Nathan Monroe demonstrate that the majority leadership can use the "motion to table" to keep unwanted amendments off the Senate floor, thereby exercising a loose form of agenda control. Lawrence, Maltzman, and Smith (2005) examine roll rates at the individual level (how often individual legislators are on the winning and losing side of roll calls) and likewise find evidence of party effects in the Senate. These effects were evident during the nineteenth century, however—well before the emergence of centralized party leaders in the chamber. As a result, Lawrence and his colleagues conclude that party influence in the Senate probably does not derive *primarily* from leadership agenda prerogatives. More generally, Krehbiel (2002, 2007) has argued that none of the leading vote-based indicators of member preferences are sufficient for disentangling the effects of parties and preferences in either chamber.

The whip system, we believe, provides a useful window for examining the impact of party leaders in the days and weeks prior to major floor actions. Data pertaining to whip counts can help researchers look beyond the roll-call record and isolate the mechanisms through which party leaders exert influence on other members. This article is part of a broader project that uses the records of more than 750 whip counts conducted by House and Senate leaders from 1955 to 1993 to examine how member positions and preferences develop on significant legislative matters.[2]

Whip Operations in the Senate

The whip process typically begins with a request from the majority or minority leader for a count of the leanings of rank-and-file legislators on a matter that has been placed (or soon will be placed) on the floor calendar. The party whip then communicates the request to members of the extended whip system for the party. In 1989–90, for instance, Alan Cranston (CA) served as the Senate Democratic whip, and Alan Dixon (IL) was Cranston's chief deputy.[3] Members of the Senate Democratic Caucus were divided into four regional groups for the purposes of conducting nose counts (West, South, Midwest, and East), and each group was headed by an elected deputy whip (Timothy Wirth, CO; Bob Graham, FL; Tom Harkin, IA; and Patrick Leahy, VT, respectively). The four regional groups were each divided into two zones, one led by the relevant deputy whip and the other by an assistant deputy whip (Brock Adams, WA, in the West; Charles Robb, VA, in the South; Thomas Daschle, SD, in the Midwest; and Barbara Mikulski, MD, in the East). The zones ranged in size from five to eight members and were organized along geographic lines. The deputy and assistant deputy whips are selected by the Democratic senators from the relevant states. The whip and chief deputy whip are chosen by the full Democratic Caucus at the beginning of each Congress.

In the Senate, the role of party whip dates to 1913, when Democrats created the position to help their floor leader monitor attendance in the full chamber.[4] Republicans followed suit two years later. The structure of the whip system has changed over time. Democrats, for instance, relied on just four deputy whips during the 1960s and 1970s until the number was increased to nine after Cranston became whip in 1977. During the tenure of his successor, Wendell Ford (KY), the number of deputies was cut in half. Over the past three decades, the number of GOP deputy whips has varied from zero to fifteen, depending on the operating style of the Republican floor leader.

The duties performed by the party whips typically include some combination of the following:

- poll members on their preferences prior to major floor votes;
- persuade wavering or opposing party members to stay loyal to the party position;
- provide members with policy information about legislative matters;
- communicate to rank-and-file legislators about the floor schedule;
- work with the floor leader to formulate and implement party strategies;
- stand in for the floor leader when this individual cannot be on the floor;
- act as a party spokesperson; and
- manage and run regular meetings of the extended whip system.

As Democratic whip, Cranston was widely recognized for his abilities as a vote counter. In 1977, Majority Leader Robert Byrd (D-WV) described the Californian as "the best nose-counter in the Senate, he is absolutely superb when it comes to knowing how the votes will fall in place on a given issue."[5] Cranston emphasized that the job "isn't just counting votes, it's figuring out how to influence the outcome by finding out what Senator could go one way or the other" on a pending matter.[6] In both parties, the deputy whips also play an important role in coalition building.

At the beginning of a whip count, the whip's office often produces an issue summary featuring the specific questions being polled and a synopsis of the arguments for the party position. The left panel of figure 5.1 is a copy of a May 1989 issue summary for a major child-care measure, including three questions for the whip count.[7] The nose-counting process starts when the deputy whips contact the half dozen or so members of their zones, asking for feedback about their positions. The deputies report the results back to the main whip's office, either directly or through staff. The internal operations of the Senate whip process are much less formal and routinized than is the case on the House side. In the House, zone or regional whips usually are responsible for tracking the preferences of a dozen or more members. Initial positions are tabulated on zone sheets or cards that are sent to the whip's office. Staff to the House whip transfer the information on the zone tallies to computerized lists that are regularly updated as roll calls near, often multiple times per hour (Evans 2004). The whip process is more fluid in the Senate, because of the smaller membership, greater emphasis placed on personal relationships, and far less predictable floor agenda. Often, initial responses on a count are communicated via a brief note or conversation. The right panel of figure 5.1, for example, contains a note that Cranston scratched to his top aide, Ron Greenaway, reporting on an exchange with Tom Harkin (then deputy whip for the Midwest region) about the preferences of three members on the three polled questions for the child-care bill. In the note, a "+" indicates a response in favor of the leadership position and a "?" means undecided. Still, party whips in the Senate do attempt to make the polling process as systematic as possible. Time permitting, they use zone sheets and caucus tallies. The left panel of figure 5.2 is a 1989 zone sheet from Brock Adams (an assistant deputy whip in the Western region) denoting the positions of five members on the child-care counts. Cranston's office tabulated the results from the deputy whips on a caucus tally sheet included in the right panel of figure 5.2.

Interestingly, the Republican whip's office was not responsible for conducting nose counts during the 1980s. Often, GOP leaders were willing to defer to the legislative liaison operations of the Reagan and Bush

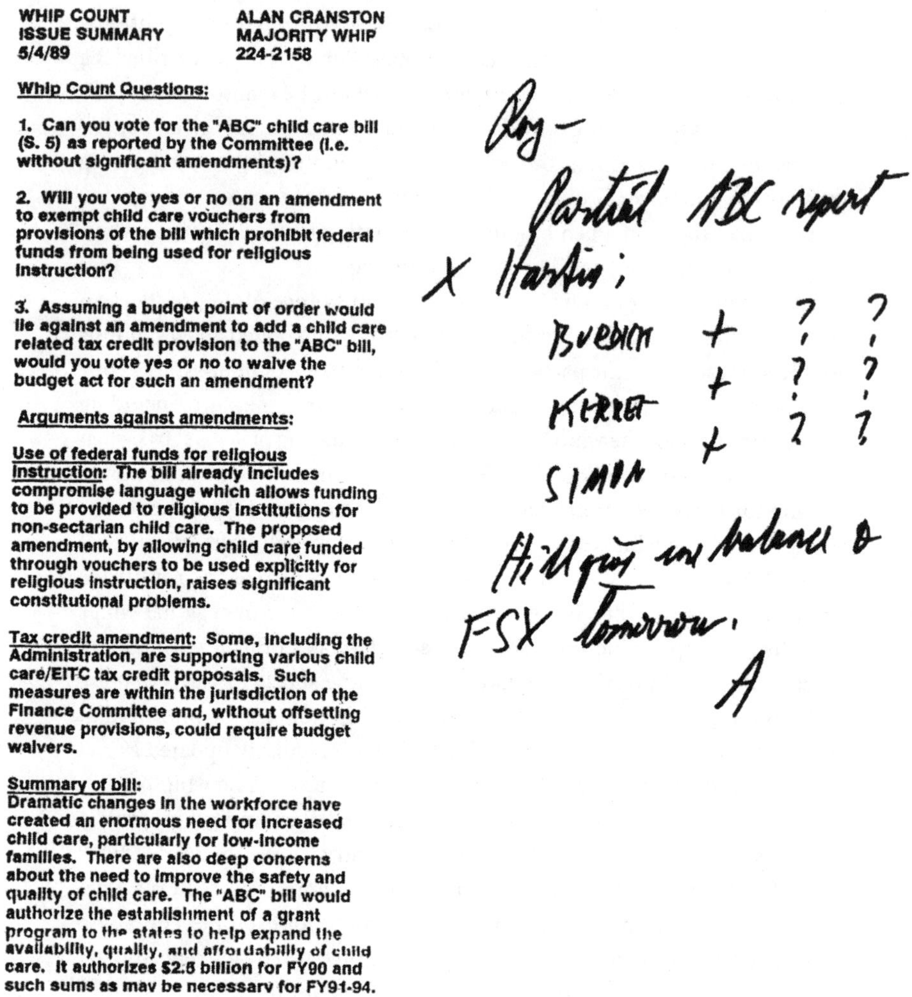

WHIP COUNT   ALAN CRANSTON
ISSUE SUMMARY   MAJORITY WHIP
5/4/89   224-2158

Whip Count Questions:

1. Can you vote for the "ABC" child care bill
(S. 5) as reported by the Committee (i.e.
without significant amendments)?

2. Will you vote yes or no on an amendment
to exempt child care vouchers from
provisions of the bill which prohibit federal
funds from being used for religious
instruction?

3. Assuming a budget point of order would
lie against an amendment to add a child care
related tax credit provision to the "ABC" bill,
would you vote yes or no to waive the
budget act for such an amendment?

Arguments against amendments:

**Use of federal funds for religious
instruction:** The bill already includes
compromise language which allows funding
to be provided to religious institutions for
non-sectarian child care. The propposed
amendment, by allowing child care funded
through vouchers to be used explicitly for
religious instruction, raises significant
constitutional problems.

Tax credit amendment: Some, including the
Administration, are supporting various child
care/EITC tax credit proposals. Such
measures are within the jurisdiction of the
Finance Committee and, without offsetting
revenue provisions, could require budget
waivers.

Summary of bill:
Dramatic changes in the workforce have
created an enormous need for increased
child care, particularly for low-income
families. There are also deep concerns
about the need to improve the safety and
quality of child care. The "ABC" bill would
authorize the establishment of a grant
program to the states to help expand the
availability, quality, and affordability of child
care. It authorizes $2.5 billion for FY90 and
such sums as may be necessary for FY91-94.

Fig. 5.1: Issue summary and partial zone returns, child-care bill, May 1989 (Courtesy of
The Bancroft Library, University of California, Berkeley)

administrations, as well as Republican committee leaders, for intelligence
about member preferences. The internal polling that was conducted by
Senate Republicans during this period was managed by Howard Greene,
a longtime senior aide to the Republican Conference. Greene would sit in
the cloakroom and speak to members personally about their positions on
upcoming roll calls. From various memoranda and notes in the personal
papers of Alan Simpson (WY), Senate GOP whip from 1985 to 1994, it is
apparent that Simpson considered asking for the responsibility for con-

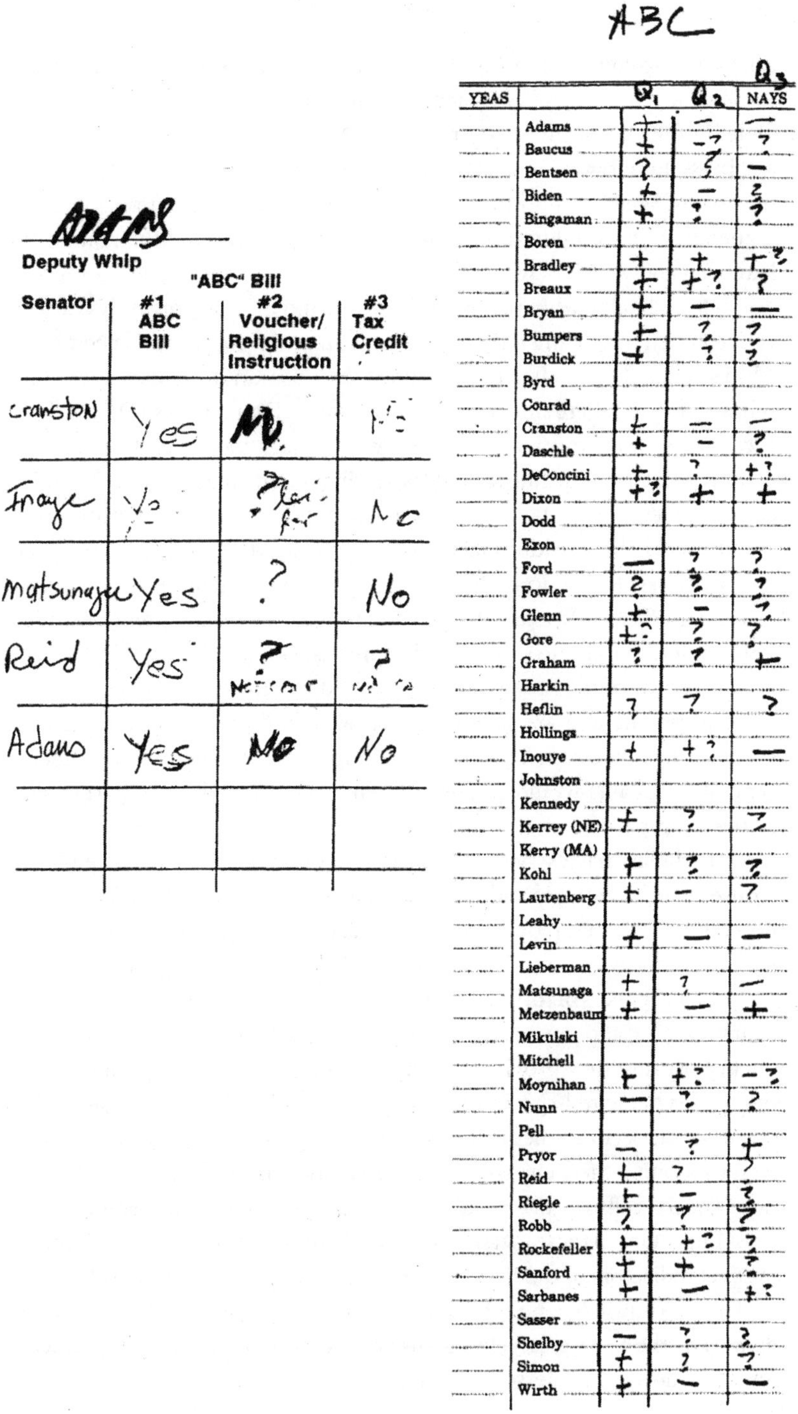

Fig. 5.2: Zone and tally sheets, child-care bill, May 1989 (Courtesy of The Bancroft Library, University of California, Berkeley).

ducting nose counts after his election as whip.[8] However, Simpson chose to defer to Greene and (implicitly) to incoming majority leader Robert Dole on the matter. In 1994, Trent Lott (MS), who had previously served as House Republican whip (from 1981 to 1988), challenged Simpson for the post of Senate Republican whip. During the leadership campaign, Lott argued that he would be a more active and aggressive whip than Simpson had been and would play a more significant role in nose counts.[9] Simpson was defeated in the whip race by the younger and more aggressively conservative Lott. The responsibility for conducting nose counts returned to the whip's office shortly after Lott assumed the position in January 1995, and it has remained there under Lott's successors—Don Nickles (OK), Mitch McConnell (KY), and again (beginning in January 2007) Trent Lott.

According to a top aide to Nickles, during the late 1990s Senate Republicans conducted about two dozen formal counts per year. More impromptu counts were held on additional matters. Typically, the leadership knew that only five or six Republicans would be "in play" on an issue and would contact those offices informally for information about voting intentions. The staffer referred to these abbreviated counts as "bobtails."[10]

The results of the nose counts conducted by House and Senate leaders are kept private and are seldom shared with individuals outside the relevant leadership circle. The reasons are obvious. Making the intelligence generally available would create disincentives for members to participate in the whip process and to accurately report their views. Over the years, several scholars have served as "participant-observers" in the office of the House Democratic whip and produced noteworthy studies of partisan coalition building that employed whip-count data (e.g., Ripley 1964; Dodd 1978; Dodd and Sullivan 1981). In addition, such data have been gathered from the personal papers of former House party leaders (Burden and Frisby 2004; Evans 2004). Whip-count data are potentially useful for analyzing party influence because they provide systematic information about member positions *prior to the roll-call decision*. With these data, scholars can gauge the changes that occur in member positions during the lobbying endgame and discern whether these changes are toward or away from the leadership position. The roll calls subject to whip counts also are precisely the items that are most important to the leadership. As a result, these data improve upon more indirect indicators of the significance of a vote to the party agendas.[11]

To our knowledge, no scholarship exists that makes use of whip-count data from the Senate, largely because of the difficulties entailed in tracking them down. The personal papers of Alan Cranston, however, contain extensive records of the whip counts conducted by Senate Democrats during 1989, the first session of the 101st Congress, along with related contextual material about the leadership lobbying process.[12] In the remainder of this chapter, we use these data to explore the efficacy of partisan coalition building in the chamber.

The 101st Congress, it should be noted, was part of the transition between the cross-partisan cleavages that characterized the 1960s and 1970s and the high partisan polarization of the contemporary Senate. Early in 1989, Robert C. Byrd (WV), a moderate Democrat steeped in the folkways of the traditional Senate, was replaced as majority leader by George Mitchell (ME), an aggressive liberal who first entered the chamber in 1980. As the Democratic whip, Alan Cranston stepped up his coalition-building activity during 1989, in part because of an aborted challenge he had faced for the position from Wendell Ford. The first session of the 101st Congress was also the first year of the George H. W. Bush administration. Coming off the 1988 campaign, the Republican White House sought to advance a broad legislative agenda through the Democratically controlled Congress. There were fifty-five Democrats in the Senate that year, roughly the average size for Senate majorities during recent decades. The first session of the 101st Congress, in other words, is a useful period for exploring leadership influence in the Senate.

Targets of Opportunity

Table 5.1 lists the items on which Senate Democrats conducted whip counts during 1989. Included are twenty-seven polled questions across fourteen legislative issues and one executive nomination. The number of counts is consistent with the informal comments of knowledgeable staff.[13] It also resonates with analogous evidence collected for the House (see Evans 2004 for details). The specific items upon which Senate Democrats polled in 1989 also make sense. Of the twenty-seven whip counts in table 5.1, fifteen occurred on legislation on *Congressional Quarterly*'s "key vote" list for the year. And of the sixteen *CQ* key votes for the Senate in 1989, half were the subject of at least one whip count by Senate Democrats.

Congressional party leaders exert care when considering whether to initiate a whip count. The time and political capital of the whips and deputy whips constitute scarce resources. Organizing the polling process, contacting members, feeling them out for their views, engaging in persuasion—these activities all require a nontrivial investment of effort that could be allocated

TABLE 5.1. Items subject to majority whip counts in the Senate, 1989

Item	Date	Question	Winner
Minimum wage	March 15	Amendment	Ambiguous
Minimum wage	March 15	Passage	Democrats
Social Security earnings	April	Amendment	Ambiguous
Savings and loan regulation	April 18	Amendment	Ambiguous
Budget resolution	May 3	Procedure	Bipartisan
Budget resolution	May 3	Passage	Bipartisan
Budget resolution	May 3	Amendment	Bipartisan
Child care/committee bill	May 4	Passage	Ambiguous
Child care/tax credits	May 4	Procedure	Ambiguous
Child care/vouchers	May 4	Amendment	Ambiguous
FS-X aircraft	May 9	Passage	Ambiguous
Child care/Dem. substitute	June 16	Substitute	Democrats
Child care/GOP substitute	June 16	Substitute	Democrats
Drug programs	September 12	Amendment	Bipartisan
Eastern Airlines	September 13	Cloture	Democrats
Catastrophic health	September 20	General	Neither
Legislative-branch appropriations	October	Conference	Ambiguous
Legislative appropriations/ disclosure	October	Conference	Democrats
Legislative appropriations/ mailings	October	Conference	Democrats
Reconciliation	October	Substitute	Bipartisan
Flag burning	October 3	General	Bipartisan
Flag burning	October 3	Passage	Bipartisan
Hatch Act	October 24	Passage	Democrats
Cason nomination	November 14	Nomination	Democrats
Pay raise/ethics	November 14	Passage	Neither
Pay raise/ethics	November 14	Substitute	Neither
Pay raise/ethics	November 14	Procedure	Bipartisan

to other politically valuable endeavors. Party leaders will only initiate the whip process when the potential benefits to the party countervail the opportunity costs.

What factors are considered by Senate leaders (and House leaders) in deciding whether to conduct a whip count? First, the issue usually must be important to the party agenda. Minor matters or measures that are irrelevant to the party program are less likely to be the subject of counts. There are exceptions. Occasionally, party leaders will poll on cross-partisan or secondary issues at the request of a committee chair or if the item is a personal interest of a member of the leadership. Usually, however, the whip process focuses on party priorities.

Second, the issue should have at least the potential for producing a high degree of intraparty unity. If an item badly divides the party rank and file, there may not be an accepted party position, and the whip process likely will not be engaged. Although abortion roll calls are highly salient and receive ample media attention, for example, they are almost never the subject of whip counts in either chamber, because the policy area divides both parties internally.

Third, whip counts typically are conducted when the outcome is in doubt. In the House, nose counts are not conducted on the organizational votes that occur at the beginning of each new Congress, because these roll calls are settled along straight party lines. Whip counts tend to occur on matters where, within the relevant caucus, there is a shared underlying goal or viewpoint but there also exists significant ambivalence or potential opposition among some members about specific policy alternatives. The leadership uses the intelligence from nose counts to decide whether to push for a vote; whether to mobilize a full-scale lobbying and public relations effort; whether to target particular members for lobbying; and whether substantive modifications in the party position are necessary to prevail on the floor.

Tables 5.2 and 5.3 provide information about the incidence of whip activity across issue areas and the degree of partisan polarization on the targeted roll calls. For the exploratory purposes of this paper, we utilize the policy-categorization scheme developed by Clausen (1973).[14] In the rightmost column of both tables, we include information for all 312 roll calls that occurred on the Senate floor during 1989.[15] The middle columns are for roll calls on bills that were the subject of at least one whip count by Senate Democrats. Often, individual counts can be associated with multiple roll calls. Including all votes on "whipped" legislation in this category strikes us as the best and most conservative approach for discerning whether differences exist across roll-call categories.[16]

As indicated in table 5.2, almost half of the roll calls on whipped measures took place on social welfare issues—policies that traditionally have defined the core differences that exist between Democrats and Republicans. Overall, almost two-thirds of the social welfare votes were associated with whip activity. Included are a major child-care bill, legislation to increase the minimum wage, a repeal of the catastrophic health-care program, and an anti–drug abuse initiative. In public opinion polls, citizens tend to express greater confidence in the ability of Democrats to handle such matters. Put differently, these issue areas are more likely to be "owned" by the Democratic Party and are disproportionately likely to appear on the "message"

TABLE 5.2. Roll calls and majority whip activity in the Senate, 1989

	"Whipped" measures	All measures
All issue areas	80 (25.6)	312
Government management	27 (27.3)	99
Social welfare	38 (63.3)	60
Agriculture	0	0
Civil liberties	12 (29.3)	41
Foreign policy and defense	3 (2.8)	109
Miscellaneous	0 (0)	3

Note: Cell entries are the number of roll calls in each category. The row percentages are in parentheses.

TABLE 5.3. Partisan conflict and majority whip activity in the Senate, 1989

	Average party difference across roll calls*	
	"Whipped" measures	All measures
All issue areas	.387	.283
Government management	.244	.236
Social welfare	.516	.435
Agriculture	n.a.	n.a.
Civil liberties	.257	.204
Foreign policy and defense	.559	.271
Miscellaneous	n.a.	.262

*"Party difference" is the absolute value of the difference between the percentage of Democrats voting "yes" on a roll call and the percentage of Republicans voting "yes."

agendas of congressional Democrats (Petrocik 1996; Sellers 2002; Evans 2001).

Civil liberties matters were also disproportionately represented among the polled items. The twelve roll calls in this category dealt with anti–flag burning legislation and a measure to reform the Ethics in Government Act. Twenty-seven of the polled items concerned government-management issues: these matters are included at roughly their percentage of roll calls in general. Among the government-management measures that drew whip activity were the annual budget resolution and legislation to bail out the savings and loan industry.

Although foreign policy and defense issues account for more than one-third of all recorded votes in 1989, there were only three roll calls from this category among the whipped measures, all relating to a U.S.-Japanese agreement to develop the FS-X fighter plane. Public opinion data indicate that citizens usually have far more confidence in the Republicans on defense matters (Petrocik 1996). Defense issues tend to divide Democrats and are less likely to appear on the party's message agenda (Sellers 2002; Evans 2001). Indeed, Senate Democrats were somewhat divided on the FS-X issue in 1989; there was no party position, and the item likely was subject to a whip count because of the personal interest of Alan Dixon (IL), the chief deputy whip.[17]

Table 5.3 provides data about the extent to which the roll calls on whipped matters were more likely to divide senators along partisan lines. For each roll call, we calculated the "party difference," that is, the absolute value of the difference between the proportion of Democrats and the proportion of Republicans voting in the affirmative. The scale ranges from 1.0 (every Democrat voted one way and every Republican voted the other) to zero (Democrats and Republicans supported the motion in exactly the same proportions). Obviously, the lower portions of the scale fail to distinguish between consensual and divisive votes, but overall it does tap the degree of conflict between parties, which is our primary interest. Not surprisingly, partisan conflict is more pronounced on the roll calls on whipped measures. The difference is most striking on the three defense votes, even though there was not a party position on the FS-X question. Differences in party polarization between the subset of whipped votes and all roll calls are least striking on the government-management issues. The highest level of partisan conflict is on social welfare matters, although partisan cleavages were common here regardless of whether or not the whip process was engaged.

The contents of table 5.3 need to be interpreted with care. We cannot be sure whether the higher partisan conflict that occurred on polled measures was a result of whip activity or whether these items were singled out for attention by the whips precisely because they were more likely to divide the parties. But these data do reveal that whip efforts are disproportionately allocated to party priorities and that polled measures are disproportionately likely to be characterized by deep partisan cleavages.

Whip Counts and Roll Calls

Our attention now turns to the responses of Democratic members to whip polls and the ability of the leadership to retain or convert wavering legislators. Here, it is important to consider the broader partisan context of a measure. Was there a formal party and leadership position before the whip process began? Was there a clear conflict of interest between Democratic and Republican leaders? We reviewed media accounts of the legislative activity that occurred prior to floor action and separated the polled items into three groups: for category A, no Democratic leadership position existed; for category B, there was a Democratic leadership position but not a clear and divergent position for Republican leaders; and for category C, unambiguous and divergent positions were taken by Democratic and Republican leaders. For each category, the whip-count results for the relevant items are summarized in table 5.4.

In addition to the FS-X aircraft, the Democratic leadership did not have a position on the savings and loan roll call nor on an amendment that William Armstrong (R-CO) offered to the minimum wage bill aimed at relaxing the Social Security earnings test. However, there was a clear party position on all of the other items—the vast majority (88.9%). For thirteen of the questions, there was a Democratic Party position but Republicans either were cooperating with the majority leadership or were relatively inactive (category B). The budget resolution and reconciliation bills, for instance, were structured by a bipartisan agreement between congressional leaders and the Bush White House. Categorizing catastrophic health care is a closer call. The momentum to repeal the Medicare Catastrophic Coverage Act of 1988 came largely from rank-and-file members of both parties, who were concerned about the highly negative reaction to the act from senior citizens. At various points during the yearlong struggle over repeal, Democratic and Republican leaders were on different sides of specific issues, but positions on both sides of the aisle were in flux, and both leaderships were on the defensive. Conflict over the legislative-branch appropriations bill and the proposed pay raise/ethics reform was more bicameral than partisan. Indeed, on the pay-raise issue, Democratic and Republican leaders worked together but were basically rolled by backbench members of both parties.[18] The lack of a clear-cut conflict of interest between Democratic and GOP leaders on slightly more than half of the polled items in our sample may reflect the transitional nature of the 101st Congress.

The remaining eleven items were explicitly partisan fights in which Democratic leaders were arrayed in opposition to the GOP leadership (category C). Not surprisingly, the average level of party support ("yes" plus "leaning yes" responses) on whip counts was highest on these items (34.7 votes). Average party support among Democrats was next highest for category B, the items with a Democratic position but lacking a clear conflict of interest at the leadership level (29.1 votes). It was lowest (23.3) for the three items without a clear Democratic position. The average number of party opponents exhibits the reverse trend. The number of opponents ("no" plus

TABLE 5.4. Responses to majority whip counts in the Senate, 1989

Item	Question	Y	LY	U	LN	N	NR or other
No leadership position (A)							
Social Security earnings	Amendment	11	8	5	8	7	16
Savings and loan regulation	Amendment	25	4	7	0	5	14
FS-X aircraft	Passage	18	4	7	5	11	10
Average		18.0	5.3	6.3	4.3	7.7	13.3
Leadership position but no clear partisan conflict (B)							
Budget resolution	Procedure	31	2	7	1	9	5
Budget resolution	Amendment	32	4	7	2	6	4
Budget resolution	Passage	31	3	7	1	8	5
Catastrophic health	General	14	9	10	4	16	2
Legislative-branch appropriations	Conference	47	3	1	0	4	0
Legislative appropriations/ disclosure	Conference	32	5	10	1	6	1
Legislative appropriations/ mailings	Conference	36	3	11	1	3	1
Reconciliation	Substitute	33	6	4	0	0	12
Flag burning	General	24	2	0	0	3	26
Flag burning	Passage	13	3	5	0	0	34
Pay raise/ethics	Passage	11	3	8	4	28	1
Pay raise/ethics	Substitute	19	0	8	0	9	19
Pay raise/ethics	Procedure	13	0	6	0	8	28
Average		25.8	3.3	6.5	1.1	7.7	10.6
Leadership position and clear partisan conflict (C)							
Minimum wage	Amendment	15	1	14	2	9	14
Minimum wage	Passage	32	4	4	0	1	14
Child care/committee bill	Passage	28	2	5	0	4	16
Child care/tax credits	Procedure	8	1	23	3	4	16
Child care/vouchers	Amendment	12	1	19	4	3	16
Child care/Dem. substitute	Substitute	44	1	9	0	0	1
Child care/GOP substitute	Substitute	43	3	5	1	1	2
Drug programs	Amendment	34	9	4	0	2	6
Eastern Airlines	Cloture	48	1	3	1	2	0
Hatch Act	Passage	41	3	2	0	0	9
Cason nomination	Nomination	49	2	1	2	0	1
Average		32.2	2.5	8.1	1.2	2.4	8.6

Note: Y = yes; LY = leaning yes; U = undecided; LN = leaning no; N = no; NR = nonresponsive.

Note: Responses have been recoded so that "yes" reflects the position of the leadership. For category A (no leadership position exists), coding reflects the way the question was phrased by the whips.

"leaning no" responders) ranges from 3.6 (category C) to 8.8 (category B) to 12.0 (category A). For undecided responders, the averages were roughly similar across the three categories (ranging from six to eight members). The average number of nonresponders (members who failed to report a position) varied with the partisan context, ranging from 13.3 on the non-leadership matters to 10.6 in category B and just 8.6 for category C. Efforts to discern member positions apparently were more intensive (and non-responses less tolerated) on major Democratic priorities that divided the parties at the leadership level.

Notice, however, that even in the most polarized category, the outcome of the relevant roll calls was generally not a foregone conclusion. If we assume that all the nonresponders were closet leadership supporters—which is highly unlikely—Democratic leaders could be confident of fifty-one Democratic votes on only four of the items (and one dealt with the volatile issue of flag burning and had twenty-six nonresponders). On none of the items was the leadership within range of the sixty votes necessary to invoke cloture. The minimum wage and child-care measures were two of the top domestic priorities for congressional Democrats during the 101st Congress, yet support for the party position was mixed on all of the relevant whip counts. On two possible amendments to the child-care bill, almost half of the Democratic Caucus reported as "undecided" or "leaning." Even on major party priorities, then, the roll-call outcome is seldom settled by the beginning of the process of endgame lobbying. The activities that occur between the whip count and the vote can matter a great deal.

Table 5.5 presents information about retention rates on the roll-call votes associated with the polled items. It was possible to link the polled question to a specific roll call for eighteen of the twenty-seven nose counts. The percentage of counts that could be linked with a floor vote is somewhat lower here than is the case for ongoing research about the House whip process, reflecting the less predictable nature of the Senate floor agenda (Evans 2004). Once again, items are categorized by whether there was a Democratic position and whether the leaderships embraced divergent positions. Categories B and C are of particular interest. Across all of the polled items, the leadership was remarkably successful at holding onto the "yes" responders on whip counts. Still, when we compare categories B and C, across all of the poll responses the leadership retention rate was highest for category C, the items with divergent leadership positions. The largest difference was for members who initially signaled opposition during the nose counts ("leaning no" or "no"). While most of the likely opponents in category B ended

TABLE 5.5. Senate roll-call results by whip-count position, 1989

Count position	No leadership position (A)			Leadership position but no clear partisan conflict (B)			Leadership position and clear partisan conflict (C)		
	Yes	No	% Yes	Yes	No	% Yes	Yes	No	% Yes
Yes	53	0	100	227	20	91.9	232	6	97.5
Leaning yes	16	0	100	26	7	78.8	20	1	95.2
Undecided	16	3	84.2	41	22	65.1	24	3	88.9
Leaning no	7	5	58.3	5	5	50.0	2	0	100
No	4	18	18.2	6	54	10.0	5	1	83.3
Nonresponsive	29	9	76.3	59	15	79.7	30	1	96.8
Total	125	35	78.1	364	123	74.7	313	12	96.3

Note: For categories B and C, poll positions and votes have been recoded so that "yes" reflects the position of the Democratic leadership. For category A, responses and votes are coded as they were cast (e.g., a "yes" code for the roll call means that the member actually voted "aye").

up voting against their leaders, the vast majority of initial opponents in category C stayed on the partisan reservation. In other words, Democratic leaders were especially successful in retaining their members on the items most important to the party "name brand" (Cox and McCubbins 1993).

We also conducted an individual-level analysis of whip-count positions and roll-call choice to identify the member-specific characteristics associated with greater or less support for the leadership. Eight explanatory variables are of particular interest.

1. *Member ideology.* More-liberal members should be more likely to support the leadership on whip counts and roll calls. We captured member ideology with DW-NOMINATE values, which range from −1 (extreme liberalism) to +1 (extreme conservatism).[19]

2. *Constituency ideology.* The more liberal the state that a senator represents, the more likely that she will support the leadership on whip counts and roll calls. We use the percentage of the vote won by Democratic presidential nominee Michael Dukakis in 1988 to proxy for constituency liberalism.

3. *Electoral proximity.* The further a member is from running for reelection, the more discretion the legislator should have to support party over constituency, interest groups, and other competing pressures. Our proximity measure ranges from two years (term ends in 1990) to six years (term ends in 1994).

4. *Electoral margin.* The safer the seat, the more likely a senator should be to support the leadership. Electoral margin is measured by the percentage of the vote that the member received in the most recent campaign.

5. *Population.* The size of a senator's state has consequences for many aspects of legislative behavior (Lee and Oppenheimer 1999). Larger states tend to be more diverse politically, broadening the range of interests that a legislator must confront. There may be incentives for senators from large states to respond disproportionately as "undecided" or "leaning" on whip counts, reducing leadership support.

6. *Committee membership.* Members of the committee with jurisdiction over an issue should be less likely to be undecided during the floor lobbying process. Given the relatively small number of open opponents of the leadership on polled items, we expect a positive association between committee membership and support for the leadership on whip counts.

7. *Chairs and seniority.* Senators chairing a standing committee are part of the extended leadership circle and should be especially supportive of the party position on polls and votes. Similarly, more-senior members of the Democratic Caucus have relatively more to gain institutionally from maintaining majority control and should therefore exhibit higher levels of party support.

8. *Zone whip.* Finally, the members of the extended whip system (although selected by other members of their regions) tend to work closely with the leadership during the whipping process. Their status as members of the extended leadership may result in higher party support on polled items.

To evaluate these hypotheses, we conducted separate probit analyses for poll responses and roll-call choices for each of the item categories. For the analyses of whip-count responses, the dependent variable is a dichotomous measure that takes the value of 1 if a member responded as "yes" or "leaning yes" and is zero otherwise.[20] For the roll-call regressions, the dependent variable is 1 if the member voted with the leadership and zero for "no" votes. If there was no discernible Democratic position, the dependent variable is 1 for "yes" votes and zero for "no" votes on the motion as offered.

The results for the six regressions are reported in table 5.6. Once again, our primary interest is in categories B and C, because of the presence of a clear Democratic position. Although the results are mixed, most of the hypotheses have a degree of support in one or more of the regressions. For both sets of issues, ideological liberalism is strongly associated with

TABLE 5.6. Probit analysis of majority whip polls and votes in the Senate, 1989

Variables	No leadership position (A)		Leadership position but no clear partisan conflict (B)		Leadership position and clear partisan conflict (C)	
	Poll (n = 125)	Vote (n = 160)	Poll (n = 534)	Vote (n = 435)	Poll (n = 510)	Vote (n = 325)
DW-Nom	−.084	.113	−1.137**	−.777	−2.160***	−3.067
Dukakis	.019	−.010	.000	.036	.0279**	.104**
Proximity	−.047	−.079	.105***	.133**	.032	.121***
Margin	−.028	−.024	.004	−.006	−.021***	−.008
Population	−.029*	−.036***	.009	.016	−.020**	−.024
Committee	.029	−.584	.235	−.177	.317**	.234
Chair	.324	.174	.064	.448	.012	.223
Service	−.025	−.018	.004	.005	.021**	−.043
Zone whip	−.036	−.232	.176	.175**	.557***	−.204
Constant	1.427**	3.522***	−.887	−1.652	−.314	−2.856***
% correct	0.568	0.819	0.665	0.747	0.776	0.963
PRE	0.018	0.171	0.077	0.068	0.109	0
Log likelihood	−81.889	−76.562	−336.509	−233.850	−254.835	−37.554
McKelvey-Zavoina R^2	0.093	0.155	0.079	0.165	0.233	0.419

Note: The number of observations varies somewhat across whip-count and roll-call equations because of different levels of member participation and whether a count can be linked to a specific roll-call vote. Standard errors are adjusted for clustering on the item being polled.

$*p < .1$; $**p < .05$; $***p < .01$ (two-tailed tests)

leadership support on whip counts. More-liberal members are more likely to respond as "yes." The relationship also occurs on roll calls but is not statistically significant, probably because of the high levels of party support overall at this stage. Constituency liberalism is strongly associated with party support on polls and votes for category C items. The results for the "electoral-connection" variables are somewhat inconsistent. For the items in categories B and C, the further a senator is from running for reelection, the more supportive that member is of the party position, which is consistent with expectations. This relationship is statistically significant in three of the four regressions. Higher electoral margins, however, appear to be associated with less, rather than more, leadership support, although the relationship is only statistically significant for the whip-count regressions for category C. The parameter estimates for the remaining explanatory variables have the appropriate sign for the category C poll regression

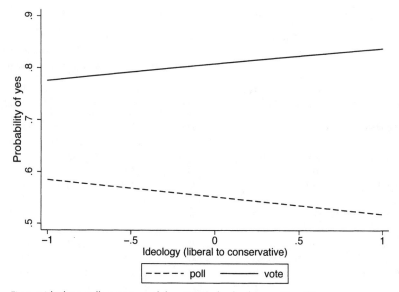

Fig. 5.3: Ideology, poll position, and the vote: No leadership position (A).

and for the most part achieve statistical significance. With the exception of the zone-whip variable for the vote equation in category B, remaining coefficients are not statistically significant.

The substantive relationship between member ideology and leadership support is portrayed in figures 5.3 to 5.5. With other explanatory variables held to their means, the figures show changes in the predicted probability of a "yes" position on polls and roll calls for the three categories. Although the "yes" position on the nonleadership items (category A) had more Democratic support than the "no" position, there was no consistent relationship between member ideology and poll or roll-call behavior here. Decision making on these issues did not track the liberal-conservative ideological dimension, complicating efforts by Democratic leaders to devise a consistent position for the party. The relationships portrayed in figures 5.4 and 5.5, however, do track member ideology. For both sets of items, the likelihood of leadership support increases markedly as DW-NOMINATE values tend toward −1 (the liberal end of the continuum). The probability of leadership support also increases from poll to roll call, as members break from undecided or potentially against on the whip count to "yes" on the vote. The shift toward leadership support is especially marked in the −.5 to .5 range of the ideology scale, where most moderate to conservative Democrats were located during the 101st Congress. The shift also is especially

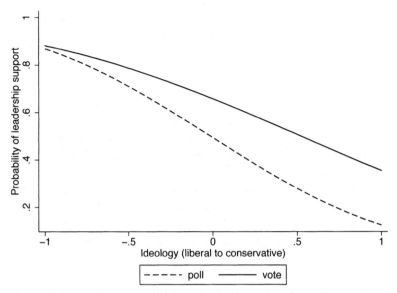

Fig. 5.4: Ideology, poll position, and the vote: Leadership position but no clear partisan conflict (B).

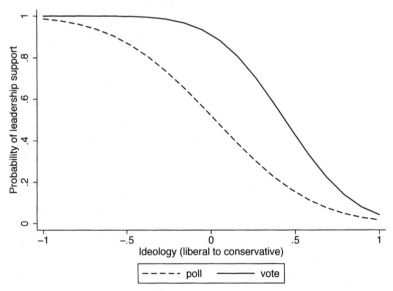

Fig. 5.5: Ideology, poll position, and the vote: Leadership position and clear partisan conflict (C).

large in figure 5.5, precisely where we would expect the coalition-building efforts of Democratic leaders to be most intensive.

Do Whip Efforts Matter?

The whip system fulfills an important informational function for party leaders and rank-and-file members. Leaders uses whip-count results to avoid being caught by surprise on the floor: nose counts serve as an early-warning system for potential problems in the full chamber. The whip process also addresses the informational needs of rank-and-file lawmakers. The whips inform their colleagues about scheduling plans and provide background information about pending legislation. Indeed, the fact that a count is being conducted on a question provides useful information to rank-and-file legislators. Members usually can infer from the whip process itself the contents of the party position and that the targeted matter is significant to the leadership.

However, party theories of Congress generally maintain that the impact of leadership activity is more than informational—that is, that leadership behavior has an independent and significant impact on the coalition-building process and legislative outcomes. Does our exploration of the Senate whip system suggest that these functions make a difference? The answer is a qualified "yes."

First, consider the level of leadership success on polled items. In table 5.1, the identity of the winner in each legislative fight is denoted in the column to the far right. These entries are based on the extent to which party positions prevailed on the floor, the contents of the whip counts, and the associated roll-call record. On eight of the items (29.6%), the majority Democrats prevailed. On eight more, the outcomes are best characterized as a joint win for both leaderships. For almost 60 percent of the polled questions, then, the Democratic leadership was fairly successful on the floor. On three of the items (dealing with pay raise/ethics and catastrophic health care), neither leadership was successful. And for the remaining eight questions, the best characterization of the outcome is "ambiguous," because we cannot discern with confidence which side won or lost. For example, the outcomes for the three items with no leadership position are in this category. Interestingly, none of the polled items in table 5.1 resulted in an unambiguous GOP win and Democratic loss. Given that the final outcomes of the measures were all in play at some point during the endgame lobbying process and that initial support for the Democratic position was often tenuous, the overall success rate for the majority leadership is fairly high.

It is also important to take into account the tactics that the leadership used in response to polling information, especially decisions to moderate proposals because of potential opposition. Some of the Democratic successes in table 5.1 were possible only because of the leadership's willingness to ratchet down its demands following problematic nose counts. Consider, for example, certain of the items in category C, with a Democratic position and clear partisan differences at the leadership level. On the highly salient minimum wage and child-care initiatives, the Democratic leadership modified its positions in order to build support on the floor and reduce the likelihood of an administration veto. A brief review of the relevant legislative history is instructive.[21]

On January 5, 1989, Edward Kennedy (D-MA), chair of the Committee on Labor and Human Resources, introduced S. 4, which would have increased the minimum wage to $4.65 per hour over four years. The Bush administration countered with a proposal to increase the minimum wage to $4.25 over three years and to implement a 180-day subminimum wage for new employees. The following month, House Democratic leaders endorsed, and the chamber passed, a minimum wage hike to $4.55 over three years and a sixty-day training wage. The modifications were aimed at increasing support for the measure among conservative Democrats and moderate Republicans.

The White House responded with a veto threat, and on March 7 Bush met personally with Republican members of Kennedy's committee, urging them to oppose the Democrats' revised position and enhance the administration's negotiating leverage on Capitol Hill. The following day, the Labor Committee reported the Kennedy proposal to the full Senate. A week later, Senate Democrats conducted whip counts asking members whether they could support the committee bill and whether they intended to vote for certain floor amendments.[22] Thirty-six Democrats responded as "yes" or "leaning yes" on the committee bill. Four members (Jeff Bingaman, NM; Howell Heflin, AL; Frank Lautenberg, NJ; and Daniel Moynihan, NY) were undecided, and Richard Shelby (AL) was a "no." However, fourteen Democrats did not respond to the whip count, and fourteen also were undecided about whether they would support amendments aimed at weakening the bill.[23] The Kennedy measure obviously faced significant political difficulties on the floor.

As a result, a compromise proposal resembling the House-passed bill (that is, calling for an increase in the minimum wage to $4.55 and a two-month training wage) was offered as a floor amendment by Bob Graham (D-FL) and David Pryor (D-AR). The amendment was adopted on April 11 by a margin of 61–39, with only two Democrats (Ernest Hollings, SC, and Bennett Johnson, LA) voting no. The amended bill passed the next day by a vote of 62–37. The increase in party support from whip count to floor action was substantial. But one reason was the decision by Democratic leaders to moderate the party position.[24]

Similar dynamics characterized the ABC bill (Act for Better Child Care). Child care was a major issue during the 1988 presidential campaign. In March 1989, the Labor Committee reported a Democrat-backed child-care measure to the full Senate. The legislation authorized federal grants for families to subsidize child care. In exchange for federal funds, child-care providers would have to meet certain health and safety standards. The White House and most congressional Republicans opposed the new standards and instead favored child-care tax credits targeted to low-income families. There were also jurisdictional squabbles between the Labor panel and the Finance Committee, mostly concerning tax matters.

The committee-passed measure was itself a compromise: Democrats accepted adjustments in the health and safety standards to secure the support of Orrin Hatch (UT), the ranking Republican on the Labor Committee. Even with Hatch's support, however, the Labor Committee bill drew significant partisan opposition, and the nation's governors preferred a Finance Committee alternative that placed greater emphasis on tax incentives. Negotiations continued. On May 4, Democratic leaders polled their members on three questions: Can you support the child-care bill as reported by the Labor Committee? Will you vote yes or no to an amendment exempting child-care vouchers from provisions of the bill prohibiting the use of federal funds for religious instruction? Will you vote to waive budget-act points of order, allowing the Senate to vote on an amendment to add a child-care tax credit to the legislation? Thirty members responded as "yes" or "leaning yes" on the question about passage of the Labor Committee proposal. But nine Democrats were either undecided or opposed, and sixteen did not respond at all to the nose count. Moreover, almost half of the caucus was undecided on the other two questions, reinforcing sentiments at the leadership level that the legislation was in trouble.

As a result, Democrats coalesced behind a substitute crafted by Majority Leader Mitchell that contained a streamlined version of the Labor Committee bill, a tax-credit package authored by Finance chairman Lloyd Bentsen (D-TX), and a provision from Wendell Ford and David Durenberger (R-MN) permitting federal funding for religious organizations. Minority Leader Robert Dole (R-KS) responded with a GOP substitute focusing on tax incentives. On June 16, Democratic leaders conducted whip counts on the competing substitutes from Mitchell and Dole. Forty-five members were "yes" or "leaning yes" on the Mitchell proposal, and there was only one nonresponse. But nine members reported as "undecided," primarily party conservatives such as David Boren (OK), Sam Nunn (GA), and Richard Shelby. The following week, amid veto threats from the administration, the Senate adopted the Mitchell substitute by a vote of 63–37. Only Nunn voted no.[25] Although the Democratic leadership made substantive adjustments to gain support for the bill, the fact that eight of nine undecided Democrats broke toward the leadership is highly suggestive of consequential endgame lobbying by Mitchell and the whips.[26]

Conclusion

This chapter is the first scholarly description of the Senate whip system in action. It provides a degree of support for contentions that majority-party leaders in the chamber influence member behavior and legislative outcomes. The portrait of party influence that emerges from this study, however, diverges in important ways from what we know about leadership influence in the House. By most accounts, majority-party leaders in the House have the procedural prerogatives and other formal advantages necessary to control the floor agenda, typically enabling them to keep items that would divide the majority caucus from appearing on the floor agenda (Cox and McCubbins 2005). For the most part, the majority leadership in the Senate lacks these prerogatives (but see Den Hartog and Monroe, forthcoming).

Still, Senate party leaders do play critical roles as negotiators and bargainers on legislation, nominations, and other chamber business. Especially on significant party issues that deeply divide Democrats from Republicans, the compromises and bargains necessary to manage the flow of legislation in the Senate are made or heavily influenced by the top party leaders. Within this context of negotiation and compromise, the whip system can provide the majority leadership with important tactical advantages in the bargaining game. Whip counts enable majority-party leaders to gauge which alternatives are likely to prevail on the floor; to make adjustments in the timing and content of party initiatives; to signal to rank-and-file members about which initiatives are central to the party agenda; and to persuade wavering members to stay on the partisan reservation. The tactical impact of the whip system, then, reflects and reinforces the tactical nature of majority leadership in the U.S. Senate more generally.

Notes

Preparation of this article was assisted by financial support from the National Science Foundation (Award SES-0417759) and the Roy R. Charles Center of the College of William and Mary. Mark Oleszek and David Kessler gave valuable assistance with archival research. We also appreciate the comments of Mat McCubbins, Barbara Sinclair, Charles Stewart, Randy Strahan, and especially Lee Rawls.

1. Party unity votes are roll calls in which at least half of Democrats oppose at least half of Republicans. Data about the incidence of these roll calls have been gathered by Joseph Cooper and Garry Young and are available at http://www.jhu.edu/polysci/faculty/cooper/. For an analysis of several measures of party unity as they relate to the role of party in congressional voting, see Cooper and Young 2002.

2. For an overview of the project, see Evans 2004.

3. Cranston served as Democratic whip from 1977 to 1991, when, in the aftermath of an ethics investigation about his involvement with financier Charles Keating, the Californian was replaced by Wendell Ford of Kentucky.

4. See various papers by Steven Smith and Gerald Gamm (especially Smith and Gamm 2002) regarding the emergence of party leadership structures in the Senate. See also Oleszek 1971. Ripley 1964 is an excellent study of the emergence of the whip's role in the House.

5. Glenn R. Simpson, "Is Cranston Vulnerable to Whip Challenge? Ford Said to Be Ready for Rematch in 1990; Other Possibilities: Dixon, Pryor, Breaux," *Roll Call*, December 11, 1989.

6. Timothy J. Burger, "Cranston Says He'll Be Back as Whip, but His Campaign Is on Hold for Now," *Roll Call*, July 23, 1990.

7. The reproductions in figures 5.1 and 5.2 are of materials in the Alan MacGregor Cranston Papers, 88/214 C, series 8, carton 59, Whip Files/Leadership, 1977–91, Bancroft Library, University of California, Berkeley.

8. Folder 8, box 624, Alan Simpson Congressional Collection, American Heritage Center, University of Wyoming, Laramie.

9. "Some Thoughts on the Whip Election," memo to Alan Simpson, November 25, 1994, box 610, folder 10, Alan Simpson Congressional Collection.

10. Not-for-attribution interview conducted by C. Lawrence Evans and Walter J. Oleszek in Washington, DC, December 8, 1999.

11. Terry Sullivan has authored a number of important studies using data from presidential head counts, which resemble whip counts in certain ways (e.g., Sullivan 1990a, 1990b). See also Covington 1987.

12. The whip-count materials are all included in the Cranston Papers, series 8, carton 59, Whip Files/Leadership, 1977–91.

13. Not-for-attribution interview (see n. 10 above).

14. Similar patterns are apparent if we use the policy categories formulated by Peltzman (1984), Poole and Rosenthal (1997), or the Policy Agendas Project (http://www.policyagendas.org).

15. Results do not change appreciably if unanimous and near-unanimous roll calls are dropped, so we include the entire population of votes.

16. The issue codes for specific roll calls were secured from Voteview (http://voteview .com/). We thank Keith Poole and Howard Rosenthal for making this remarkable resource available to the research community.

17. Dixon authored the resolution of disagreement for the FS-X deal.

18. On the flag-burning issue, there was clear conflict at the leadership level over a proposed constitutional amendment banning the behavior. The whip counts conducted on the issue, however, concerned statutory language to restrict flag burning. The statutory proposal did not evoke clearly divergent positions from Democratic and Republican leaders in the Senate.

19. DW-NOMINATE values were downloaded from Voteview (http://voteview.com/).

20. The whip-count regressions were also conducted with a five-point categorical measure serving as the dependent variable ("yes," "leaning yes," "undecided," "leaning no," and "no") and using an ordered probit routine. Estimates of the cut points between categories were not statistically significant, however, and we instead report the results for the dichotomous dependent variable.

21. The following material is mostly from the Cranston Papers and various issues of *CQ Weekly Report*.

22. According to the issue summary produced by the Democratic whips, possible major amendments to the committee bill included an administration substitute with a lower wage hike ($4.25 instead of $4.65), an administration proposal allowing for a 180-day subminimum wage, and a compromise thirty-day "first job" training wage.

23. The Cranston Papers also include references to a second set of whip counts (scheduled to be conducted on April 4) that would have asked members their views about the House-passed measure. There are no results for such a poll, however, and it may not have been conducted.

24. Still, Bush vetoed the measure in June, and congressional Democrats failed in their override attempt. After months of additional negotiations, the White House and congressional Democrats agreed to compromise language raising the minimum wage to $4.25 over two years and providing for a three-month training wage for teenagers. The measure was signed into law on November 8, 1989.

25. Earlier in the day, the Dole proposal had been defeated 44–56.

26. The measure later became embroiled in bicameral conflict. Portions were adopted as part of a reauthorization of the Head Start program, but the tax-credit provisions were dropped.

6

Party Loyalty and Discipline in the Individualistic Senate

KATHRYN PEARSON

The Republican leader has very few carrots and no sticks. He leads by the power of the position and personal persuasion, which is wonderful if you can do it, but it doesn't always work with some of these good ol' boys around here.

Former Senate majority leader TRENT LOTT (R-MS), September 2004

In June 2001, Senator James Jeffords (VT) denounced his Republican Party allegiance, declared himself an independent, and gave Democrats majority-party control of the Senate by joining them for organizational purposes. In explaining his decision, Jeffords cited his growing alienation from his party. In particular, he suggested that when leaders shelved his legislation to help Vermont dairy farmers, it was a means of punishing him for his frequent votes against his party. To what extent do Senate leaders exert party discipline by allocating resources and legislative opportunities on the basis of party loyalty?

In the aftermath of Jeffords's defection, party discipline in the Senate received considerable media attention—more so than it has in the House of Representatives. Given the shift in majority-party control, this is hardly surprising. Party leaders' opportunities to exert discipline through decisions affecting the resources and opportunities of their rank-and-file members, however, are more limited in the Senate than they are in the House.

In this chapter, I explore how senators have increased their party loyalty in their roll-call voting and with their fundraising efforts to help their party's candidates. I then analyze Senate leaders' potential mechanisms of discipline—the resources, positions, and opportunities that party leaders allocate to senators—and identify instances where leaders have and have not been willing to use them to reward loyalty or punish disloyalty. Although

I find that Senate leaders' carrots and sticks are limited, Senate norms are slowly changing, and senators have shown increasing willingness to cede power to their leaders. The chamber's membership is also changing, and partisans are replacing the "good ol' boys" whom Senator Lott bemoaned (quoted in Stevens 2004). This chapter reveals that although norms of individualism, combined with institutional features of the Senate, protect senators from most attempts by leaders to exert party discipline, even "individualistic" senators have greater incentives to toe the party line.

Increasing Partisanship in Congress and Its Consequences

In the 1990s, in the wake of the institutional and political changes that increased the centrality of parties in Congress during the 1970s and 1980s, a sea change occurred in the literature on Congress. As party voting in Congress increased, so did attention to congressional parties—particularly in the House—among scholars and congressional observers alike. Scholars focused on testing two leading theories of congressional parties: the conditional party government theory (Rohde 1991; Aldrich and Rohde 1998, 2000a) and the party cartel model (Cox and McCubbins 1993, 2002, 2005). Although there are important differences between these two partisan models, implicit in both is the potential for majority-party leaders to shape legislative outcomes and to discipline members.

When Keith Krehbiel (1993b, 2000) challenged scholars to explain why parties, not preferences, explained outcomes in the House of Representatives, scholars began a "hunt for party discipline" (see, e.g., McCarty, Poole, and Rosenthal 2001). Engaging Krehbiel over the last decade in the debate on party effects, many scholars demonstrated that parties in the House exert influence in postreform congressional politics (see, e.g., Aldrich and Rohde 1998, 2000a; Ansolabehere, Snyder, and Stewart 2001b; Binder, Lawrence, and Maltzman 1999; Snyder and Groseclose 2000; McCarty, Poole, and Rosenthal 2001; Cox and Poole 2002; and Sinclair 1995, 1999). What explains these party effects?

As parties became more internally homogeneous and polarized along partisan lines, rank-and-file House members ceded more legislative prerogatives to their leaders (Rohde 1991; Sinclair 1995). As a result, party leaders in the House have several mechanisms available to reward the faithful and, by omission, to punish the disloyal. There are three central domains in which party leaders may discipline their members when allocating scarce benefits and opportunities: legislative preference, committee positions, and campaign assistance (Pearson 2005). Leaders determine whose bills, amendments, and resolutions will be considered on the House floor; whose requests for committee transfers to honor and, increasingly, whom to elevate as committee chairs; and whose campaigns to fund. Through statistical analyses of leaders' decisions beginning in 1987 and through qualitative interviews, I showed (2005) that leaders exert discipline by rewarding members in the legislative and committee domains for their party loyalty when they need party unity to pass their legislative program. When they prioritize electoral goals, they help the electorally vulnerable with legislative opportunities and campaign resources.

The central debates adjudicating between preference-based and partisan theories on the one hand and conditional party government theory and cartel theory on the other hand were waged over votes, committees, agendas, rules, and organization in the majoritarian House of Representatives. These theories do not travel well across the Capitol to the Senate, a chamber characterized by its lack of rules that constrain individual participation and by a sixty-vote requirement to end a filibuster. Senate party leaders exercise less power than their House counterparts, which means that party leaders in the Senate have considerably less control over the policy agenda and the careers of their rank-and-file members. Not surprisingly, the party leadership system in the Senate emerged long after it did in the House: party "floor leaders" in the Senate gradually assumed scheduling and organizational responsibilities between 1900 and the 1930s (Smith 2005).

Nonetheless, scholars have recognized that partisanship infuses the individualistic Senate as well. Barbara Sinclair (2005) traces the Senate's transformation from the chamber described by Donald Matthews in the 1950s—a body characterized by institutional patriotism and apprenticeship (Matthews 1960)—to an individualistic and partisan chamber. Sinclair notes that "by the mid-1970s the individualist Senate had emerged" (2005, 3), and senators now regularly exploit their ability to participate in and obstruct the legislative process. The combination of increased individualism and partisanship is potent. Senators—typically those in the minority party—have increasingly employed filibusters, holds, and other individualistic Senate prerogatives for partisan gain (Sinclair 2005). Senate leaders have adapted, too, bolstering their own responsibilities and reach and the influence of their party organization. Each party's floor leader is responsible for scheduling, directing party strategy, serving as the party spokesperson, communicating with the White House, and fundraising (Smith 2005). With this expanded role, senators have approved increased appropriations to fund the party leadership in the contemporary era (Lee 2006).

In considering parties in the individualistic but increasingly partisan Senate, then, a key question is the extent to which party leaders are able and willing to exert discipline by punishing defection or rewarding loyalty, and in what domains.

Increasing Party Loyalty

How do senators express party loyalty, and how do Senate leaders assess it? Across several indicators, party loyalty is on the rise in both chambers. There are doubtless many reasons for this, including the increase in ideological homogeneity within both parties in both chambers (see, e.g., Rohde 1991; and Poole and Rosenthal 1997) and the increase in electoral competition between the parties. In this volume, Erin M. Bradbury, Ryan A. Davidson, and C. Lawrence Evans provide compelling evidence that under the right conditions, a party's whip system can move vote outcomes its way through vote counting, coalition building, and targeting wavering senators.

An obvious litmus test of a member's loyalty is his or her voting record in support of the party on legislation considered on the floor. Such loyalty is particularly valuable to leaders in an era of tight competition for party control of Congress, when both parties want to be able to point to a record of legislative accomplishment. An extra-legislative test of loyalty is a member's willingness to raise money to help the party fund its candidates. Both measures of loyalty—voting and fundraising—are important to both majority- and minority-party leaders. Minority-party leaders strategize to become *majority-party* leaders, and funding quality candidates is critical to attaining that goal. Minority-party leaders need their members' support to block as much of the majority party's legislative agenda as possible, which is naturally easier to do in the Senate because of the filibuster. As Sean Gailmard and Jeffery A. Jenkins show in this volume, minority parties in both chambers, but especially the Senate, indeed have some success in blocking agenda items that a majority of their members oppose. In this section, I demonstrate the rise in loyalty in voting and fundraising, and I highlight the ways in which disloyalty in the contemporary era can be particularly irksome for Senate party leaders.

Floor Votes

Leaders in both the Senate and the House value support for their party's policy program. At the end of each session, *CQ Weekly Report* publishes members' party unity scores, the percentage of votes in which a member of

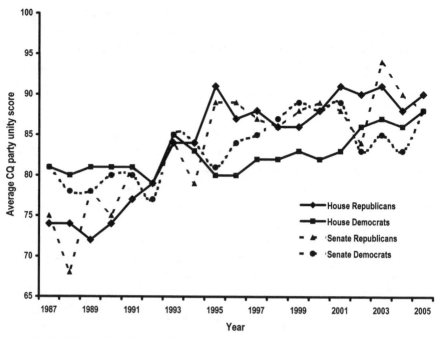

Fig. 6.1: Rising party unity in the House and Senate

Congress votes with his or her party on roll-call votes where the majority of each party opposes the majority of the other, adjusted for participation.

Party loyalty in policy voting has increased in both chambers. Figure 6.1 plots each chamber's average *CQ* party unity score from 1987 to 2005, by party. Over this period, the average level of party loyalty in roll-call voting increased significantly in both parties on both sides of the Capitol, although not in a strictly linear fashion. The Republicans' minority-party loyalty in the House and Senate averaged only 74 percent and 71.5 percent, respectively, in the 100th Congress; by comparison, their majority-party scores in the 108th Congress were 89.5 percent and 92 percent, suggesting that with majority-party status comes the responsibility—and pressure—to pass a party program. After an initial drop in loyalty in 1995, Democrats in both chambers responded to Republican majority control by becoming more unified in opposition. As loyalty increases, standard deviations decrease: members are increasingly clustered at the loyal end of the continuum.

Some might argue that the increase in party-line voting exhibited in figure 6.1 alone demonstrates an increase in party discipline. If members vote with their party more frequently, does this mean their leaders have tightened party discipline through a system of rewards and punishments?

There may be a correlation, but high party unity is not in and of itself evidence that leaders effectively worked to produce loyalty among their members (see, e.g., Krehbiel 1993b). The increase in party-line voting is concomitant with the increasing homogeneity of members' policy preferences within each party (see, e.g., Rohde 1991; and Poole and Rosenthal 1997). The continuing partisan realignment in the South has reduced the share of conservatives in the Democratic Caucus and increased the share of conservatives in the Republican Conference in both chambers.

The rise in party loyalty among senators is a function of both member replacement and increased loyalty at the individual level in an increasingly partisan climate. For example, moderate Republican senator Arlen Specter (R-PA) voted with his party 56 percent of the time in 1994 compared to 84 percent of the time in 2005; and the party-loyalty score for Senator Robert Byrd (D-WV) increased from 74 percent to 93 percent during the same period.

Votes on cloture motions are included in senators' CQ party unity scores. Although these votes are procedural in nature, they have clear policy implications and are visible to constituents, unlike most procedural votes in the House. Party leaders cannot bring their legislative priorities to a vote if they are subject to endless debate. Rule 22 (adopted in 1917 and modified in 1975) stipulates that the support of three-fifths of all senators present and voting is necessary to invoke cloture to end a filibuster. These votes are important to both the majority and minority leaders in the Senate. As filibusters have become more common and more partisan, majority-party leaders are increasingly frustrated when their agenda items are held up because they cannot attract sixty votes. The minority party, for its part, does not want any of its members to defect and thus help the majority attain the necessary sixty. From the minority leader's perspective, those who break party ranks by supporting a cloture motion deny the minority party one of its greatest institutional rights in the Senate—the ability to foil the majority party's agenda with a minority of forty-one votes. By contrast, in the House, party leaders can rely entirely on majority-party members to pass a special rule to bring legislation to the House floor. For this reason, House majority-party leaders are particularly concerned about keeping all of their members in line on procedural votes on special rules, whereas House minority leaders realize they will rarely succeed in stopping the majority party from bringing their key items to the floor.

Fundraising Loyalty

As party loyalty in voting increases among all senators, fundraising provides them a way to distinguish themselves by expressing their loyalty above and beyond their voting record. Members of Congress have incentives to raise money for their own campaigns and their war chests to ward off future challengers. Beyond that, they have typically lacked incentives to raise money, posing a collective-action problem for their parties. Why should members in electorally safe districts or states spend their time fundraising for other candidates when they will still share in the benefits of majority-party status? Beginning in the 104th Congress, following the change in the majority party in both chambers, leaders of both parties recognized that majority control rested on election outcomes in a handful of states and districts. Party leaders provide incentives—and directives—to help overcome this collective-action problem.

Members of Congress contribute to their party's congressional campaign committees—the Democratic Congressional Campaign Committee (DCCC), National Republican Congressional Committee (NRCC), Democratic Senatorial Campaign Committee (DSCC), or National Republican Senatorial Committee (NRSC)—which in turn contribute money to congressional candidates in the form of direct contributions; coordinated expenditures; and independent expenditures on behalf of candidates or against their opponents. Chaired by senators or representatives who make up part of the party's leadership team, congressional campaign committees also provide a variety of resources to help candidates, including staff, recruitment, research, polling, communications, fundraising assistance, and grassroots activities. Before the ban on soft money, congressional campaign committees used it to run party issue-advocacy ads.

Leadership PACs (political action committees) provide elected officials a high-profile way to express their commitment to the party's electoral team, and more and more senators and House members form them with each election cycle. Members of Congress began to form leadership PACs in the 1980s (Baker 1989), although many members were already contributing to fellow partisans from their own campaign coffers. Leadership PACs allow members to contribute up to $10,000 per cycle ($5,000 in the primary and $5,000 in the general election) to their colleagues and would-be colleagues. Initially, leadership PACs were formed mainly by the congressional leadership or aspiring leaders, but they have become increasingly common among ambitious members of Congress anxious to demonstrate their loyalty. Additionally, an increasing number of members of Congress help their colleagues with contributions of up to $1,000 per election from their own campaign funds.

Tables 6.1 and 6.2 reveal that senators' contributions to their colleagues and their party committees from their campaigns and leadership PACs have increased significantly in the last several election cycles. By this measure,

TABLE 6.1. Republican senators' contributions to Senate candidates and party committees, 1988–2004 (in dollars)

	100th Congress (1988)	101st Congress (1990)	102nd Congress (1992)	103rd Congress (1994)	104th Congress (1996)	105th Congress (1998)	106th Congress (2000)	107th Congress (2002)	108th Congress (2004)
Average senator's contribution to NRSC	22 (147)	0	0	398 (2,638)	4,091 (18,907)	21,555 (45,944)	47,402 (166,599)	29,608 (75,524)	57,149 (82,244)
Number of senators contributing	1	0	0	1	5	31	19	14	30
Total contributions made to NRSC	1,000	0	0	17,500	225,000	1,185,500	2,654,500	1,510,000	2,971,750
Average senator's contribution to Senate candidates	0	0	0	1,519 (1,900)	1,270 (3,681)	2,834 (6,667)	1,188 (2,184)	3,053 (5,988)	1,345 (2,229)
Number of senators contributing	0	0	0	25	17	21	21	21	23
Total contributions made to candidates	0	0	0	66,843	69,842	155,879	66,500	155,700	69,929
Average senator's leadership PAC contributions	4,205 (16,450)	3,287 (15,764)	2,314 (13,485)	17,537 (85,952)	40,313 (104,435)	45,094 (98,063)	52,770 (97,152)	79,043 (109,330)	100,336 (128,770)
Total leadership PAC contributions made to colleagues	193,426	151,203	104,116	771,648	2,217,189	2,480,171	2,955,133	4,031,194	5,217,475
Number of leadership PACs	8	8	5	10	15	23	28	31	38

Source: Data are from the Federal Election Commission and the Center for Responsive Politics 2004; entries are calculated by the author.

Note: Standard deviations are given in parentheses. NRSC = National Republican Senatorial Committee.

TABLE 6.2. Democratic senators' contributions to Senate candidates and party committees, 1988–2004 (in dollars)

	100th Congress (1988)	101st Congress (1990)	102nd Congress (1992)	103rd Congress (1994)	104th Congress (1996)	105th Congress (1998)	106th Congress (2000)	107th Congress (2002)	108th Congress (2004)
Average senator's contribution to DSCC	840 (4,169)	418 (2,720)	776 (4,373)	3,353 (6,851)	5,031 (7,116)	19,130 (48,066)	25,340 (26,155)	29,196 (48,800)	160,166 (377,379)
Number of senators contributing	3	2	2	16	23	25	34	29	35
Total contributions made to DSCC	45,375	23,000	45,000	194,500	246,500	880,000	1,191,000	1,459,810	7,687,978
Average senator's contribution to Senate candidates	0	0	0	1,909 (3,822)	1,143 (2,236)	1,489 (2,540)	1,490 (3,035)	2,799 (2,799)	2,355 (3,836)
Number of senators contributing	0	0	0	29	18	18	18	39	24
Total contributions made to candidates	0	0	0	110,733	56,000	68,500	70,000	139,954	113,035
Average senator's leadership PAC contributions	4,719 (20,368)	3,296 (12,963)	2,956 (11,326)	1,051 (3,809)	2,093 (8,939)	5,692 (18,166)	29,521 (7,961)	82,268 (152,955)	76,830 (156,080)
Total leadership PAC contributions made to colleagues	254,838	181,272	171,475	60,960	102,550	261,843	1,387,477	4,113,387	3,687,849
Number of leadership PACs	9	8	8	8	4	7	14	23	25

Source: Data are from the Federal Election Commission and the Center for Responsive Politics 2004; entries are calculated by the author.

Note: Standard deviations are given in parentheses. DSCC = Democratic Senatorial Campaign Committee.

expressions of partisanship have dramatically increased. From 1988 to 1992, the average senator was barely contributing to his or her party's campaign efforts. In the 100th Congress, only nine Democratic senators and eight Republican senators formed leadership PACs. Collectively, they contributed $448,264 to other candidates. The totals were even smaller in the 1990 election cycle: in the 101st Congress, eight Democrats and eight Republicans ran leadership PACs, contributing $332,475 to other candidates. Not much had changed by the 1992 cycle. In the 102nd Congress, the leadership PACs of eight Democrats and five Republicans contributed a total of $275,591.

Republican senators stepped up their leadership PAC activity well before Democratic senators did. The number of Republican senators with leadership PACs increased from five to ten between 1992 and 1994, and the contribution dollars nearly tripled. By the 1998 election cycle, twenty-three GOP senators' leadership PACs contributed $2,480,171 to their Republican colleagues. By 2004, well over half of Republican senators (thirty-eight) had leadership PACs, contributing a total of $5,217,475.

While Democratic senators were slower to contribute from leadership PACs, by 2004, twenty-five had leadership PACs that contributed $3,687,849 to their Democratic colleagues up for reelection. Only two cycles earlier, Senate Democrats' fourteen leadership PACs had contributed $1,387,477, considerably less than their GOP counterparts.

Leadership PAC activity was increasing simultaneously on both sides of the Capitol. In the 1988 election cycle, only sixteen House Democrats and five House Republicans formed leadership PACs. By 1998, those numbers were twenty-two and fifty-one, respectively, and Democratic House candidates received $2,600,000; Republican House candidates received $5,996,000 from their colleagues' leadership PACs.[1] Majority-party status is clearly correlated with leadership PAC activity. In the House, just as in the Senate, Republicans took the lead once they controlled the majority beginning in the 1996 cycle.

The steep increase in contributions from senators to the party campaign committees mirrors the increase in leadership PACs, as seen in tables 6.1 and 6.2. Only three senators contributed to the DSCC in 1988, making contributions totaling $45,375; and only one senator contributed to the NRSC ($1,000) in this cycle. In 1990, no Republicans contributed to the NRSC, and only two Democrats contributed to the DSCC, totaling $23,000. In 1992, two Democrats contributed a total of $45,000 to the DSCC; no Republicans contributed to their congressional campaign committee. The shift in majority-party control in 1995 and the heightened competition generated by close margins engendered a more partisan, dynamic fundraising mentality among senators. By 1998, twenty-five Democratic senators contributed a total of $880,000 to the DSCC, and thirty-one Republican senators raised $1,185,500 for the NRSC. Six years later, thirty-five Democratic senators contributed $7,687,978, and thirty Republican senators contributed $2,971,750. Fundraising for the party had clearly become an important part of rank-and-file senators' careers.

In the early 1990s, senators did not contribute to their colleagues' campaigns from their own individual campaigns. By the mid-1990s, senators were contributing generously to their colleagues' campaigns. Republicans were most active in this domain in the 1998 cycle and the 2002 cycle, when they contributed a total of $155,879 and $155,700, respectively. Democratic senators helped the team most in 2002, making contributions totaling $139,954.

House leaders have been particularly aggressive in soliciting their members to raise funds for the party in upcoming elections (Kolodny 1998; Sabato and Larson 2002). Majority-party House Republican leaders formed the Retain Our Majority Program (ROMP), setting quotas for some incumbents to contribute to the NRCC to help their more vulnerable colleagues (Eilperin 1999). While Senate leaders may be less explicit, it is clear that by the mid-1990s, members in both chambers were responding to increasingly competitive elections and increasingly demanding leaders. Raising money for the party, which usually requires more effort than voting with one's party, began to set the fundraisers apart from their colleagues whose party loyalty was expressed only in their voting records.

Disloyalty in the Senate

Disloyal senators can do much more damage to their party's agenda or image than disloyal House members can. Senators command and receive much more public attention. The press spills more ink covering senators, and they have higher name recognition among the public. The damage that a senator's public dissent does to the party agenda is therefore more than simply casting a roll-call vote against the party, and it provides more cover to minority-party senators voting against the majority's position. Such damage to the party reputation is not easily detected in roll-call analyses.

In April 2003, Majority Leader Bill Frist (R-TN) was forced to make a deal with Senate moderates to pass President Bush's proposed tax cuts. Frist reached an agreement with House Republican leaders and the White House on tax cuts totaling $550 billion—but Senators Olympia Snowe (R-ME) and George Voinovich (R-OH) refused to support tax cuts at that level. Their opposition generated a great deal of attention, provided cover for moderate Democrats, and proved costly for Frist. On the Senate floor, Frist promised Snowe and Voinovich that the final amount for tax cuts would not exceed $350 billion, which infuriated GOP House leaders and opened Frist up to charges that he had reneged on his promise to the House (Stevens and Taylor 2003). The public leadership of Senator John McCain (R-AZ) on campaign-finance reform (among other issues) over the course of several years—and over the opposition of party leaders—generated much more ill will among Republican leaders than can be captured by his votes on the issue. In his first year as majority leader, Senator Frist appeared on the Sunday morning talk shows only half as often as McCain (Stevens and Taylor 2003). And in the 109th Congress, majority-party members of the "Gang of 14" dashed Frist's chances of passing the so-called constitutional option to end the minority's ability to filibuster judicial nominees.

Senate Leaders' Disciplinary Tools

When Republican Senate leaders pressured Jeffords to support their legislative program in 2001, it had an effect opposite to what the leaders anticipated. They had overreached, and the consequences—losing majority-party control—were costly.

House Republican leaders, despite their thin margin of 221–210 at the time of Jeffords's defection, did not react to it with the concern that observers had expected (and moderate Republicans in the House had hoped for), stating that they did not intend to make any changes within their own chamber to appease moderates.[2] Given their power in the majoritarian House, they did not need to. Majority Whip Tom DeLay (TX) told reporters that he did not plan to change how Republicans ran the House and that party loyalty should always trump disagreements within the party: "It's disappointing that Senator Jeffords doesn't understand what it means to be a member of the party. You work within a structure and you get things done."[3]

Senators have many more individual prerogatives than their House counterparts, but Senate leaders do have some instruments of discipline at their disposal. In the pages that follow, I outline the leaders' disciplinary tools and compare them to those of their House counterparts.

The Legislative Agenda

House leaders have more opportunities than their Senate counterparts to exert party discipline by shaping policy alternatives and denying legislative opportunities to their dissenting members and to minority-party members.

Nonetheless, to the extent possible, Senate floor leaders have capitalized on their scheduling prerogatives (Smith 2005). The Senate majority leader has the right of first recognition. The majority leader is guaranteed the privilege of offering a bill or amendment, or addressing the Senate, before any other senator, and the leader schedules votes. This allows him or her to move that a bill be taken from the calendar and considered, although this motion to proceed can be filibustered. If a leader brings up a bill by unanimous consent, any senator may object.

Two *CQ Weekly* articles highlight the importance of the floor leader's scheduling power. "The power to keep the Senate in session—through the night, the weekend, the August recess—is perhaps the majority leader's most potent weapon in the struggle to impose order on a body with few rules and 100 free spirits" (Donovan 1994). To impose "discipline" on the Senate when seven Democrats missed important votes scheduled on a Friday in 1987, Majority Leader Robert Byrd retaliated by scheduling two more votes that day that they would be embarrassed to miss and publicly chastised the absent Democrats (Calmes 1987).

To what extent does scheduling matter when it comes to the overall Senate agenda or specific policy content? Unlike his or her House counterpart, the majority leader cannot effectively keep legislation off the Senate floor. There is no Senate equivalent of the House Rules Committee; bills in the Senate are not preceded by special rules that structure debate and limit members' opportunities to amend legislation. Further, unlike the House, the Senate does not have a rule stipulating that amendments must be germane, except under limited conditions (e.g., pursuant to a unanimous consent agreement, when considering appropriations and budget bills, and when cloture has been invoked). Senators, then, have ways to circumvent gatekeeping by party leaders or committees. Of course, the Senate leader cannot force a vote on party priorities either. With the rise in filibusters, it often takes sixty votes to bring important legislation to a vote.

To impose some order and efficiency in the legislative process, Senate party leaders will often negotiate a unanimous consent agreement (UCA). UCAs set the terms of debate for a bill, and they may set a time for a final vote. UCAs accommodate senators' specific interests and have the support of all members of both parties. In the Senate, a single member may derail a UCA by objecting. If a senator demands a vote on his or her amendment as a condition of supporting the UCA, leaders have incentives to agree rather than to subject the bill to a possible filibuster.

Majority-party leaders in the House wield considerable agenda control compared to their Senate counterparts. After using their agenda-setting power to determine which bills will be considered on the House floor—and their gatekeeping power to determine which bills won't be considered—they use their influence over the House Committee on Rules to determine which amendments are considered during debate over legislation. Restrictive rules are now the norm, whereby amendments acceptable to party leaders are permitted and all others are barred. The Speaker determines whose noncontroversial bills are considered under the suspension of the rules. The legislative calendar therefore provides party leaders in the House opportunities to exert discipline when they allocate legislative opportunities to their rank-and-file members. In the contemporary era, leaders largely decide which members' bills, amendments, resolutions, and "suspensions" are considered on the House floor, and under what conditions. When leaders are pursuing a partisan agenda, they are willing to reward loyal partisans and fundraisers (Pearson 2005).

Party leaders in the Senate lack these legislative mechanisms of discipline enjoyed by their House counterparts on the floor. It is possible, however, that when party leaders in both chambers finalize the details of major legislation, they have opportunities to reward loyalty. The increasing number of earmarks added in conference committee or during budget summit negotiations may provide limited opportunities to reward loyalty that are worth further investigation.

Lacking the agenda power of their House counterparts, Senate leaders have demonstrated increasing willingness to resort to arcane procedural tactics to try to shape the agenda. When Senate Armed Services Committee chair John Warner (R-VA) announced his plan to mark up a draft of a military-commissions bill supported by three maverick GOP senators—Warner, McCain, and Lindsey Graham (R-SC)—instead of the bill introduced by Frist and supported by President Bush, Frist retaliated. Employing an "obscure Senate rule," GOP leaders had an anonymous senator block the Armed Services Committee markup (Donnelly 2006). The markup continued after the block was removed, but Senate leaders had sent a signal to the three maverick Republicans and their colleagues.

Committee Assignments and Chairmanships

Committee assignments have a relatively dull edge as an instrument of discipline in the Senate, but recent changes suggest that they may soon provide party leaders with more opportunities to reward loyalty and, by omission, punish defection.

Senate rules prohibit members from serving on more than two "A" (major) committees, which include Agriculture, Appropriations, Armed Services,

Banking, Commerce, Energy, Environment, Finance, Foreign Relations, Governmental Affairs, Judiciary, and Health, Education, Labor, and Pensions. Senators may also serve on one "B" committee: Budget, Ethics, Indian Affairs, Rules and Administration, Select Aging, Select Intelligence, Small Business, and Veterans' Affairs. Many senators have received waivers to circumvent these limits. Republican Conference rules bar senators from serving on more than one of the following four "A" committees: Appropriations, Armed Services, Finance, and Foreign Relations.

Senate leaders have little leverage over rank-and-file senators when it comes to committee assignments. Until recently, Republican rules stipulated that seniority dictated all membership on "A" panels. (The Republican leader appoints members to all "B" committees.) The list of committee vacancies circulated from senator to senator, in descending order of seniority, until all seats were filled. In determining seniority, in addition to Senate service, a senator's time in the House or as governor is considered. No other government experience matters. If two senators have equal experience, their names are drawn from a hat. Otherwise, senators are ranked according to the population of their state (Pierce 2002).

At the beginning of the 109th Congress, Senate Republicans voted to change their rules to cede more (but still limited) power to party leaders. Half of the seats are still allocated on the basis of seniority, but now the Republican leader has the power to appoint half of the senators on the "A" committees. In deciding between two task-force recommendations, Republican senators narrowly chose the option giving more power to the leaders. The unsuccessful proposal would have given the party leader the power to fill two slots on each "A" committee as they became available. The leader would then have made another appointment only when one of the leader-appointed members departed the committee or gained enough seniority to get on the committee anyway.

The proposal to allow the Republican leader to appoint half of all open seats on "A" committees passed in 2004 by a secret vote of 27–26. Former majority leader Trent Lott said that the vote was an attempt to fix a "hidebound, muscle-bound, dysfunctional institution" by giving Frist more weapons to prevent Republican senators from going their own way. Indeed, *CQ Weekly*'s analysis referred to this as a "potentially powerful party discipline tool for a leader who is at times caught between the conservative and moderate wings of his caucus." In the same article, moderate Republican senator Olympia Snowe reacted, "I think it's a punitive measure, by any interpretation" (Ota 2004).

In changing the party's rules, Senate Republicans adopted the same assignment process for "A" committees that Democrats already had in place. The Democratic leader factors in how long a senator has waited for a seat on a particular panel and the regional and ideological balance of the panel's Democrats (Pierce 2002). A *CQ Weekly* article describes how this power can be used:

> During his decade as the Democratic leader, Tom Daschle used his power to influence committee assignments, among other factors, to maintain party discipline and block GOP efforts to confirm controversial judicial nominees, change laws governing malpractice and other damage suits, and overhaul federal welfare programs. He also used his power to give a leg up to fellow Democrats with political problems—once even giving his own seat on the tax-writing finance committee to Carol Moseley Braun of Illinois, who was about to begin a tough battle for a second term (Stevens 2004).

In addition to maintaining party discipline, doling out assignments for the purpose of pursuing electoral goals also occurs in the Senate. For example, Minority Whip Harry Reid (D-NV) gave Senator Charles Schumer (D-NY) a position on the Finance Committee to entice him to stay in the Senate and serve as chair of the DSCC instead of running for governor in 2006 (Ota 2004).

To ascertain whether party leaders systematically use committee assignments to pursue their goals, it would be necessary to analyze all committee assignments made by party leaders. Disentangling those assignments made according to seniority from those made by the Democratic leader, however, is complicated. Further, the Democratic leader doesn't always get his way: Kent Conrad (D-ND) won a prized seat on the Finance Committee in 1993 without anointment from Majority Leader George Mitchell (Donovan 1994).

When it comes to committee assignments, Senate leaders' powers are much weaker than those of their House counterparts. When filling vacancies, party leaders in the House have the ability to exert discipline by rewarding loyalty, and they are willing to do so (see, e.g., Cox and McCubbins 1993; and Pearson 2005). Leaders, in conjunction with the parties' Steering Committees, determine which members receive transfers to better committees and waivers to serve on more committees than the rules allow.

Even with recent steps by Senate Republicans to assert more leadership control over committee assignments, institutional differences render committee assignments a less effective disciplinary tool for Senate leaders than for House leaders. Committee membership in the Senate is less central to a legislator's influence in the policymaking process—and in turn to his or her career—than it is in the House. Senators can offer floor amendments to legislation that is reported from committees on which they do not serve. Further, with more committee positions available, the competition for positions is less fierce, and senators serve on more committees than their House counterparts (Sinclair 2005). In the House, a larger membership and a more restrictive amendment process mean that committees provide members their main opportunities to influence legislation.

Seniority and Committee Chairmanships

Up until the 1970s, a strict seniority system determined committee chairmanships in the House of Representatives. During the 1970s, Democratic rule changes meant that committee seniority was no longer a guarantee of a chairmanship. Automatic Democratic Caucus votes on committee chairs at the start of each Congress provide incentives for increased party loyalty among chairs and those who hope to become chairs. In Democratic-controlled Congresses, the Democratic Caucus has occasionally asserted its power to depose sitting committee chairs who strayed too far or to violate seniority in the selection of chairs. During twelve years of Republican control, the seniority system was eclipsed by rules changes that prioritized party loyalty and fundraising, and majority-party Republican leaders were far more willing than Democrats to violate seniority. In 1995, Republicans enacted six-year term limits on committee chairs, enhancing leaders' ability to exert control over the selection process. In the Congresses that followed, seniority became but one of many factors in the selection of committee chairs—factors that also included party loyalty, fundraising prowess, and legislative skill.

When it comes to criteria for selecting committee chairs in the Senate, the paramount importance of committee seniority is clear: in nearly one hundred years, there has been no deviation from it. There have, however, been recent cases where committee chairs' posts have been in peril because they deviated from their party's position in a significant way; but typically it has been the party membership—not party leaders—that have led (unsuccessful) efforts to depose committee chairs. In 1995, Senator Mark Hatfield (R-OR) broke with his party over the balanced-budget amendment, casting a decisive vote against it on the Senate floor. Although Hatfield frequently voted against his GOP colleagues, this vote compelled newer, conservative Republicans, including former House members Rick Santorum (R-PA) and Connie Mack (R-FL), to lead an unsuccessful effort to strip him of the Appropriations Committee chairmanship. Republican leaders opposed this move, and after a meeting in which the Republican Conference discussed it, leaders did not bring it to a vote (Cassata 1995).

Two years after House Republicans adopted six-year term limits for their committee chairs, Republican senators followed suit. Under a conference rules change in 2002, Republican Senate chairs who were demoted to ranking members when Jeffords switched parties did not have any of their service in the 107th Congress count against their six-year limit. Term limits forced Orrin Hatch (R-UT) to relinquish the chairmanship of the Senate Judiciary Committee after the 108th Congress. Seniority dictated that the gavel would go to Arlen Specter (R-PA) in the 109th Congress. Specter is a moderate Republican who supports abortion rights, and the Senate Judiciary Committee can prevent judicial appointments from receiving a vote on the Senate floor. In this case, the nominees of Republican president George W. Bush were at risk—something conservatives were particularly aware of. The morning after the 2004 election, Specter suggested that the Senate would probably not confirm an anti-abortion nominee to the Supreme Court: "When you talk about judges who would change the right of a woman to choose, overturn *Roe v. Wade*, I think that is unlikely" (Perine 2005). Activists from the religious right quickly mobilized against Specter, casting serious doubts in the media about whether he would become chairman. Other outside conservative groups jumped into the fray; for example, the National Taxpayers Union expressed concern that he could derail legislation to limit liability lawsuits (Bettelheim 2004). Specter quickly retreated, publicly denying that he would apply a litmus test to deny confirmation to pro-life nominees to the federal courts and pledging his loyalty to the Bush administration and to his party. This was enough for most committee Republicans and Senate Republicans, and Specter held on to his chairmanship. And in the year that followed, Specter supported President Bush's conservative, pro-life Supreme Court nominees.[4]

Senate precedent and a long history of honoring the seniority system helped Specter retain his position, just as they had enabled Mark Hatfield to retain his chairmanship of the Appropriations Committee. However, Specter was forced to conduct an extensive media tour to reassure conservatives that he would support Bush's nominees, and Majority Leader Frist did not publicly support Specter. The seniority system was not violated, but cracks in what was considered an inviolate system emerged. It is clear that this change means that advancement within the Senate has become more difficult for those who buck the party and that the incentives for toeing the party line in the Senate have intensified.

Assistance on the Campaign Trail

In the words of former House Speaker Thomas P. "Tip" O'Neill Jr. (D-MA), "all politics is local." The campaign trail—far from Washington, D.C.—is not the most obvious place to search for evidence of party discipline. According to conventional wisdom, congressional candidates build their own election constituencies and power bases, which may or may not be linked to local, state, and national parties.[5] Once elected, incumbents can be removed only by their constituents, not by party leaders. Yet despite the relative autonomy of individual candidates, an increasing number of members of Congress, including congressional leaders and rank-and-file members, contribute to their colleagues' campaigns, as seen in tables 6.1 and 6.2.

Given the nature of their mission and leadership, congressional campaign committees are very much a part of the party-in-government, despite their distinct organizational function. Unlike the national party committees, congressional campaign committees—the National Republican Senatorial Committee, Democratic Senatorial Campaign Committee, National Republican Congressional Committee, and Democratic Congressional Campaign Committee—are chaired by members of Congress who, by virtue of this role, are in the inner circle of party leadership. Contribution decisions are therefore made in a context where party leaders possess full knowledge of a member's record and current electoral circumstances. Despite this potential tool of discipline, party leaders prioritize electoral goals when they distribute campaign funds. In both the Senate and the House, the majority of this money goes to the most vulnerable incumbents.

According to Federal Election Commission data, the largest expenditures by the party campaigns in 2004 were in the form of independent expenditures. The DSCC focused its independent expenditures on the nine most vulnerable candidates, including one incumbent, Tom Daschle (D-SD). Four of the contributions totaled over $1 million each. Senators' campaign funds come from many sources, but when they do receive funding from the party and fellow partisans, it is not used as a mechanism of discipline in the Senate.

Conclusion

Party loyalty as expressed in roll-call votes and by fundraising for one's party colleagues is increasing in both chambers of Congress. While the increase in party-line voting reflects, at least to some extent, growing intraparty homogeneity in Congress, the growth in fundraising reflects an increase in the team-sport mentality of congressional parties in both chambers and the ongoing fight for majority-party control in an evenly divided electorate.

Senate individualism is a powerful force that constrains leaders' power relative to that of their House counterparts. Rank-and-file senators have not been willing to cede the same level of power to their leaders that their House counterparts have. The results were aptly summarized by George Mitchell during his bid for majority leader after Robert Byrd stepped down in 1988: "It states the obvious to say that the job of leadership is difficult in a body comprised of 100 equals" (Hook 1988).

Unlimited debate shapes the context in which majority-party leaders in the Senate pursue their goals. The sixty-vote requirement to invoke cloture has necessitated up to ten minority-party votes for legislation in recent Congresses[6] (assuming all majority-party members vote with their party), except on budget resolution and reconciliation votes. Party leaders in the House are most likely to exert party discipline when they need nearly every vote to pass a partisan policy agenda over united minority-party opposition. Such circumstances make it less likely that leaders will attract minority-party votes in the Senate. The "Republicans-only" partisan strategy employed by House leaders in recent Congresses is unworkable in the Senate.

Individualism also protects senators' rights to offer amendments and circumvent gatekeeping, even over the opposition of party leaders or committee chairs. Unlike in the House, the legislative agenda does not provide real opportunities for exerting discipline. Individual rights and a long-standing seniority system have protected senators from discipline in some prominent cases, such as the threatened committee chairmanships of GOP dissidents like Mark Hatfield and Arlen Specter.

Senate leaders' potential tools of discipline, then, are seemingly weak. But they are sharpening, and norms are changing. A slim majority of Republican senators voted to give the party leader more power at the outset of the 109th Congress. Senator Tom Coburn (R-OK) praised the change, claiming that it is "going to give our party more cohesion" (Ota 2004). A near majority expressed support for Majority Leader Bill Frist when he publicly contemplated the "nuclear option." Frist's plan would have changed Senate rules with a procedural vote requiring only fifty-one votes to allow for an up-or-down vote on judicial nominees, effectively ending the minority's right to filibuster judicial nominees. In the 109th Congress, there were fifty-two former House members serving in the Senate, including thirty Republicans; many of these entered Congress after the 1994 elections, in an era of close margins and bitter partisan divides. Socialization is a potent process, and as more new senators are socialized as partisans first and institutionalists second, they may continue to cede power to party leaders, making systematic party discipline easier to identify in the future.

Notes

1. Data are from the Federal Election Commission and the Center for Responsive Politics 2004.
2. *CongressDaily*, "Politics—House Caucuses Differ on Fallout from Switch by Jeffords," May 25, 2001.
3. Ibid.
4. Bush's nominee Harriet Miers withdrew without any Judiciary Committee votes, lacking support from conservatives and liberals, including Specter.
5. Party leaders are increasingly likely to support likely winners in primaries in competitive races (Dominguez 2005).
6. This was the case when Republicans held fifty Senate seats but, with the vice president's vote, still effectively had a majority.

7

Make Way for the Party: The Rise and Fall of the Senate National Security Committees, 1947–2006

LINDA L. FOWLER AND R. BRIAN LAW

As the United States entered its second year of conflict in Iraq, the chair of the Senate Foreign Relations Committee proposed hearings regarding the conduct and objectives of the war. House Majority Leader Tom DeLay (R-TX) quickly attacked the proposal for its disloyalty to the Republican Party and its potential harm to President Bush's electoral fortunes, while none of the administration's top-level decision makers appeared at the modest inquiry that eventually took place in April 2004 (Rosenbaum 2004). A month later, the Senate Armed Services Committee chair, John Warner (R-VA), received a similar rebuke from his Republican counterpart in the House: that hearings regarding the treatment of prisoners at Abu Ghraib in Iraq were unnecessary (Dewar and Hsu 2004). To add insult to injury, the heads of the two committees played a secondary role to party leaders in crafting the politically charged resolutions regarding support for continuation of the Iraq war that came to the floor under Republicans in the summer of 2006 and again in the winter and spring of 2007 when the Democrats gained the majority. These incidents highlight the diminished independence and relevance of the two once formidable Senate committees and raise larger questions about institutional change in Congress and its consequences for the role of parties in national security affairs.

Committees have traditionally been the linchpin of the institutional power and policy expertise of Congress (Wilson [1885] 1973; Sundquist 1981; Fenno 1973), although they have been less central to the operation of the Senate than the House (Aldrich and Rohde 2005) and are currently less independent of the parties than in the past (Rohde 2005). Scholars have focused on their role in bargaining and logrolls (Shepsle and Weingast 1981b), their informational functions (Krehbiel 1991), their gatekeeping role in the emergence of conditional party government (Kiewiet and McCubbins 1991; Aldrich 1995b; Aldrich and Rohde 2001; Cox and McCubbins 2005, 2007), and their activities as agents of both the floor and the party caucus (Maltzman 1997). Committees did more than carry out particular functions, however: they fostered a decentralized system of power in Congress that constrained the influence of party leaders and presidents.

Despite their importance, surprisingly little discussion of the changing status of Senate committees has arisen in the current literature. The neglect is understandable, because changes regarding the prerogatives of Senate committees have been episodic, seemingly modest, and often informal. The consequences have been substantial, however: first, by adding to the collective-action problems in the Senate that powerful committee barons once handled; and second, by diminishing the incentives for committees to protect their turf from party leaders. The implication for U.S. foreign and defense policy is a potential de-emphasis of the informational role of committee experts in favor of the political calculations of party leaders.

This chapter develops a logic of unintended consequences regarding the flattening of the committee hierarchy and argues that the national security committees are a particularly significant venue to examine the workings of such broad trends. It develops a new measure of committee attractiveness—the seniority ratio, based on the distribution of senior senators—to illuminate the evolution of committee rankings over time. Comparisons of the seniority ratio for all Senate committees provide a context for the more detailed descriptions of patterns for Foreign Relations and Armed Services. The analysis then shifts to an examination of the relative importance of internal influences, such as the mean number of committee assignments and the polarization of the parties, compared to exogenous disturbances, such as public opinion, war casualties, budget priorities, and the end of the Cold War. The conclusion considers the implications of the results for the role of committees and parties in shaping U.S. foreign and defense policy.

Thinking about Senate Committees

The changes in the Senate committee system arise from two different but complementary trends. First, the Senate democratized the committee system in response to pressure from members seeking greater opportunities for influence and policy entrepreneurship (Sinclair 1989, 2001b). Beginning with the "Johnson rule" in 1953 and accelerating with the Legislative Reorganization Act in 1970, individual senators were guaranteed a spot on one

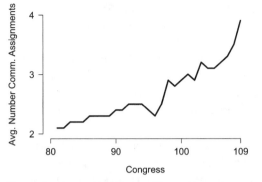

Fig. 7.1: Average number of committee assignments per senator (data are from Ornstein, Mann, and Malbin 2002, supplemented by the *Congressional Directory* through the 109th Congress)

of the Super A committees—Foreign Relations, Appropriations, Finance, and Armed Services.

Party leaders and caucuses facilitated access by expanding the size of the committees. Consequently, the average number of committees per senator rose from 2.1 in 1947 to 3.9 in 2005–6, as indicated in figure 7.1. Over the same period, major reorganization efforts to streamline committee jurisdictions failed,[1] and subcommittees proliferated to the point that every member of the majority party chaired at least one (Ornstein, Mann, and Malbin 2002). These trends compounded the collective-action problems that plague the highly individualistic Senate, because senators had fewer incentives to invest in any one committee and more opportunities to buck powerful chairs (Sinclair 1989, 2001b; Evans 1991; Deering and Smith 1997).

Amid spiraling transaction costs within and among committees, members had good reason to seek greater coordination through the parties (Aldrich 1995b), even though the Senate lacked the procedural tools available to House leaders. Paradoxically, democratization of the committee system was so successful in promoting the influence of individual senators that fewer could claim the mantle of power broker. The Senate continues to have powerful committees, notably Appropriations and Finance, but the fiefdoms of the old "textbook" Congress have diminished in influence. Parties were the unintended beneficiaries of a process that reduced the capacity of committees to protect their turf.[2]

The second trend affecting the Senate committee system was change in the external environment because of the rise of interest groups, the emergence of new issues, and the polarization of party activists (Sinclair 1989, 2001b). Fenno's classic study (1973) indicates that members' goals and strategic premises are highly sensitive to the conditions in which the committees operate. In addition, contextual effects shape committee leadership (Evans 1991), while issue salience affects the relationship between parties and committees (Maltzman 1997). It seems inevitable, therefore, that the attractiveness of specific committees would vary with broad political trends and transformative events.

Capturing external influences on congressional committees is problematic, however, because the environmental constraints vary so considerably by policy domain, institutional actors, and constituency pressures (Fenno 1973). For example, war casualties will affect service on Foreign Relations, but not Banking. To weigh the impact of such factors on committee attractiveness, therefore, requires limitations on the scope of the analysis.

We focus on the Senate's national security committees, Foreign Relations and Armed Services, because they have useful similarities and differences.[3] Both committees' jurisdictions involve high stakes of war and peace; and both contend with powerful executive prerogatives. Yet they vary in their relevance to domestic constituencies, and until the mid-1970s, Foreign Relations enjoyed greater status in the Senate, despite the fact that both were on the Super A list.

The national security committees were, and continue to be, particularly susceptible to external pressures from the executive. As Fenno (1973) noted, the interplay of member goals and strategic premises was particularly strong for what was then the House Foreign Affairs Committee, and he expressed concern about the capacity of Foreign Relations to maintain the high level of prestige it enjoyed at the time of his study. Senators, he observed, had "done nothing to give their Foreign Relations Committee any special operating autonomy," and such "ambivalence" might have an effect on the future behavior of committee members (155–56).

Scholars have described the shifts in the prestige of the Senate national security committees. For example, the committee ranking system known as the Grosewart index placed Foreign Relations as the top Senate committee from the early twentieth century through the end of World War II (Canon and Stewart 2002), a dominance that continued from the 81st to the 93rd Congresses (Stewart and Groseclose 1999). During the 94th to 102nd Congresses, however, the Grosewart index revealed Foreign Relations dropping to fifth place, behind Finance, Rules and Administration, Appropriations, and Armed Services (Stewart and Groseclose 1999).

Similarly, Deering's depiction (2001, 2005) of the environmental pressures on Foreign Relations and Armed Services highlighted the inability of the two national security committees to meet the challenges of executive prerogatives. Although Deering credited Armed Services with more effective leadership and more sophisticated use of annual authorizations than Foreign Relations, his analyses concluded on a pessimistic note regarding the capacity of either committee to carve out a meaningful role in the conduct of war or diplomacy. Given these constraints, ambitious lawmakers have had incentives to gravitate toward the committees that still offer institutional power with the added benefit of constituency payoffs—Appropriations and Finance—and to maximize their scope of influence by adding other, less significant committees to their portfolios.

Theoretical and methodological issues have limited explanations of the causes of such institutional changes, however. First, scholarly theories of legislative institutions derive from assumptions about member goals but treat these objectives as exogenous.[4] Rohde (1995) has argued that the distinction between preferences and decisions is often problematic and that legislators' choices may not match their first priorities, for a variety of reasons. He maintains further that preferences will vary with the political contentiousness and salience of issues. Consequently, members' committee preferences may be endogenous to the institution, depending upon the opportunities available, as well as highly sensitive to political context (134). A complementary line of reasoning underlies Cooper and Rybicki's argument (2002) for the inclusion of external factors as influences on particular institutional choices.

In addition, Schickler has demonstrated that institutional choices are often suboptimal, disjointed, and "full of tensions and contradictions" (2001, 267). The resulting rules and structures may be intentional but may also be inadvertent, producing consequences that legislators did not anticipate. Party theory predicts subordination of congressional committees to caucus control in the House (Kiewiet and McCubbins 1991; Aldrich 1995a; Cox and McCubbins 2005, 2007). Yet the case of the Senate is particularly vexing, because the need for supermajorities tends to foreclose formal revision of rules. Thus, the rise of party unity in the Senate, which so closely resembles conditional party government in the House, has taken place without the obvious procedural antecedents that enhanced the powers of the party leaders over representatives. Committee democratization, by creating multiple venues to pursue legislative ambitions, appears to have reduced the need for senators to protect individual committee jurisdictions. The increased visibility of party leaders in the Senate (Evans and Lipinski 2005) thus encountered surprisingly little resistance from the committee chairs whom they supplanted in the press.

The second constraint in understanding alteration of the Senate committee system is more practical, involving questions of measurement. The Grosewart index, which constructs committee rankings on the basis of transfers, is highly aggregated across decades, which makes it difficult to track changes or to pinpoint their origin. To address this constraint, we develop a new measure of committee attractiveness based on the distribution of senior senators.[5]

Although most of the findings are specific to two committees, an understanding of the unintended nature of institutional adaptation to the external environment in the case of Foreign Relations and Armed Services should shed light on congressional parties and committees more broadly. Overall, the analysis suggests that pursuit of individual member goals may push the Senate in directions that can undermine its long-term capacity to balance the executive branch, because of the substitution of partisan calculation for committee expertise. Independent-minded committees in the past have spoken truth to power in the White House, even when the Congress and the president shared a party label. Contemporary observers have faulted Congress for neglecting its basic responsibilities, for producing sloppy legislation, and most importantly for dereliction of duty in restraining presidential power (Mann and Ornstein 2006b; Rohde 2005; Fisher 2005). At least some of this criticism reflects members' diminished investment in committee expertise and responsibility.

Measuring Attractiveness of Senate Committees

Past scholarly measures of committee attractiveness have built primarily upon lawmakers' decisions to transfer off and onto committees, although Adler and Lapinski (1997) employed district interests to explain assignment to constituency committees in the House. Groseclose and Stewart (1998) developed a technique for the House that built upon earlier work by Bullock and Sprague (1969) and Munger (1988), incorporating information about the committees lawmakers transferred to, as well as the ones they left.[6] The Grosewart index that they subsequently calculated for the Senate tracked shifts in committee desirability from the 14th to the 79th Congresses (Canon and Stewart 2002) and for the contemporary Senate in the 80th to 102nd Congresses (Stewart and Groseclose 1999). Their findings proved consistent with the official Senate categorical hierarchy in ranking the Super A committees—Appropriations, Finance, Foreign Relations, and Armed Services—

with Foreign Relations in first place and Armed Services in fifth place for most of the twentieth century. By the mid-1970s, however, the Grosewart index and the Senate Super A list began to diverge, as Foreign Relations slipped to fifth place behind Armed Services, and Rules moved into the second spot. These shifts over time are difficult to investigate without a continuous measure of committee attractiveness, as noted above.

Other factors complicate the ranking of committee choices beyond individual lawmakers' strategic considerations. Norms generally prevent senators representing the same state from serving together on a committee, while ensuring states with relevant constituency characteristics at least one seat (Deering and Smith 1997). By the same token, senators from the same state use their committee assignments to differentiate themselves from each other (Schiller 2000a). Such constraints suggest that Rohde's caution about the endogeneity of preferences (1995) seems particularly apt in the context of committee decisions in the Senate. For many reasons, then, senators' choices may not reflect an underlying institutional preference ordering.

The Grosewart index provides evidence to this effect when we compare the committee scores for the Senate and the House, indicating that the index is less effective for the Senate. These scores show less consensus among senators than among representatives about the most desirable committees in their respective chambers; and they reveal smaller differences among senators than among House members in the size of the coefficients between the top committees and the least attractive ones, as well as higher numbers of so-called burden committees in the Senate than in the House (Stewart and Groseclose 1999, 967, 971).

At the same time, committees' external environments changed with the rise of new issues on the policy agenda, such as the environment, the shift in budget priorities toward entitlements, the eventual winding down of the Cold War, and the explosion of interest groups. Democratization of the committee-assignment process enabled senators to appeal to more diverse constituencies and to acquire committee seniority and influence in more policy domains (cf. Sinclair 1989, 2001b; Deering and Smith 1997). In other words, committees remained vital to Senate careers, but the emphasis shifted to breadth rather than depth. Taken together, internal constraints on senators' preferences and external stimuli should flatten the differences in desirability for most committees across time and reduce the commitment of lawmakers to any one committee.

Where did parties fit in the changing patterns of committee status? Party caucuses were the vehicles for expanding committee access, beginning with the Johnson rule, as noted above. A critical ingredient was not only caucus approval for increasing the numbers of assignments, but the mutual collaboration of Democratic and Republican leaders to expand the size of individual committees in order to accommodate the burgeoning portfolios of individual senators. There is little evidence that party leaders were doing anything other than responding to the desires of their members, but disruption of the power of old-style committee barons had consequences once the parties became more polarized. By dividing their attention across committees, senators had less at stake in any single committee on which they served and therefore less incentive to protect the committee's turf. Democratization of the committee system thus seems to have contributed to the mix of individualism and partisan polarization characteristic of the current Senate (Sinclair 2005).[7]

To measure shifts in the attractiveness of individual committees across time, we exploit the fact that seniority factors heavily in the award of committee requests. Senate Republicans use a formula based strictly on seniority, although Democrats weigh other factors on a case-by-case basis (Schneider 2003). Generally, senators' personal and political characteristics have mattered only in "tiebreakers," when members of equal seniority are competing for the same seat (Deering and Smith 1997, 106; Kiewiet and McCubbins 1991; Cox and McCubbins 1993, 2005). If some committees continue to be more desirable than others, even within the less hierarchical Senate, they should accumulate higher percentages of members with long service. The same phenomenon is observable in football stadiums, where longtime ticket holders end up dominating the choice seats on or near the fifty-yard line. If we think about this in terms of probability and randomly choose a person from the midfield section, there is a very good chance that the person is a long-standing ticket holder. Similarly, if we randomly choose a lawmaker from a Super A committee, there should be a high probability that the senator has served in the Senate for many years. Note that, like the Grosewart index, the seniority ratio makes no a priori assumptions about committee desirability and merely depends upon each senator's years of service in the Senate and the specific committee assignment.

Calculating the index of committee attractiveness is straightforward. Seniority is measured as the number of continuous years of service in the Senate. Summing the seniority of all committee members and dividing the total by the number of senators on the committee generates the average seniority for that committee. This measure permits comparison of committees' average seniority *within* a given Congress.[8] For example, Appropriations and Agriculture had average seniority of 12.9 and 10.3 years, respectively, in the 86th Congress (1959–60). However, simple averages do not allow comparison *across* time and Congresses, because the level of seniority in the Senate in any given year depends on the number of retirements and electoral defeats. A flood of freshmen lowers most or all committees' average seniority compared to the prior Congress, but not because of any shifts in senators' strategic decisions to add assignments to their portfolio. To control for the fluctuating level of seniority in the Senate, we divide each committee's average seniority by the average seniority of the entire Senate to get the seniority ratio.[9]

$$\text{seniority ratio} = \frac{\text{committee's average seniority}}{\text{senate's average seniority}}$$

The seniority ratio has a simple substantive interpretation such that a committee's attractiveness is reflected in how much the seniority ratio differs from the number one. For example, the Armed Services Committee had a seniority ratio of 1.25 in the 105th Congress, which means that the committee's average seniority was 25 percent greater than if the Senate had filled the committee by lottery.

Figures 7.2a to 7.2d depict the seniority ratio for all Senate standing committees, with the exception of Post Office and District of Columbia, from 1947 to 2006.[10] We use the Deering and Smith (1997) classification scheme to categorize the committees that are not on the Super A list, although we include Rules with the Super A group because of its recently elevated status. The seniority ratio varies considerably across time, but the trend has been a steady narrowing of the gap between high-seniority committees and low-seniority ones, with a few exceptions, such as Banking. Among the Super A committees plus Rules in figure 7.2a, only Appropriations has consistently been above the threshold of one for the entire period, while Finance dropped below one during the 1970s and has recovered to slightly above one today. Armed Services has been the most consistent committee in terms of its concentration of long-serving members, tracking very close to one for the entire period, but in recent years it has dipped below one. Foreign Relations has dropped precipitously; it boasted the greatest concentration of senior lawmakers before falling below Armed Services and even below several of the policy committees in figure 7.2b.

The policy committees reveal a general increase in their attractiveness to senior lawmakers over time. The big winner appears to be Judiciary, which has increased its seniority ratio substantially since the 98th Congress; it now outranks Armed Services and Foreign Relations, while drawing even with Finance. The other four policy committees are at or close to one for recent Congresses. In contrast, all of the constituency committees, with the exception

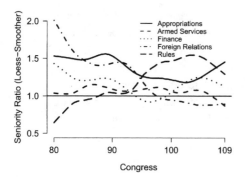

Fig. 7.2a: Changes in seniority ratio: "Super A" committees

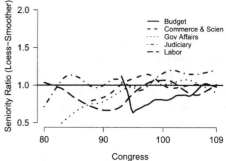

Fig. 7.2b: Changes in seniority ratio: "Policy" committees

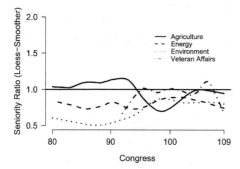

Fig. 7.2c: Changes in seniority ratio: "Constituency service" committees

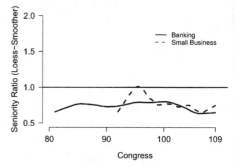

Fig. 7.2d: Changes in seniority ratio: "Mixed" committees

of Agriculture, continue to be disproportionately packed with junior senators. With respect to the two "mixed" committees, Banking has proved consistently undesirable.

Figure 7.3 reveals further evidence of the committee hierarchy's leveling in a series of box plots that show the distribution of seniority-ratio scores for all committees over time. Each box shows the 25th, 50th, and 75th percentile values (the interquartile range), while vertical dotted lines mark the minimum or maximum value within 1.5 times interquartile range. Open circles designate outliers beyond the maximum and minimum values. The vertical line at the 94th Congress is consistent with the dividing point for the Grosewart index and captures changes in the postreform era. The compression of the box plots over time highlights the fact that democratization diminished, but did not eliminate, the segregation of junior senators on less desirable committees and also spread senior members more broadly across most committees.

The seniority ratio, however, moves at different rates across time for Republicans and Democrats on the two national security committees. Figure 7.4a indicates, for example, that senior Republicans placed a significantly higher valuation on Foreign Relations than did Democrats until the 100th Congress. After that time, Foreign Relations gained favor among senior Democrats, while it continued to lose appeal among Republicans.[11] Indeed, the seniority ratio indicates that GOP decisions to shun the committee have been a major factor in its declining fortunes. The partisan valuations of Armed Services have also diverged, after converging briefly in the 1960s. Senior Democrats found the committee increasingly attractive in the mid-1990s but began to avoid it in recent years, while longer-serving Republicans have been increasingly unwilling to serve. As with Foreign Relations, the diminished attractiveness of Armed Services seems to be an artifact of changes in Republican decisions. Such partisan differences raise interesting questions about how members react to changes in the committees' political context.

The seniority ratio's results are consistent in many ways with the Grosewart index. In the interests of saving space, we summarize the similarities and differences rather than presenting additional tables and direct the reader to Law (2007) for a full discussion. For the pre-reform period, both measures picked the same top five committees and ranked them similarly in agreement with the Super A list, with the exception of Agriculture and Commerce and Science, which ranked just ahead of Armed Services on the seniority measure. In addition, both measures tapped into the dramatic change in the status of Rules and of Foreign Relations in the mid-1970s.

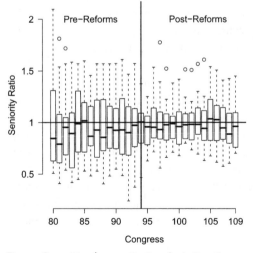

Fig. 7.3: Committee democratization: Seniority ratio

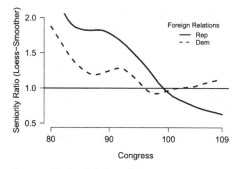

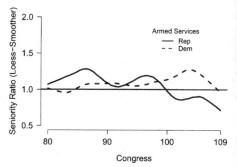

Fig. 7.4a: Foreign Relations Committee seniority ratio, by party

Fig. 7.4b: Armed Services Committee seniority ratio, by party

The major differences are in the postreform rankings. The Grosewart index includes the 94th to the 102nd Congresses, but the seniority ratio indicates that the democratization process began a few years earlier with the 92nd Congress (1971–72), immediately following the 1970 Legislative Reorganization Act. To make comparisons, however, we average the seniority ratio across the 94th through the 109th Congress to obtain the following ranking: Rules, Appropriations, Judiciary, Finance, and Armed Services, with Foreign Affairs quite far down the pecking order. In contrast, the top five for the Grosewart index are Finance, Rules, Appropriations, Armed Services, and Foreign Relations. The seniority ratio, as expected, is more sensitive to variation over time. For example, the Grosewart index appears to have underestimated the overall decline of Foreign Relations in recent years and failed to pick up the fluctuating status of Finance. Most important, the seniority ratio suggests a slightly different view of committee desirability, as follows: Appropriations consistently at the top in terms of desirability; a fairly large cluster that includes two of the Super A committees (Finance and Armed Services), as well as several policy and constituency committees (Judiciary, Government Affairs, Agriculture, and Commerce); and another cluster that includes Foreign Relations and the remainder of the policy and constituency-oriented committees.

If we view these trends more broadly, it appears that democratization not only helped junior senators, but also benefited senior senators by enabling them to diversify. Lessening the differences among committees, moreover, indicates a serious mismatch between the Senate rules regarding Super A committees and senators' observed behavior. More important, it may have diminished senators' interest in protecting individual committees from party influences.

External versus Internal Influences on Senate Committee Prestige

The relatively flat hierarchy of committee assignments has responded to external incentives as well. For the national security committees, similarities and differences are readily apparent in their respective environments. Both committees cope with asymmetries in information and overwhelming executive prerogatives, but they differ in the size of their budget authorizations and their relevance to constituency concerns. For example, Foreign Relations has a significantly smaller portfolio of programs to authorize than Armed Services, including the perennially unpopular foreign aid budget. In addition, its domestic constituencies pay attention to aid in the Middle East and Africa, as well as global trade, but Foreign Relations' jurisdiction typically involves smaller and less concentrated benefits than is the case for Armed Services Committee members (see Rundquist and Carsey 2002). Finally, Armed Services' responsibility for military personnel may make it more attuned to casualties. Thus, we expect that both committees will reflect external environmental influences but will respond to different variables. The net effect, however, is to reduce their prestige as institutional actors.

To evaluate the influences on the changing status of the national security committees, we run separate regressions for Foreign Relations and Armed Services with explanatory variables for both internal and external covariates. The dependent variable in the analysis is the numerator of the seniority ratio—the committee's average seniority for a given Congress. The ratio's denominator, the average seniority of the chamber, becomes a "control" on the right-hand side. In other words, we predict the mean seniority for each committee (*commsen*) and deploy the mean seniority for the chamber as a control (*chambsen*). This rearranging does not change the substantive results and allows us to use ordinary least squares, which makes interpretation of the coefficients more intuitive for the reader.

The key internal explanatory variable for committee seniority is the mean number of committee assignments (*commassign*). In addition, the analysis controls for the polarization of the parties within the Senate, using the difference in medians of first-dimension DW-NOMINATE scores for Republicans and Democrats (*chambpol*). The party-polarization variable is a standard way of operationalizing the development of conditional party government. Law (2007) reports an inverse relationship between the seniority ratio and partisan polarization for all committees. Thus, this variable appears to be a good proxy for any increase in partisan influence over the committee-assignment process.

With respect to external influences on committee attractiveness, two types of variables are relevant. The first concerns the salience of foreign and defense policy generally, which we capture with measures of public opinion and military casualties. Public opinion varies significantly across the post–World War II time series in terms of the salience of foreign and defense policy, and it is a chronically volatile issue in attitude surveys (Holsti 2004; Jones and Baumgartner 2005). The variable (*public opinion*) is the percentage of respondents who designate foreign and defense policy as the most important problem in Gallup surveys. Major conflicts also increase interest among citizens in international events, although the effect of casualties on public opinion has varied with the nature of the conflict (see Karol and Miguel 2007; Berinksy 2005; Gartner and Segura 1998; Jentleson 1992). The log of the number of U.S. and foreign casualties is used in the analysis, *casualties(ln)*. Given the domestic economic benefits that draw senators to Armed Services, we expect that both measures of salience will be less important for the attractiveness of the committee than is the case for Foreign Relations.

Finally, the end of the Cold War was a watershed in the nation's security posture. We use a dummy for 1989 and subsequent years, marking the fall of the Berlin Wall.

The second type of external constraint is budget authority, which differs dramatically for the two committees, as noted above. Immediately following the end of World War II, the disparity between federal expenditures on foreign aid and diplomacy and those for military personnel and equipment was relatively modest. Since then, both categories have shrunk as a percentage of all federal budget outlays, because of the growth of entitlements spending. Military expenditures have dwarfed those related to foreign policy but have been more volatile, with big increases during the Korean and Vietnam wars followed by shrinkage during peacetime and, most recently, an escalation after 9/11. The variable *budget* takes different values for Foreign Relations and Armed Services; it is the authorized amount for international affairs and defense, respectively, as a percentage of total authorized funds in the federal budget. Again, we expect that downward shifts in the budget will have different consequences for the two committees. Senior senators will be deterred from serving on Foreign Relations as its unpopular budgetary authority becomes more limited. Expectations for Armed Services are unclear: on the one hand, senior senators might find the committee less attractive when defense budgets shrink relative to domestic programs; on the other hand, senators might seek to move to the committee to protect vital constituency interests.

TABLE 7.1. Descriptive statistics of variables, 1947-2006 (by Congress)

Variable	Brief description	Mean	Median	St Dev.	Min	Max	N
Dependent variable	Commsen (each committee's average seniority, in years)						
Foreign Relations		12	12	3	8	17	30
Armed Services		11	11	2	7	14	30
Independent variables							
budget (defense)	Percentage of federal budget	34%	27%	15%	16%	69%	30
budget (int'l affairs)	Percentage of federal budget	3%	2%	3%	1%	16%	30
casualties	Raw number of casualties	120,000	7,995	210,000	0	640,000	29
chambpol	Difference in median party DW-NOMINATE	0.62	0.61	0.10	0.43	0.89	30
chambsen	Senate's average seniority (in years)	10	11	2	7	13	30
Cold War (1989)	Cold War dummy	0.73	1.00	0.45	0.00	1.00	30
commassign	Average committee assignments per senator	2.65	2.50	0.47	2.10	3.90	30
public opinion	Most important problem (%)	15%	13%	13%	0%	43%	30

Several of the independent variables use values lagged by one Congress in the expectation that members rely on past experience to evaluate the future desirability of a committee. All variables are aggregated by Congress, but because of the lagged variables, the analysis has an N of 29 (81st to 109th Congresses) for the full models. For the annual budget allocation and the public opinion variable, we used the mean for each two-year Congress. For the casualties variable, we used the sum of the two years within each Congress. Table 7.1 gives a summary of the independent variables and descriptive statistics.

Ordinary least squares regression with robust standard errors is used to estimate the relative strength of internal and external factors on committee attractiveness. The analysis for each committee produces separate estimates for internal and external effects and then combines them in order to highlight the impact of each set of regressors. Diagnostic checks for heteroskedasticity, autocorrelation,[12] and influential outliers did not call for a more elaborate specification. Significance tests are two-tailed.

Results

For the Foreign Relations Committee, table 7.2 presents regression results predicting changes in the committee's attractiveness to senior senators by breaking out the internal and external covariates and then examining their combined effects. The model restricted solely to internal variables shows that both the mean number of committee assignments and party polarization in the Senate reduced the attractiveness of the committee to senior members, controlling for the overall change in the mean seniority of the chamber. In substantive terms, if every senator took one more committee assignment, the average seniority on Foreign Relations would decrease by nearly five years (−4.92), a strong indication that expansion was a major factor in the loss of prestige of the Senate committee.

With only the external variables, increased casualties and greater concern within the public about foreign and defense policy led to significantly greater committee attractiveness. For example, if the percentage of the public concerned about foreign and defense policy increased by one standard deviation, which is nearly 13 percent, then the Foreign Relations committee's average seniority would increase by 0.8 years, all else equal.[13]

The last column in table 7.2 presents the complete model, in which the coefficients for mean number of assignments, public opinion, and casualties are all significant and the signs are in the hypothesized direction. Interpretation of the log of the casualties variable indicates that a 100 percent increase in the number of casualties in any given time period should result in a 0.20 increase in the committee's average seniority in the following Congress. In other words, it would require an enormous increase in casualties in order to change members' career incentives to serve on Foreign Relations, while relatively modest shifts in public opinion hold great weight.

The patterns are somewhat different for the Armed Services Committee, as expected (see table 7.3). For the internal variables, only chamber seniority is significant, and it has a modest positive effect on committee seniority. With respect to external influences, only the log of the casualties variable is significant, but the sign is in the *wrong* direction, such that more casualties are associated with lower average committee seniority. As with Foreign Relations, its substantive effect is very small.

TABLE 7.2. Foreign Relations Committee prestige, 1949–2006, by Congress

(Dependent variable = committee average seniority, Commsen)

	Internal covariates	External covariates	Combined
Commassign	−4.92***		−3.35***
	(1.38)		(0.99)
Chambpol	−13.76*		−4.66
	(7.01)		(3.89)
Chambsen	1.74***	0.69**	1.11***
	(0.39)	0.32	(0.29)
Public Opinon (L)		6.32**	6.87***
		(2.80)	(2.42)
Cold War dummy		1.34	−0.53
		(1.01)	(0.99)
Budget (L)		0.83	0.24
		(0.63)	(0.58)
Casualties (ln) (L)		0.23***	0.20***
		(0.06)	(0.05)
Constant	16.04***	4.73*	11.44***
	(2.63)	(2.56)	(2.73)
N	30	29	29
R^2	0.55	0.78	0.88

Note: OLS regressions; robust standard errors are given in parentheses. (L) indicates variables lagged by one Congress. $N = 29$ in models with lagged variables, starting in 81st Congress (1949).

*$p <. 1$; **$p < .05$; ***$p < .01$ (two-tailed test)

The combined model yields a slightly different pattern. Most notably, the mean number of committee assignments is significant, and it is negatively correlated with committee attractiveness. If every senator took one more committee assignment, the committee's average seniority would decrease by 1.8 years, slightly more than one standard deviation. As expected, the desirability of Armed Services among senior members is not responsive to public opinion. The results, however, do not confirm our hypothesis that changes in the defense budget would affect senators' decisions to build careers on this committee.

In sum, committee career decisions for the Senate national security committees appear responsive to the democratization of the chamber's committee hierarchy, as well as to changes in the external environment. Foreign

TABLE 7.3. Armed Services Committee prestige, 1949–2006, by Congress

Dependent variable = Committee average seniority, Commsen

	"Internal" Covariates	"External" Covariates	Combined
Commassign	−1.28		−1.94*
	(1.04)		(1.02)
Chambpol	8.38		4.27
	(5.38)		(4.84)
Chambsen	0.65**	0.91***	0.98***
	(0.27)	(0.18)	(0.22)
Public Opinon (L)		−0.40	0.05
		(2.32)	(2.47)
Cold War dummy		0.09	−0.27
		(0.76)	(0.81)
Budget (L)		0.83	0.22
		(0.81)	(0.80)
Casualties (ln) (L)		−0.14***	−0.15***
		(0.04)	(0.04)
Constant	2.46	3.57*	4.85**
	(1.54)	(2.02)	(2.06)
N	30	29	29
R^2	0.63	0.70	0.74

Note: OLS regressions; robust standard errors are given in parentheses. (L) indicates variables lagged by one Congress. $N = 29$ in models with lagged variables, starting in 81st Congress (1949).

$*p < .1; **p < .05; ***p < .01$ (two-tailed test)

Relations, however, proved more susceptible to both, and thus emerged as potentially more susceptible to party influence.

Conclusion

This chapter demonstrates a significant change in the Senate committee system overall and examines in detail the impact of this shift on Foreign Relations and Armed Services. In the aftermath of the 1970 Legislative Reorganization Act and pressures by junior members to spread influence more widely within the chamber, the committee hierarchy became flatter as members added committee assignments to their portfolios. Both the Grosewart index and the seniority ratio capture changes in senators' committee preferences, but the seniority ratio highlights considerable variation in the attractiveness of committees over time and enables us to pinpoint the onset of democratization in the 92nd Congress. Moreover, by providing a continuous measure of committee status, it allows us to put committee prestige "on the left-hand side" as a dependent variable and to examine the impact of external influences on members' decisions regarding their careers within the Senate.

Much of the change was intentional, in order to satisfy members' demands for expanding their scope for policy influence. But as Schickler (2001) might have predicted, some of the shift was an unintended byproduct, as environmental factors reinforced internal incentives. The group of top committees, for example, no longer coincides with the chamber's designated Super A list. Moreover, the consequences of these trends have been particularly detrimental to Foreign Relations. If White House officials had conspired to undercut the president's chief rival in foreign affairs, they could not have done a better job.

Since the invasion of Iraq in 2003, public criticism of Congress has intensified (Mann and Ornstein 2006b; Fisher 2005). From its failure to ask hard questions before passing a blanket authorization in the fall of 2002, to its refusal to engage in oversight during the years of GOP control, to its inability to oppose an unpopular president in the aftermath of an election that repudiated his policies, Congress has sunk in public esteem. Missing from the national debate are senators with the stature of a J. William Fulbright or a Sam Nunn to speak authoritatively to the nation about the direction of U.S. security policy. To be sure, both the past and present chairs of Foreign Relations and Armed Services have been active legislatively, and both Republican ranking members made headlines briefly when they broke with the president in July 2007 about remaining in Iraq. But the voices of committee members are merely few among many, with no apparent special claim to shaping elite discourse about the war.

Instead, the initiative and the spotlight have been on the Senate party leaders and their counterparts in the House. To the outside observer, both Republican and Democratic leaders appear more concerned with the reputational effects of the Iraq war than with the difficult policy choices entailed in either its continuation or its termination. In light of the historic importance of the Foreign Relations and Armed Services committees in crafting and sustaining the largely successful policy of containment during the long years of the Cold War, their marginalization today is troubling. Yet reversal of the declining fortunes of the national security committees is unlikely under the current incentive system, and the substitution of partisanship for expertise in U.S. foreign affairs seems likely to persist.

Notes

The authors acknowledge support from the John Simon Guggenheim Foundation for a fellowship year for Fowler and from the Nelson A. Rockefeller Center at Dartmouth College for funds to collect data. The article has evolved from an early version presented at the 2005 annual meeting of the American Political Science Association and has benefited from the comments of too many helpful scholars to acknowledge individually.

1. The Senate did eliminate the Post Office and District of Columbia committees.
2. The decision by the Republican caucus in 1995 to limit committee chairs to three terms is symptomatic of the subordination of the Senate committee system to party leaders.
3. We do not examine the Senate Intelligence Committee because it was not created until the mid-1970s, and we are not able to obtain sufficient observations for statistical analysis.
4. This is different from the issue of multiple goals and principals raised by Maltzman (1997).
5. The Grosewart index calculates a value for the 80th to the 93rd Congresses and another for the 94th to the 102nd. In addition, the index is substantively difficult to interpret.
6. Stewart and Groseclose compare their measure to its two predecessors as follows: "(1) [the earlier methods] do not use all the information available about *which* committees are acquired and *which* committees are relinquished in the course of each transfer; (2) they do not deal with 'many-for-many' transfers satisfactorily, nor with 'null transfers' (i.e., uncompensated departures from committees); (3) the transfer dominance method is sensitive to the 'sparse cell problem;' (4) neither method solves for committee power simultaneously; (5) neither method provides goodness-of-fit measures with known statistical properties; (6) neither produces estimates with cardinal meaning; and (7) neither method can identify 'burden committees'" (1999, 964).
7. The imposition of term limits on Republican chairs by the party caucus in the 104th Congress is consistent with this view.
8. This calculation used the data on committee assignments compiled by Nelson and Bensen (1993) and Stewart and Woon (2005). These data are available on Charles Stewart's Web site at http://web.mit/17.251/www/data_page.html, including a recent update by Stewart and Woon in 2006. Seniority was compiled from the *Congressional Directory*, 80th–109th Congresses.
9. Law (2007) discusses the differences between the seniority ratio and the Grosewart index at length in a paper available from the author.

10. Established in 1958, the Aeronautics and Science Committee was merged with the Commerce Committee in 1977.
11. The Grosewart index for the 81st to 102nd Congresses gives Foreign Relations coefficients of 1.38 and 2.58 for Democrats and Republicans, respectively, and Armed Services coefficients of .86 and 1.59 (Stewart and Groseclose 1999, 970).
12. Lagrange multiplier tests and comparisons to the AR(1) model ruled out concerns regarding autocorrelation (Greene 2003).
13. This increase in seniority was calculated by multiplying the independent variable's standard deviation by the estimated coefficient ($6.32 * 0.1287 = 0.8$).

8

Agenda Influence and Tabling Motions in the U.S. Senate

CHRIS DEN HARTOG AND NATHAN W. MONROE

The rules of the Senate . . . reflect an egalitarian, individualistic outlook. The right of individuals to debate at length, and to offer amendments on any subject, is generally protected. Only extraordinary majorities can limit debate or amendments. And for reasons of practicality, most scheduling is done by unanimous consent. The majority party usually must negotiate with minority party members to schedule floor action and to bring important measures to a vote.

STEVEN S. SMITH, JASON M. ROBERTS, AND RYAN J. VANDER WIELEN, *The American Congress*

My proposed amendment ought to get 100 votes in the U.S. Senate, but it will not. People will walk up to the door and up to the manager and say, "What is our vote on this?" Well, they will not have to ask, they know what their vote is. They know there has been a motion to table every single amendment. What kind of democracy is that?

SENATOR DALE BUMPERS (D-AR)

Conventional wisdom, as laid out succinctly in the quotation above from Smith, Roberts, and Vander Wielen (2006, 112), holds that party influence in the U.S. Senate is limited or absent. From this perspective, party leaders seem little more than servants of the chamber's rank and file, shackled by procedures such as the filibuster and the Senate's open amendment process (Davidson 1985, 1989; Sinclair 1989, 2001a; Smith and Flathman 1989; Binder 1997; Binder and Smith 1997; Smith and Gamm 2001). Indeed, such constraints force the chamber to operate largely by unanimous consent, whereby individuals and minority coalitions can extract significant benefits (Krehbiel 1986; Smith and Gamm 2001). As Evans and Lipinski (2005) summarize this view, "The procedural prerogatives extended to individual senators undercut the central prerogative of leadership in a representative assembly—control over the chamber agenda" (242).

But the quotation above by Senator Dale Bumpers—made during the 104th Congress just prior to a motion to table one of his amendments—clashes with this conventional view. He seems to suggest that members do not vote strictly on their policy preferences on motions to table (MTTs), which usually propose to kill amendments that have been offered during consideration of a bill. Instead, the quotation suggests, members vote on MTTs on a basis other than whether they prefer the given bill with or without the amendment.[1] In fact, a number of Senate procedural experts and congressional scholars describe votes on motions to table as instances in which senators feel at least some level of compulsion to vote the party line (Tiefer 1989; Marshall, Prins, and Rohde 1999; Gold 2004; Oleszek 2004). In this sense, MTTs are somewhat akin to procedural votes in the House—such as votes on special rules—on which party members display high cohesion and feel compelled to vote with their party independently of their preferences on the underlying bill or the amendment. If this is indeed the case, then senators' much-touted ability to *offer* amendments may not actually undermine the majority party's ability to influence the agenda, because offering an amendment would not be equivalent to getting a vote based strictly on members' policy preferences over that amendment.

After summarizing the standard view as excerpted above, Evans and Lipinski go on to express a sentiment at odds with that view, but very much in line with the point we make in this chapter: "As a result, majority party leaders have developed strategies and tools to help them maintain a semblance of control" (2005, 242).[2] Also, a number of recent studies provide evidence of majority-party influence in the Senate.[3]

Our purpose here is to study the majority party's use of motions to table as a means of killing unwanted amendments. We do so, however, as part of a larger project in which we propose a new theoretical framework for thinking about legislative parties' influence over legislative decisions generally—one that is particularly well suited to the Senate, inasmuch as it leads to important modifications of the conventional wisdom. This framework revolves around the premise that the majority and minority parties face costs in getting measures onto the legislative agenda (by which we mean getting a final-passage vote) and that these costs are higher for the minority party than for the majority party. These costs grant the majority party some level of influence over the legislative agenda, and thus outcomes, despite the majority's not having the ability to unilaterally dictate what is or is not on the agenda. With this approach, we move away from the all-or-nothing character of scholarly debate over majority-party agenda setting in Congress. We instead conclude that although agenda-setting costs sometimes prevent majority parties from getting what they want, such costs do not prevent them from systematically getting what they want more often than do the minority parties against whom they compete for policy influence.

The link between this costly-agenda-setting framework and motions to table is that if majority-party senators vote the party line rather than their own preferences on MTTs, then MTTs impose an agenda-setting cost on the minority party that the majority party does not have to pay. In short, this chapter is intended to demonstrate one type of extra cost faced by the minority party. Using data from the 103rd and 104th Congresses, we find support for this claim. We find that motions to table offered by majority-party members are more likely to be accepted than those offered by minority-party members, and that motions to table kill minority-party amendments far more often than they kill majority-party amendments.

In what follows, we first present our theoretical framework for thinking about legislative parties' influence over outcomes, placing it within the broader literature on congressional organization. We then present related hypotheses, which we test in the following sections. We conclude with a summary and discussion of the implications of our findings.

A Costly-Agenda-Setting Theory of Legislative Influence

In line with other work on parties in Congress, we believe that the main mechanism through which parties influence outcomes is by affecting the legislative agenda, rather than by maintaining high voting cohesion on key substantive votes. In discussing our theoretical framework, we begin by positing that what the literature calls "agenda control," which is usually conceptualized as dichotomous, can be more fruitfully conceptualized as a continuous concept.[4] We therefore think "agenda influence" is a better descriptor—especially in the case of the Senate. Indeed, in even the strongest responsible-government parliaments, the majority party sometimes fails to dictate the agenda. Conversely, we can think of few examples of legislative bodies in which access to the agenda is perfectly divided among the members of the body, with all members having identical opportunities to influence the agenda. In short, influence over the agenda is rarely, if ever, either entirely concentrated or equally distributed to all members.

The gist of our cost-based approach is straightforward.[5] In most legislatures, floor time for consideration of bills is scarce (that is, there is not enough time for every bill to be considered). Some form of rationing is thus necessary to determine which bills are and are not on the legislature's agenda. Such rationing mechanisms take many different forms, but all share a characteristic: they determine what costs various actors in the legislature must pay to get a bill onto the agenda.[6] These costs may be relatively evenly distributed among legislators and/or parties, or there may be great disparities in the costs paid by different actors. Our central point is that actors paying lower costs will find the cost worth paying—and will enjoy greater influence over the agenda—more often than will actors paying higher costs, all else constant.[7]

Typically, all actors face some agenda-setting costs, even if only in the form of opportunity costs that follow from spending scarce floor time on some bills rather than others. But there are often costs faced only by non-majority-party members or coalitions. For instance, in the House it is possible to circumvent the majority and put something onto the agenda via a discharge petition, but the high cost of this procedure ensures that it is used infrequently (Beth 1997a, 1997b; Oleszek 2004). The disparity created by these extra costs serves as a source of leverage for the majority party and gives it the ability to bias outcomes in its own favor—even if, as seems to be the case in the Senate, the disparity is not large and the majority party itself faces significant agenda-setting costs.[8]

Agenda-Setting Costs in the Senate

We surmise that one reason many people find it difficult to accept the idea of agenda manipulation in the Senate is that this manipulation manifests itself in different ways in the Senate than it does in the House, and that upon finding that the Senate lacks some of the House majority party's agenda-setting tools, many people conclude that Senate agenda setting is not feasible. In the House, agenda influence (especially the "negative" variety) takes place almost entirely at the pre-floor stage, through the majority party's control of committees, the careful crafting and dispensing of special rules, and the Speaker's discretion on the order of business.

In the Senate, on the other hand, agenda influence requires a judicious mix of pre-floor and floor tactics. One might say that agenda influence is cobbled together on an almost case-by-case basis in the Senate. While the Senate majority party controls committees, and the majority leader takes the lead in setting the order of business, such agenda-setting advantages may not be significant if the majority party cannot "plug the holes" that are potentially punched in its agenda-setting apparatus by the ease with which amendments may be offered on the floor. Put another way, it may be the case that senators who disagree with the majority party can get their proposals onto the agenda at low cost. In addition, the need for unanimous consent and the ever-present threat of filibusters may make it costly for the majority party to put its own proposals onto the agenda. This is another way of stating the conventional view—agenda influence is no less costly for majority-party senators than it is for non-majority-party senators.

However, there are reasons to suspect that both parts of this conventional view understate the majority party's advantage. The minority party may face significant costs in attempting to get *pure policy votes* on amendments (by which we mean votes on which senators choose strictly on the basis of their policy preferences, without regard for other considerations such as loyalty or obligation to party). In addition, the magnitude and significance of the costs imposed on the majority by dilatory tactics are often overstated. These tactics are sometimes treated, at least implicitly, as though they give the minority party a veto over majority-party proposals. In other words, they are seen as imposing prohibitive agenda-setting costs on the majority.

We agree that this is sometimes the case but emphasize that it is not usually the case. Denial of unanimous consent is not equivalent to a veto. Rather, it means that to put a bill onto the agenda, the majority must make a motion to proceed, have it approved, and overcome any filibuster that might be mounted against the bill—and filibusters create agenda-setting costs for the majority party. This is certainly a more costly way for the majority to put a bill on the agenda than is unanimous consent, but in many cases the cost is not prohibitive.

In addition, the use of dilatory tactics is not necessarily an attractive option for those who oppose the majority party's efforts, since it can be costly to refuse consent (Krehbiel 1986; Ainsworth and Flathman 1995) or to filibuster (Koger 2004, 2007; Wawro and Schickler 2004)—as evidenced by the fact that senators frequently agree to unanimous consent agreements and do not filibuster bills that they ultimately vote against. Further, the conventional view overlooks the fact that the majority party can also take advantage of the low costs of proposing amendments, and that dilatory tactics can be used to impose the same agenda-setting costs on minority-party senators that can be imposed on majority-party senators.

Beyond those just mentioned, there are several important mechanisms that leave the majority party facing lower costs than the minority. For instance, control of committee chairs and committee majorities makes it easier for the majority party to push its measures out of committee. Also, the majority leader's right of first recognition makes it at least marginally less costly for the majority leader to bring about consideration of bills, to propose amendments,[9] and to make procedural motions than is the case for anyone else in the chamber. This right can also give the majority leader advantages in bargaining over unanimous consent agreements (Ainsworth and Flathman 1995).

These types of lower costs have typically been overlooked in studies of the Senate, no doubt in large part because of the widespread belief that the Senate is an institution defined by decentralization and individualism. But if, as we argue, costs imposed on the majority by dilatory tactics are often not very high, and if MTTs make the cost of getting pure policy votes on amendments higher for minority-party senators than for majority-party senators, then there is a clear cost disparity in favor of the majority party. When we also consider the advantages conveyed by the majority party's control of committees and the leadership, a picture of significant majority agenda-setting advantages in the Senate emerges.

Expectations about Motions to Table

In 1989, Senator Jesse Helms (R-NC) colorfully expressed what happens with tabled amendments: "Mr. President, the Helms amendment, which apparently will be tabled, is pretty much in a fix that a rustler would get into if he was hung and thereafter given a fair trial" (*Congressional Record*, October 5, 1989). Motions to table provide the Senate with a mechanism whereby a simple majority can effectively kill a motion, amendment, or bill. Their use presents an interesting question: in the absence of a tabling motion, the next step in the legislative process is typically an up-or-down vote on the amendment under consideration. Given that the amendment could be voted down at that point, why bother to offer a motion to table an amendment rather than simply vote on the amendment itself?

We think MTTs likely appeal to the majority party for two reasons. First, the motion is nondebatable and thus is not subject to filibuster. This means that what is essentially an up-or-down vote on the amendment can be forced immediately. Without an MTT, there is the possibility that debate—and potentially a filibuster—will ensue before the vote on the amendment, thereby imposing opportunity costs on the majority party by consuming scarce floor time.

The second reason is that votes on motions to table and votes on amendments are not equivalent in the public eye, because a vote on a tabling motion is less visible to the public, and less easy to interpret, than is a direct vote on an amendment or a bill. In other words, as is often claimed to be the case with special rules votes in the House, votes on motions to table are procedural votes that allow members to act in a partisan fashion while taking smaller electoral risks than would be the case if they achieved the same goals via partisan voting on substantive votes. This point is also made by Marshall, Prins, and Rohde (1999) and is supported by a quotation from Senator Robert Byrd (D-WV):

A motion to table is a procedural motion. It obfuscates the issue, and it makes possible an explanation by a Senator to his constituents . . . that his vote was not on the merits of the issue. He can claim that he might have voted this way or might have voted that way, if the Senate had voted up or down on the issue itself. But on a procedural motion, he can state he voted to table the amendment, and he can assign any number of reasons therefore, one of which would be that he did so in order that the Senate would get on with its work or about its business. (*Congressional Record*, September 23, 1975, 29814; cited in Oleszek 2004, 236)

Oleszek (2004) adds, "If a procedural vote can be arranged to kill or delay a controversial bill, it is likely to win the support of senators who may prefer to duck the substantive issue. Moreover, senators generally support the party leadership on procedural votes. As one senator has pointed out, on a procedural vote, members 'traditionally stick with the leadership'" (236).

Though we do not undertake a systematic analysis here, we have done a brief analysis of roll-call data and found evidence consistent with claims that senators do not always cast tabling-motion votes strictly on the basis of their policy preferences regarding the amendment in question. We have examined all twenty cases from the 101st through 109th Congresses in which a tabling motion failed and was followed by a roll-call vote on the amendment. If tabling-motion votes are nothing more than votes based on policy preferences over the amendment, senators should, for each such pair, always vote either against the motion to table and for the amendment, or for the motion to table and against the amendment. In 17 percent of the cases (332 out of 1,928) in which a senator voted on both votes in a pair, the senator did not vote as predicted—that is, the senator either voted for the tabling motion *and* for the amendment, or voted against both. This seems to indicate unequivocally that MTT and amendment votes are not always based on identical considerations.

To get at whether something like partisan loyalty is a factor, as claimed, we examine the same vote pairs from a different angle. We code whether each vote in a pair was a party unity vote, defined as more than 50 percent of one party voting against more than 50 percent of the other party. In twelve of the twenty pairs, both the MTT vote and the amendment vote are party unity votes; in such cases, we cannot distinguish between party- and preference-based voting. In another five pairs, however, the MTT vote is a unity vote but the amendment vote is not, consistent with the claim that senators are at least somewhat more inclined to vote with the party on MTTs than on amendment votes.

These claims about how the majority uses tabling motions dovetail with our argument that the minority party faces higher costs than the majority party does in trying to put proposals onto the agenda. Essentially, these figures suggest that for minority-party members to use the amendment process to put a proposal onto the agenda, they have to pay not only the cost that all senators face in doing so, but also the cost of overcoming majority-party senators' predisposition to vote with the party on motions to table. If this characterization—and our theoretical framework—is correct, then we expect to see the following things:

Hypothesis 1: Motions to table offered by majority-party members are more likely to pass than those offered by minority-party members, ceteris paribus.

Hypothesis 2: Motions to table amendments sponsored by minority-party members are more likely to pass than motions to table amendments sponsored by majority-party members, ceteris paribus.

These hypotheses are tested against the following null hypotheses:

Hypothesis 1$_{Null}$: Majority status of the motioner has no effect on the likelihood that a tabling motion will pass.

Hypothesis 2$_{Null}$: Majority status of the amendment sponsor has no effect on the likelihood that a tabling motion will pass.

Note that the null is expected under the conventional view of Senate decision making. If the Senate is an institution defined by egalitarianism, where individuals rather than parties dominate decision making, then majority status should confer no special advantage.

Research Design

To test our hypotheses that motions to table offered by majority-party senators are more likely to pass than those offered by minority-party senators, and that motions to table minority-party senators' amendments are more likely to pass than motions to table majority-party senators' amendments, we use a data set with an observation for each of the motions to table that was subject to a recorded vote in the 103rd or 104th Congress.[10]

For each MTT, we have coded whether the motion was accepted or rejected. We have also coded a series of variables dealing with the "motioner": who made the motion, whether the motioner was a majority-party member, whether the motioner was a party leader, whether the motioner was chair of the committee that reported the underlying measure, and whether the motioner was a member of the reporting committee. In addition, we have coded variables regarding the sponsor of the amendment that the motion proposes to table: who the sponsor was and whether he or she was a majority- or minority-party senator.

The intuition of our research design is that we treat majority-party membership as a treatment that makes motioners' MTTs more likely to pass, and we treat sponsors' minority-party membership as a treatment that makes amendments that are subject to a tabling motion more likely to be tabled (in each case, all else constant). We use a probit analysis to get at the effects of majority-party members' offering of MTTs and of minority-party members' amendment sponsorship. We estimate the model

$$Pass_i = \alpha + \beta_1 MajMotioner_i + \beta_2 MinSponsor_i + \beta_3 ByComm_i + \beta_4 MajComm_i$$
$$+ \beta_5 MotionerDist_i + \beta_6 SponsorDist_i + \varepsilon_i,$$

where

$Pass_i$ is a dummy variable, coded one if tabling motion i was accepted;

$MajMotioner_i$ is a dummy variable, coded one if the motion was offered by a majority-party member;

$MinSponsor_i$ is a dummy variable, coded one if the amendment was offered by a minority-party member;

$ByComm_i$ is a dummy variable, coded one if the motion was offered by a member of the reporting committee;

$MajComm_i$ is a dummy variable, coded one if the motion was offered by a majority-party member of the reporting committee;

$MotionerDist_i$ is the absolute value of the difference between the motioner's ideal point and the chamber median's ideal point on the first dimension of DW-NOMINATE; and

SponsorDist$_i$ is the absolute value of the difference between the amendment sponsor's ideal point and the chamber median's ideal point on the first dimension of DW-NOMINATE (Poole and Rosenthal 1997).

The key coefficients in our analysis are those associated with *Maj Motioner*, which we expect to be positive, and with *MinSponsor*, which we expect to be negative. We include the committee variables as controls for the possibility that committee membership makes MTTs more likely to pass and for the possibility that MTTs are actually an instrument of committee agenda influence, along lines posited by distributive models, rather than an instrument of majority-party agenda influence.

We also include the distance variables as crude controls for the effects of members' ideology on the probability that their motions to table or amendments are accepted or rejected. Preference-centered views should predict that as table motioners are more ideologically distant from the floor median, MTTs are *less likely* to pass, and that as amendment sponsors are more distant from the median, MTTs are *more likely* to pass.[11]

Results

The results of our probit analysis are shown in table 8.1. As expected, the coefficient for *MajMotioner* is positive and significant at a level just over 96 percent, indicating that majority-party members' motions to table are more likely to pass than minority-party members' motions to table, ceteris paribus. Also as expected, the coefficient for *MinSponsor* is positive and significant above the 99 percent level, indicating that motions to table amendments offered by minority-party members are more likely to pass than MTTs that propose to table majority-party members' amendments.

Interestingly, as indicated by the coefficients for *ByComm* and *Maj-Comm*—neither of which is significant—motions to table made by majority-party members of the reporting committee, and by reporting-committee members generally, are not more likely to pass than motions made by majority members generally (though, as we discuss in the next section, this belies the frequency with which these various actors offer successful MTTs). In addition, as indicated by the negative and marginally significant (93%) coefficient for *MotionerDist*, motions made by more ideologically extreme senators are less likely to pass; the coefficient for *SponsorDist*, however, indicates no relationship between the extremity of amendment sponsors' ideology and the probability of passage.

TABLE 8.1. Effects on probability of passage for motions to table offered by nonleaders

	Coefficient	Standard error	p-value
MajMotioner	.781	.375	.037
MinSponsor	.775	.217	.000
ByComm	.570	.414	.169
MajComm	−.700	.475	.143
MotionerDist	−.945	.533	.076
SponsorDist	.126	.437	.773
Constant	.100	.420	.811

Note: Coefficients are probit coefficients. $N = 409$; log likelihood = −149.81459; pseudo-$R^2 = 0.1123$.

These probit coefficients are useful for testing our hypotheses, but less useful for conveying the extent to which motions to table (dis)advantage members of each party. To illustrate the substantive impact of MTTs, in figure 8.1 we present data on the frequency of motions being offered and the rates of success, categorized by different types of senators and by the party of the amendment sponsors.

The figure shows the frequency with which senators from each of six categories offered motions to table (the categories are majority leaders,[12] minority leaders, majority members of the reporting committee, minority members of the reporting committee, majority members not on the reporting committee, and minority members not on the reporting committee). For each category, there are two columns: one that shows how often senators in that category made motions to table minority-party amendments, and one that shows how often they made motions to table majority-party amendments. Each column in the table shows how many of the MTTs in that category were approved by the Senate (the white area in each column) and how many were rejected (the black area in each column). Columns representing motions to table majority-party members' amendments have a dotted pattern in both areas.

This chart has a number of interesting features. The first thing one notices is that the largest category, by far, is motions by majority-party members of the reporting committee to table minority-party amendments, which account for 218 of the 458 MTTs in the sample and which kill 196 minority-offered amendments. The next-largest category is motions by majority-party members *not* on the reporting committee to table minority-party amendments, which account for 71 of the MTTs and kill 66 minority-offered amendments. This category is followed closely by motions by majority-party members of the reporting committee to table majority-offered amendments, which

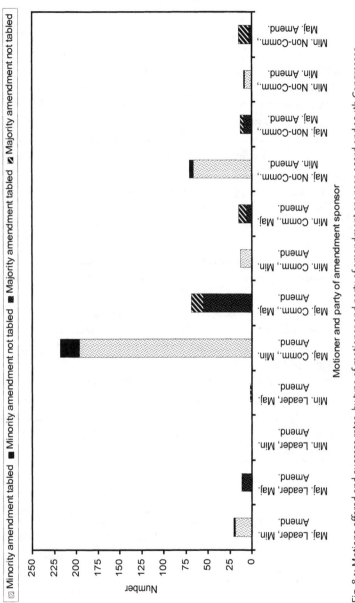

Fig. 8.1: Motions offered and success rates, by type of motioner and party of amendment sponsor, 103rd and 104th Congresses

account for 69 MTTs and kill 55 minority-offered amendments. In each of these categories, motions to table are accepted at high rates. By comparison, minority-party motioners in each category (leader, committee member, non–committee member) offer very few MTTs.

Across the board, majority-party motioners offer more motions to table minority amendments (310) than to table majority amendments (104), and they kill far more minority-party amendments (281) than majority-party amendments (71). By contrast, when minority-party members offer MTTs, they are far more likely to kill an amendment offered by a member of their own party than an amendment from the other party. Of the 51 motions offered by minority members, 19 of 20 motions to kill minority amendments are accepted, whereas only 8 of 31 motions to kill majority amendments are accepted.

Finally, note that, independent of rates of passage, the disparity in the frequency of proposed MTTs alone constitutes support for our theory. That minority-party senators offer roughly one-tenth as many MTTs as majority senators suggests that a significant cost disparity exists. Further, it may imply that the passage rate of minority-party-initiated MTTs in our sample is biased *upward*. If the minority party only offers MTTs that have the highest likelihood of success—which seems a reasonable assumption—then the *real* rate of passage is actually lower. That is, if the minority party were forced to offer the same number of motions to table as the majority, the actual majority-party advantage would likely be even larger than we have estimated here.

In sum, all the data point in the direction we expected and are consistent with our hypotheses. The results are consistent with the argument that minority-party members face an extra cost of placing proposals onto the agenda (that is, a cost not faced by majority-party members) in the form of motions to table.

Conclusion

In this chapter, we have made both a narrow empirical point and a broader theoretical point. The empirical point is that the majority party often uses tabling motions to kill amendments, whereas the minority party does not. Moreover, the majority party uses these motions to kill amendments offered by minority-party senators far more often than it uses them to kill majority-offered amendments. In fact, this same pattern holds in the relatively small number of cases in which the minority party offers tabling motions—they also succeed in killing decidedly more minority-offered amendments than majority-offered amendments.

These results, along with our probit results, support the hypotheses that majority-party senators are more successful at using MTTs to kill amendments than are minority-party members, and that motions to table minority-offered amendments are more likely to be accepted than are motions to table majority-offered amendments. This evidence is consistent with claims that majority members treat votes on tabling motions as procedural votes on which they are (at least somewhat) obliged to vote with their party. This has important implications for the conclusions one draws about the extent to which the Senate's open amendment procedures undercut majority-party agenda influence. It implies that, in at least some cases, the ability to *offer* an amendment is not the same as the ability to *get a pure policy vote* on an amendment—meaning that, notwithstanding the ease with which amendments can be offered, minority-party senators often face an uphill battle in their attempts to use floor amendments as a means of getting proposals onto the agenda.

The evidence also supports our claim that minority-party members face higher costs than majority-party members when it comes to putting proposals on the agenda. This claim is a key premise in our broader theoretical argument that Senate procedures, via the distribution of agenda-setting costs they create, give the majority party advantages that allow it to bias Senate outcomes in its favor.

We believe this costly-agenda-setting approach to thinking about legislative agenda influence is promising both as an instrument for studying the Senate and as an approach to thinking about agenda manipulation in legislatures more generally. As noted, elsewhere we have developed a formal theory along these lines; but we think a number of promising avenues for empirical research remain. First, we would like to have a more comprehensive catalog of agenda-setting costs in the Senate, which we see as including costs borne by all senators, as well as costs borne only by minority-party senators. Second, we want to explore variation in these costs (and thus variation in the cost disparity). It seems likely that there is significant variation across issues, time, and perhaps other factors also, and that the majority party thus enjoys greater advantages under some conditions than under others.

We also hope this cost-based approach provides a common theoretical framework for thinking about different legislative chambers, as well as different legislatures. Indeed, one way of explaining why majority-party agenda influence is stronger in the House than in the Senate is that the difference between majority and minority costs is smaller in the Senate than in the House, where the Rules Committee gives the majority party a low-cost way of putting things onto the agenda, and debate and amendment limitations often make it prohibitively costly for the minority party to set the agenda.

Our framework also allows us to examine other legislatures, with different cost structures, and to reconcile the long-standing view of House parties as weak with the now more widespread view that House parties exert considerable influence on decision making. From as early on as Bagehot ([1867] 1963) or Wilson ([1885] 1973), legislative scholars' skepticism about party influence in the House was based on comparisons between the House and western European parliaments (Beer 1982; Loewenberg and Jones 1986). Indeed, Mayhew's conclusion (1974, 27) that "no theoretical treatment of the United States Congress that posits parties as analytic units will go very far" stems directly from his comparison of party effects in the British House of Commons and the U.S. Congress. In most western parliaments, procedures as well as strong party discipline give the majority coalition the ability to set the agenda at very low cost and make it difficult for nonmajority legislators and parties to get pure policy votes on their proposals. This gives the parties a level of influence that is large in comparison to that of parties in the House; but, as the last fifteen years of congressional scholarship has shown, this does not imply that House parties do not matter. Ironically, in the contemporary literature on Congress, the House is now often the model of party effects against which the allegedly partyless Senate is compared. We suggest that all this reflects variation in costs across different legislative bodies.

Notes

The authors thank Mike Crespin, Erik Engstrom, Larry Evans, Chuck Finocchiaro, Sean Gailmard, Jeff Jenkins, Greg Koger, Frances Lee, Mat McCubbins, Bruce Oppenheimer, David C. W. Parker, Greg Robinson, Dave Rohde, Wendy Schiller, Barbara Sinclair, Rob Van Houweling, and an anonymous reviewer for helpful comments and conversations. We also thank Greg Robinson and Linda Mamula for excellent research assistance. Nathan Monroe gratefully acknowledges the financial support for this project provided by the Intramural Grants program at Michigan State University.

1. MTTs cannot be filibustered, are highly privileged, and need only a bare majority for acceptance.
2. Turning the conventional wisdom on its head, they make a compelling case about why holds and unanimous consent agreements are crucial components of such strategies.

3. Campbell, Cox, and McCubbins (2002) find a huge disparity in majority and minority roll rates in the modern Senate. Bargen (2003) finds that extremists on the liberal and conservative end of the Senate's ideological spectrum face different disappointment rates on roll calls and that these differences vary systematically with the party of the majority. Koger (2003) shows how the majority party has been able to enhance its power by making end runs around the two-thirds supermajority requirement to invoke cloture on rules changes, by using rulings by the presiding officer to establish precedents regarding the interpretation of the rules. We find evidence that the 2001 switch by James Jeffords (VT) from Republican to independent led to predictable changes in roll-call vote patterns (especially individual roll rates) and in the stock prices of Republican and Democratic firms (Den Hartog 2005; Den Hartog and Monroe, forthcoming).

4. We refer to our discussion as a theoretical *framework* because we discuss elements of a theory without spelling out an explicit theory. In recent work, we have presented a formal game-theoretic model built around ideas discussed here (Den Hartog and Monroe 2007).

5. We develop our costly-agenda-setting approach in more detail elsewhere (see Den Hartog and Monroe 2007, forthcoming) and merely summarize the approach here.

6. We consider proposals to be *costly* in the sense that some thing or things of value must be given up to have a proposal considered. The link between costs and procedures is that procedures determine what actions must be taken to get a proposal on the agenda and thus determine what scarce resources—such as time, staff, energy, and political capital—must be given up in order to get something on the agenda.

7. For a simple illustration of this point, imagine a one-dimensional model in which each party's ideal point is equidistant from the floor median; each party can propose to change the status quo on that dimension; a cost must be paid for making such a proposal; and if a proposal to change the status quo is made, the status quo is replaced by the floor median's ideal point. Suppose first that the status quo is at the minority's ideal point and that the majority's proposal cost is smaller than the distance between the minority's ideal point and the floor median's ideal point. In this case, the majority party will find it worthwhile to propose change, since the policy gain that will result is larger than the proposal cost. Now suppose instead that the status quo is at the majority's ideal point and that the minority's proposal cost is larger than the distance between the majority's ideal point and the floor median. In this case, the minority will make no proposal, since the resulting gain would be less than the proposal cost, and the status quo will be maintained. The only thing that varies between these two scenarios is that the minority's proposal costs are larger, and this results in the minority's not realizing gains that the majority realizes in an otherwise comparable situation.

8. We make no attempt here to explain the source(s) of agenda-setting costs, nor the extent to which they are imposed by the majority party versus the extent to which they are generated exogenously. To explain legislative decisions, we simply assume that the costs exist.

9. Indeed, Schiller (2000b) and Campbell (2004) have pointed out how the majority leader's right of first recognition helps facilitate the tactic of "filling the amendment tree" (see also Oleszek 2004 for a discussion of this tactic).

10. There were 515 MTTs in the two Congresses we examine. Of these, some are excluded from our analysis because they were motions to table committee amendments, and the *ByComm* and *MajComm* variables (see the explanation of variables in the text below) are therefore missing data for those observations. We also exclude motions made by party leaders from the probit shown in table 8.1. Theoretically, we think that leaders are actually the most likely to be successful in offering MTTs. When we include these observations, however, and add dummy variables for whether the motion was made by a party leader and for whether the motion was made by a majority-party leader, Stata will not estimate standard errors for the majority-leader dummy. Presumably, *the majority-party leader variable too accurately predicts passage.* Indeed, the data displayed in figure 8.1 support this suspicion. We could have simply thrown these observations in with the rank-and-file majority-party members, but we thought it theoretically inappropriate. To the extent that leaving out these observations biases our results, it will lead to a bias *against* our hypotheses.

11. This hinges on the assumption that table motioners and amendment sponsors offer MTTs and amendments, respectively, that reflect their preferences. In other words, as motioners are more extreme, they are more likely to want to kill a bill that the median does not want to kill; and as sponsors are more extreme, they are more likely to propose amendments that the median wants to kill.

12. We include whips along with party leaders in the majority- and minority-leader categories.

9

Filibustering and Majority Rule in the Senate: The Contest over Judicial Nominations, 2003–2005

GREGORY KOGER

On January 31, 2006, Samuel Alito was confirmed as an associate justice of the U.S. Supreme Court by a vote of 58 to 42. Like most legislation, judicial nominations are vulnerable to filibusters, and sixty votes are required to override a filibuster and force an up-or-down vote on the nomination.[1] Recent research on Senate obstruction highlights the role of filibustering as an everyday tactic in the modern Senate (Koger n.d.; Krehbiel 1998; Sinclair 2002b), and the forty-two senators opposed to Alito could have blocked his confirmation if they had all voted against cloture.[2] Instead, sixteen Democrats voted for cloture on Alito and then voted against his nomination. This chapter explores the secret of Alito's success: the endogeneity of filibustering rights in the Senate.

Alito's confirmation ended—at least temporarily—a five-year feud over the use of filibusters to block judicial nominations. The feud began as a serious disagreement about what kind(s) of judges ought to sit on the federal bench and grew into a dispute over the rules of the Senate. It led to drastic threats: the leaders of the majority party threatened to revoke the minority's right to obstruct judicial nominations, and the leader of the minority party threatened a complete shutdown of the Senate. This debate nicely demonstrated three general points about legislative parties in the Senate. First, the Senate can severely reduce minority rights if a bare majority of its members are sufficiently devious and determined. Second, the political and legislative costs of such majoritarian tactics can be prohibitively steep, making it difficult to form a majority coalition that is willing to incur these costs. Third, this case illustrates the limits of party power in the Senate. In the end, critical blocs of senators who had little to gain from a confrontation over minority rights combined to defuse the conflict. Thus, senators have the ability but (so far) not the desire to impose majority-party rule on the Senate.

This chapter begins by explaining how simple majorities can reduce minority rights in the Senate even if a minority attempts to obstruct reform. As we shall see, senators can use unconventional tactics to circumvent a filibuster against a formal change in the standing rules of the Senate. Second, I assess the frequency and partisanship of parliamentary rulings in the modern Senate. Finally, I turn to the fight over judicial nominations from 2003 to 2005, which culminated in a bipartisan agreement to preserve the right to filibuster while limiting the use of that right.

Rules, Precedents, and Filibustering

To a naive reader of Senate rules, it is obvious that a simple majority can change the rules of the Senate. Senate rules are changed by resolutions; these resolutions require a simple majority to pass; thus, Senate rules can be changed by a majority. However, resolutions can also be debated, and the Senate has no formal rule for limiting debate by a simple majority vote. Therefore, unless the Senate votes to impose cloture, a minority of the Senate can drag out debate on a rules change indefinitely. To make matters worse for reformers, Rule 22 of the Senate imposes an especially high threshold for cloture on rules changes: two-thirds of all senators voting must support cloture before the Senate can limit debate on a resolution to change the Senate's rules.[3]

What recourse is left to senators seeking to empower the majority party by restricting filibustering? Even if it is difficult for a slender majority of senators to formally alter their chamber's rules, it can be relatively easy to change the *meaning* of their rules. Like most legislatures, the Senate has a regular process for any member to challenge the manner in which the legislature is functioning by raising a point of order stating his or her objection. Ordinarily, these points of order are used to enforce current rules, such as Senate Rule 19's prohibition on speaking ill of the motives of another senator. In such cases a transgression occurs, a point of order is lodged, the chair sustains the complaint, the transgressor is admonished, and debate goes on.

Occasionally, a senator disagrees with the presiding officer's decision. Any senator can appeal the chair's decision. Appeals are debatable and are decided by a simple majority vote. Any senator can cut off debate on an appeal and force a vote by moving to table the appeal. While the vocabulary of this process is drawn from legal settings, legislators are under no obligation to adopt the "right" or "best" interpretation of a rule when they vote on appeals, nor are procedural interpretations subject to judicial review.[4]

In extraordinary cases, these procedural objections can be used to alter the interpretation of current rules or to boldly assert new prerogatives. Consider some historical precedents that empowered the Senate majority party:[5]

June 1879: The president pro tempore counts nonvoting members toward a quorum for the purpose of transacting business, but not voting. This makes it more difficult for the Republican minority to continue a filibuster against an appropriations bill (Burdette 1940).

May 1908: The presiding officer again counts a nonvoting member toward a quorum. Also, a new ruling, supported by a 35–13 vote, makes it more difficult for senators to obstruct by repeatedly demanding the counting of a quorum (Burdette 1940).

August 1937: The presiding officer formally recognizes the majority leader's priority in recognition (Riddick and Frumin 1992).

February 1975: Senators vote 51–42 in favor of limiting debate on changing the Senate's cloture rule by a simple majority vote. This test vote was subsequently reversed as part of a compromise (Binder and Smith 1997).

October 1977: Vice President Walter Mondale and Majority Leader Robert Byrd (D-WV) cooperate to limit the use of time-wasting amendments after a successful cloture vote.[6]

March 1995: The Republican majority suspends the prohibition against adding policy riders to appropriations bills (Rule 16) by a 57–42 vote (Koger 2002, chap. 9).

These examples suffice to show that Senate majorities can revise the *meaning* of its rules by raising points of order and then sustaining or overturning the presiding officer's decision by simple majority vote.

It is possible to make drastic changes in Senate decision making by *reinterpreting* current rules. Over the years, senators have considered the following

Empowering the presiding officer of the Senate to determine when sufficient debate has occurred on an issue. Republican leaders contemplated this strategy in 1891 (Koger 2002; Wawro and Schickler 2006). Some scholars point out, correctly, that senators are unwilling to allow their presiding officer to exercise this much power (e.g., Haynes 1938; Gamm and Smith 2000), but it is nonetheless *possible* for senators to employ this strategy.

Moving the previous question. The rules of the Senate do not mention the "previous question" motion used to cut off debate in the House, but the rules do not ban such a motion either. During the 1915 filibuster of the ship purchase act, the Democratic majority seriously considered asserting the right to move the previous question, but they abandoned the venture because they lacked the votes to make it work (Koger 2007).

Suspending the rules by majority vote. Motions to suspend the rules can include all of the procedural detail (restrictions on amendments, time limits) included in unanimous consent agreements in the modern Senate or special rules in the modern House; the only restriction is that the motion cannot be introduced and considered on the same day (Beth 1993). When combined with the Senate majority leader's right to be recognized before all others, this strategy would allow the majority-party leader to propose restrictive floor procedures for a simple majority vote. In order to adopt this process, a Senate majority would have to overturn a 1915 precedent requiring a two-thirds majority to suspend a rule of the Senate and, most likely, adopt a new precedent making these motions nondebatable.

Requiring the Senate to readopt rules by majority vote at the beginning of each Congress. Although this may be the most complicated strategy, it has also been the most attempted (see Binder and Smith 1997; and Wolfinger 1971). First, a majority must overturn a precedent that the Senate is a "standing body"—that is, that its rules automatically continue from Congress to Congress. Next, the Senate, like the House, would consider amendments to its rules by simple majority vote. Once freed of the current rules, a simple majority could assert its right to limit debate on rules proposals. In 1963, 1967, 1969, 1971, and 1975 (see above), senators voted on whether the Senate is a standing body.

It may be easier to implement a "reinterpretation" strategy when the presiding officer supports the reform effort. In order to win, the reform faction usually must force a vote on its appeal, but appeals are traditionally subject to debate (and hence endless discussion) in the Senate. There are three ways out of this conundrum. First, if the presiding officer makes a ruling that favors reform, then it is the defenders of the status quo who must appeal the chair's decision. These appeals can be tabled by a simple majority without debate. Second, a chair may, of his or her own authority, simply announce after some debate on an appeal that there has been adequate discussion for senators to make up their minds, so voting will commence without further deliberation. Both of these scenarios rely on the assistance of the presiding officer. Obviously, vice presidents have the constitutional authority to preside over the Senate, and some vice presidents, such as Hubert Humphrey in 1969 and Nelson Rockefeller in 1975, have been willing to intervene on behalf of reformers. Furthermore, it has often been possible for senators to place an ally in the presiding officer's chair regardless of the vice president's preferences. Prior to 1967, there was no constitutional provision for replacing a vice president, so if the vice president died, resigned, or succeeded to the presidency, the office was simply vacant and the president pro tempore presided without interruption. These gaps in vice-presidential services provided long stretches of time during which senators could carry out majoritarian schemes if they wished to do so. Furthermore, contemporary vice presidents rarely preside over the Senate, preferring to allow senators to perform this deadly dull task unless their presence is necessary to break a tie vote.

Even if there is a vice president (or some other antireform figure) acting as the presiding officer, devious majorities can circumvent this officer. First, even vice presidents are human—they must sleep, eat, and take breaks—and majorities can try to wait them out.[7] A second option is to raise a second point of order that debate on an appeal has dragged on too long. Under Senate Rule 20, the presiding officer must decide on a secondary point of order immediately, and any appeal goes to a vote without debate. Though extreme, this is the majority's trump card. A majority of the House used this strategy in February 1811 in its effort to convert the previous question motion into a limit on debate (Koger 2002).

Parties and Rule Interpretation, 1961–2000

Now that we have established the possibility of majoritarian reform, this section describes basic patterns in Senate voting on procedural rulings and tests whether the overall pattern suggests that rules are being revised for partisan advantage. I identified all the votes analyzed in this section by using codebooks for congressional roll-call votes (ICPSR 1998) and searching for the words "ruling," "chair," and "appeal." I exclude votes on whether to waive the Budget Act. For simplicity, I focus on the years 1961–2000.

First, I note that votes to interpret rules occur frequently. Figure 9.1 shows the raw number of votes on rule interpretation, including both appeals and motions to table appeals. The average number of votes on parliamentary rulings is 9.75 per Congress, with a peak in the mid-1970s, when points of order were frequently raised as a delaying tactic. The frequency of votes has decreased from a mean of 12.1 in the 1980s to 3.0 in the 1990s.

To what extent do parties enhance their procedural power by reinterpreting rules? I employ two measures of partisanship and majority control of the rules. First, I compare the mean Rice difference scores for votes to interpret rules with the mean Rice score for all other votes by Congress. A Rice difference score is the absolute value of the percentage of one party voting aye minus the percentage of the second party voting aye. A score of 0 means that equal proportions of the two parties voted aye, while a score of 100 means that each party unanimously opposed the other. If institutional

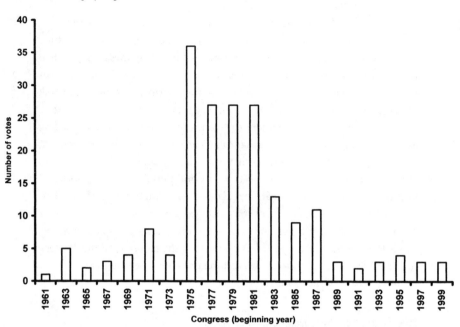

Fig. 9.1: Number of votes on parliamentary rulings, by Congress, 1961–2000

choices are less partisan than other decisions, the average Rice difference score should be lower for parliamentary decisions than for all other votes. Conversely, if parties often disagree over the proper interpretation of a rule, Rice difference scores should be higher than average on parliamentary appeals. Second, I compare the size of winning coalitions on interpretation votes versus all others. In addition to partisanship, we are also interested in whether cross-party majorities are manipulating rules for their own (presumably short-term) goals. If parliamentary votes are, on average, decided by smaller majorities than other votes, that is evidence that this form of institutional change is not based on consensus.

Voting on Senate rule interpretation is generally more partisan than other votes. Figure 9.2 shows the mean Rice difference score for interpretation votes and other votes for each two-year Congress from 1961 to 2000.

To the extent that we are curious about the *possibility* of partisan change, the disaggregated data are sufficient to resolve the question. Seventy-two votes have Rice difference scores above 50 percent; for twenty votes, the difference is in the 90–100 percent range. Parties can and do oppose each other on parliamentary votes. Furthermore, there is a pattern of elevated partisanship on interpretation votes. For the entire time series, the mean

Rice cohesion score (counting each Congress as an observation) was 42.9 for parliamentary votes and 34.4 for all other votes.[8] For the years 1979 to 2000, the mean scores increase to 52.2 for interpretation votes and 39.3 for all others—a 12.9 percent gap. Thus, these votes show an elevated level of partisanship on parliamentary votes, especially in recent years.

Of course, Rice difference scores do not necessarily indicate the size of the winning majority. A "high" Rice score of 50, for example, is possible when more than 70 percent of the chamber supports a rule interpretation. A second measure of majority control of the decision-making process is the margin of victory on key interpretation votes. If interpretation votes are more contested than other votes, we may infer that the majority of the Senate (including cross-party ideological factions) is interpreting the rules over the objections of a sizable minority. Figure 9.3 illustrates the winning-coalition size for parliamentary votes from 1961 to 2000. For comparison, the mean coalition size for all other votes is also shown.

The potential for majoritarian change is clear. Of the 210 votes, 125 are below the 66.7 percent threshold for cloture on a rule change. Any reforms achieved by these votes, we may suspect, could have been blocked by a filibuster if the majority had attempted a formal rule change. Furthermore,

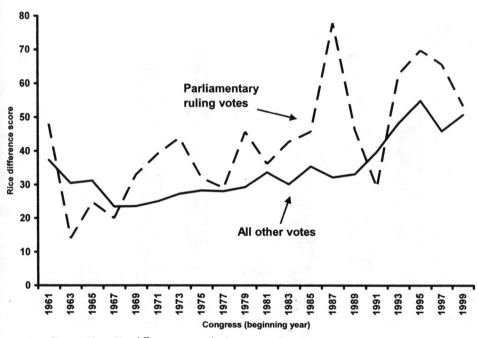

Fig. 9.2: Mean Rice difference scores, by Congress, 1961–2000

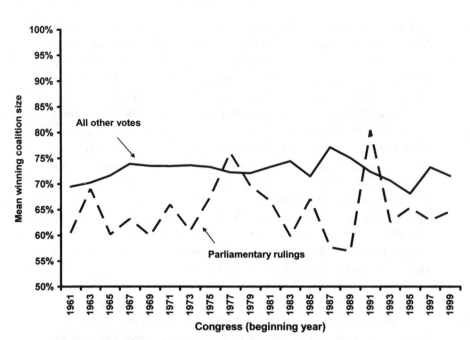

Fig. 9.3: Mean winning coalition size, by Congress, 1961–2000

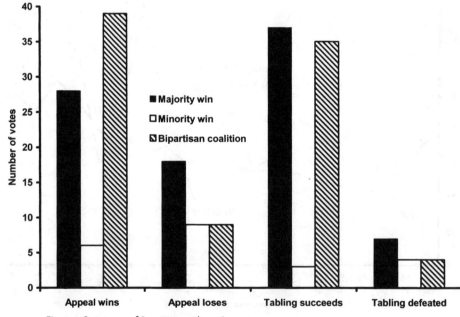

Fig. 9.4: Outcomes of Senate appeals, 1961–2000

if we take the mean of Congress-by-Congress averages, the winning side on parliamentary questions averages 65 percent of the chamber, while 73 percent is the average margin for all other votes.[9] While 65 percent is not exactly a minimal winning-coalition size, it is significantly more adversarial than other Senate votes.

The partisan potential of parliamentary decisions extends to the *outcomes* of these votes. Figure 9.4 illustrates party wins and losses parsed by vote type, outcome, and winning party for 1961 to 2000. The left-most cluster, "appeal wins," shows the distribution of party winners on votes to uphold an appeal from the ruling of the chair. Since we can fairly assume that the presiding officer typically affirms the procedural status quo when making rulings, these votes represent successful deviations from the status quo. More than half (39 of 73) of these successful appeals are supported by bipartisan majorities. The parties divided on the remaining thirty-four votes, and the majority party won 82 percent of them. Similarly, when direct votes on appeals are defeated by partisan majorities, the majority party wins twice as often as the minority party. When a motion to table an appeal succeeds, 49 percent of the time it is the majority party that successfully suppresses the appeal (37 of 75 cases), 47 percent of the time a bipartisan majority wins, and just 4 percent of such victories are won by the minority party. Finally, on the rare occasion that a motion to table an appeal fails in a partisan vote, the majority party wins 46.7 percent of the time. It is possible (but not guaranteed) that when a motion to table fails, the losing side will graciously accept the appeal from the point of order, so this category may also represent successful cases of procedural change. Taken together, these patterns suggest that the majority party has often been successful at preventing unfavorable new interpretations of chamber rules and has often imposed new interpretations of old rules by majority vote.

The next section documents a debate over whether the Senate majority party should impose a new precedent restraining obstruction against judicial nominations. This "nuclear-option" debate highlights both the fragility of Senate rules and the complex politics of institutional change.

Mutually Assured Destruction in the Senate, 2003–2005

For years, Republicans and Democrats have jousted over the partisan and ideological composition of the federal judiciary (Scherer 2005). The judicial branch is now the primary forum for a number of issues of prime importance to the members and organizations associated with each party: abortion, gay rights, civil rights, the environment, and many more. After the 2000 election, Republicans had narrow control of the White House and Senate, raising Democrats' fears that they would be able to stack the judiciary with conservative judges. For the first four years of the Bush presidency, senators fought over district- and appeals-court nominations on the basis of the notion that these positions are important in their own right (after all, the Supreme Court decides only a few dozen cases a year, so the lower courts render the final decision on all others) and are a prelude to the Supreme Court nominations to come (Dlouhy 2003).

It is noteworthy that this dispute was not simply a Senate affair. Each party acted in concert with allied interest groups. The significant role of interest groups allied with the Senate Democrats, such as People for the American Way, came to light when Republican staffers on the Judiciary Committee publicized memos written by their Democratic counterparts that detailed the coordination between Senate Democrats and interested organizations (Hurt 2003).[10] Senate Democrats used the judicial-nomination fight as a fundraising pitch (Kane 2002; Earle 2005a). On the other side, a large coalition of conservative organizations urged the nomination and approval of conservative judges, and as events unfolded, many supported drastic tactics to achieve this goal. Furthermore, President George W. Bush was a vocal critic of the Democrats' obstruction and urged the Senate to revise its rules so that every presidential nomination would be guaranteed a timely vote on approval (Allen and Goldstein 2002).

The first sign of the conflict was a low-visibility dispute over whether Democrats would be able to veto judicial nominations to posts within their own states (Eisele 2001).[11] This question became moot in 2001 after Senator Jim Jeffords of Vermont switched from the Republican Party to being allied with the Democrats, so that control of the chamber switched, Patrick Leahy became chair of the Judiciary Committee, and Democrats could block any controversial nominee.

The conflict escalated after Republicans regained majority status in 2003 and President Bush renominated several judges who had languished in committee during the 107th Congress. For the next two years, the Democrats pursued a policy of selectively blocking appellate-court nominees whom they considered too extreme; ten of thirty-four appellate nominees were defeated after cloture votes revealed that they were supported by the Republican majority but less than three-fifths of the Senate. Despite their nearly unanimous voting against cloture, some moderate Democrats were uncertain about the wisdom of confronting Bush and the Republicans on judges. As late as April 2003, a Democratic memo listed fifteen senators who were opposed to the party strategy or wavering; some Democrats' support for the strategy was contingent on whether they were fighting over process (how much information should nominees have to divulge?) or substance (is this person qualified for the federal bench?) (Bolton 2003b).

Republicans grew frustrated as the Democrats began filibustering Miguel Estrada's nomination to the D.C. Circuit Court of Appeals. On the evening of February 26, 2003, Ted Stevens (R-AK) commented that the Republicans could end the debate and approve the nomination right then if he took over as chair and ruled that filibustering nominations was out of order (VandeHei and Babington 2005). The idea gained momentum among Republicans, who considered Democrats' tactics unprecedented and unacceptable. Democrats and the press labeled Stevens's proposal the "nuclear option," since Democrats would retaliate against Republicans' assertion of the majority's ultimate power with full-scale obstruction that would bring the Senate to a halt.[12] In May 2003, Judiciary chair Orrin Hatch (R-UT) acknowledged to the press that Republicans were considering extraordinary tactics to suppress judicial filibustering (Bolton and Earle 2003), while Majority Leader Bill Frist (R-TN) proposed a formal rules change that would lower the threshold for cloture on a nomination by three votes after every defeated cloture attempt (Dewar and Allen 2003).

It was doubtful, however, that Republicans could muster a bare majority from their own members for a majoritarian strategy (Bolton 2003a), although they continued to discuss it (Bolton 2004). Instead, the Republicans continued to attempt and lose ordinary cloture votes. Moreover, they seemed to believe that they could win the war over judges by losing battles. By forcing Democrats to vote on cloture on stalled nominations (and other legislation), the Republicans hoped to build a record of Democratic filibustering and then campaign against the "obstructionist" Democrats in the 2004 elections.[13] Toward this end, they staged an anti-filibuster telethon in November 2003 to draw attention to the Democrats' obstruction (Dewar and Branigin 2003).[14]

During the 2004 election cycle, a single incumbent senator was defeated for reelection: Thomas Daschle, the minority leader from South Dakota. In a hyper-intensive campaign, Republicans characterized Daschle as an obstructionist holding up Bush's agenda and nominations. Following the election, Republicans' interest in suppressing filibusters against judicial nominations increased dramatically. President Bush, after all, had four more years to make nominations, and that would probably include one or more seats on the Supreme Court. Senator Frist criticized the Democratic filibusters as "radical" and warned that "one way or another, the filibuster of judicial nominees must end."[15]

Harry Reid of Nevada, the new leader of the Democrats, began to ne-gotiate with Frist over the ground rules for judicial nominations.[16] These negotiations, however, were hampered by two factors. First, neither leader had a unified team behind him, so it was unclear how credibly Frist could threaten reform and Reid could threaten filibusters. Senate Democrats had reason to worry about the consequences of a filibuster: "Democratic strate-gists said that some of the party's senators from states Bush carried in the presidential election could be reluctant to support a filibuster for fear of being portrayed as obstructionist—a tactic the GOP used successfully in congressional elections this year and in 2002."[17]

On the other side, Democrats speculated (and Republican aides later ad-mitted) that Frist lacked the votes to carry out his threat (Hurt 2005; Klein 2006). Senators' reluctance to engage in a high-stakes struggle reflected pub-lic opinion. A March 2005 Newsweek poll suggested public skepticism about the nuclear option; a 57 percent majority opposed the imposition of majority cloture for judicial nominations with only 32 percent supporting it, although among Republicans, a 55 percent majority supported the nuclear option and 33 percent opposed it.[18] Nor did public opinion support the Democrats' threat to retaliate; in the same poll, respondents opposed a postreform shut-down by a margin of 46 to 40 percent, although a majority of Democrats supported retaliation, by a 65 to 29 percent margin.[19] Republican-allied busi-ness interests were also fearful that they would suffer in the fallout from a struggle over the rules, as their legislative priorities might be dragged into a postreform cycle of retaliation (Bolton 2005d).

Despite this ambivalence on both sides of the party line, Reid and Frist were constrained by the keen interest of outside actors in the nomination battle. Conservative groups such as the Christian Coalition, the American Conservative Union, and Focus on the Family formed umbrella groups such as the National Coalition to End Judicial Filibusters to advocate a more con-servative judiciary at any cost.[20] Evangelical organizations held a televised "Justice Sunday" rally to urge the Senate to approve conservative judges (Babington 2005). They were joined, as before, by President Bush in advocat-ing cloture reform if necessary. On the other side, liberal groups such as the Sierra Club, Service Employees International Union, Planned Parenthood, and People for the American Way mobilized to advocate a meaningful role for Democrats—including a right to filibuster—in the judicial-confirmation process. These outside actors made it difficult to compromise, since Frist and Reid were each reluctant to disappoint the organizational core of their own party.[21] Frist, in particular, was contemplating a run for the presidency and needed to maintain his conservative bona fides (Bolton 2005c).

In April 2005, Republican threats became more intense as Frist publicly committed the Republicans to imposing reform (Bolton 2005a, 2005d; Babington 2005a), despite internal Republican polls suggesting public opposition to the nuclear option (Bolton 2005e). The threats and negotiations came to a head on May 13, 2005, when Frist announced that he planned to bring the appellate-court nominations of Priscilla Owen and Janice Rogers Brown to the Senate floor. Frist's press release stated that if Frist and Reid could not "find a way for the Senate to decide on fair up or down votes on judicial nominations, the Majority Leader will seek a ruling from the Presiding Officer regarding the appropriate length of time for debate on such nominees." Negotiations between Frist and Reid ended on May 16, with Reid decrying Frist's "all-or-nothing" approach (Hulse 2005), although a rump group of Republican and Democratic moderates continued to meet. The Senate debated Owen's nomination on May 18 and 19, then Republicans filed a cloture petition on May 20; implicitly, this meant a showdown on May 23.

On that day, hours before the Senate began to vote on cloture and, perhaps, a nuclear option, a group of fourteen senators announced a deal to resolve the conflict. These fourteen agreed to vote for cloture on three of the five nominees facing a filibuster (including Owen and Brown), leaving another two nominees exposed to a filibuster. For all future nominations—including Supreme Court nominations—the agreement stated that "nominees should only be filibustered under *extraordinary circumstances*, and each signatory must use his or her *own discretion and judgment* in determining whether such circumstances exist" (emphases added; the agreement's text is printed in the *New York Times*, May 24, 2005).

Who were the members of the "Gang of 14"? The Democrats were Ben Nelson (NE), Robert Byrd (WV), Joseph Lieberman (CT), Mark Pryor (AR), Mary Landrieu (LA), Ken Salazar (CO), and Daniel K. Inouye (HI). The Republicans were John Warner (VA), John McCain (AZ), Lindsey Graham (SC), Susan Collins (ME), Olympia Snowe (ME), Lincoln Chafee (RI), and Mike DeWine (OH). Press reports noted certain characteristics about members of the Gang of 14 that might account for why they joined this group. Some reports commented on their seniority: Byrd, Inouye, and Warner are senior senators, while Salazar, Pryor, and Graham were elected in 2002 and 2004. Other reports portrayed the members as moderates, despite members like McCain and Graham. Also, some among the Gang of 14 were up for reelection—Byrd, Lieberman, Nelson, DeWine, Chafee, and Snowe—so perhaps this was a ploy on their part to get attention as dealmakers right before the election.

I tested these claims with a probit analysis of whether a senator was a member of the Gang of 14, using seniority (number of terms), reelection, and moderation as predictors. Reelection is a trichotomous variable coded −1 for retiring senators, 1 for senators running for reelection in 2006, and 0 otherwise. Moderation is measured by senators' first-dimension DW-NOMINATE scores, which are conventionally used as a measure of ideology. In this case, I multiply Democrats' NOMINATE scores (which range from −.95 to −.021; low scores connote liberalism) by −1 so that the measure becomes an index of extremism: the higher a senator's NOMINATE score as adjusted, the more he or she is a liberal Democrat or conservative Republican. Moderates thus have low scores on this scale.

The results indicate that moderation is the best predictor of membership in the Gang of 14. There is no consistent relationship between membership and either reelection or seniority.[22] Figure 9.5 illustrates the relationship between preferences and the probability that a senator will be a member of the Gang of 14. The figure presents the predicted relationship (with a confidence interval of one standard deviation) for extremism scores ranging from −.05 (the actual minimum was −.03) to .95. The results suggest an 83 percent chance that a very moderate senator with an extremism score of 0 will be in the Gang of 14; but on the basis of these data, it appears that senators with extremism scores of .5 had a 3 percent chance of being in the Gang of 14.[23]

What did the agreement mean? "Extraordinary circumstances" is an ambiguous standard, so the key to its meaning is that a filibuster is not "justified" if a majority of the Senate is willing to suppress it. This meant that if all non-Gang Republicans were willing to vote for a nuclear option and all Democrats (plus Jim Jeffords, I-VT) would oppose such an attempt, then a filibuster was "justified" if six out of the seven Gang Republicans agreed that it was. However, the members of the Gang of 14 also committed themselves to make up their own minds on whether to suppress a filibuster—a major commitment on an issue as politicized as judicial nominations. Afterward, senators and pundits wondered whether the agreement heralded a power shift toward the responsible moderates in the Senate. Indeed, the Gang of 14 reconvened after President Bush nominated John Roberts and Samuel Alito for the Supreme Court, and in both cases the group deemed any filibuster against these nominations unwarranted.

At first glance, this contest suggests that threats of reform can deter minorities from filibustering.[24] We observe a sequence of obstruction, threat, and minority withdrawal that is consistent with deterred filibustering. Notably, all the major players in this fight—senators, staffers, reporters, interest groups—easily accepted the premise that the Republican majority could

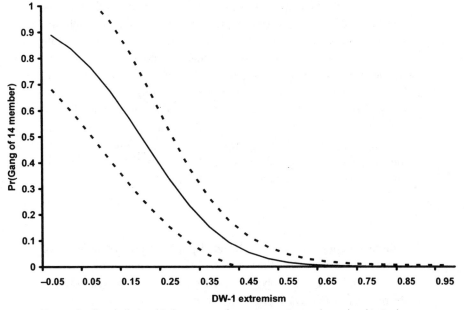

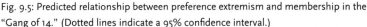

Fig. 9.5: Predicted relationship between preference extremism and membership in the "Gang of 14." (Dotted lines indicate a 95% confidence interval.)

impose majoritarian reform if it was sufficiently committed and ruthless. At no point did Democratic senators or spokespersons simply deny that reform was impossible without a preexisting right to move the previous question. At the same time, this episode illustrates the difficulty majorities face when attempting to bully minorities into acquiescence. Between May 2003 and May 2005, several Senate Republicans announced that they would not vote for a nuclear-option strategy, and several news articles expressed doubt that Frist could muster a bare majority for his strategy. For several Republicans, using drastic tactics to impose majority cloture on judicial nominations represented a major break from the comity that is necessary for the day-to-day functioning of the Senate. It would also represent a de facto transfer of power from Senate moderates, who provide critical swing votes under the current system (as embodied in the Gang of 14), to the president and interest groups who select nominees and advocate for them.

On the other side, Reid and the Democrats had a difficult time making a credible threat to "go nuclear" in a postreform Senate. The reason is simple: Democrats were presumably already filibustering in every situation where the benefits of obstruction exceeded the costs. Any punitive filibustering by the Democrats would have required obstructing in situations where the costs exceeded the benefits. Democrats could have tried to minimize the political repercussions by attributing their filibusters to the Republicans' procedural revolution, but individual Democrats would still have found themselves voting against cloture on bills that were politically popular, urgently needed, or both. For this reason, Reid had to exempt a number of bills from his threat of a legislative shutdown, including appropriations bills and legislation related to "supporting our troops," while other Democrats were reluctant to obstruct bills on highway funding or energy policy (Bolton 2005b). In the end, the Senate moderates' compromise spared both parties from trying to follow through on threats that would have been very costly to redeem and embarrassing to recant.

Discussion

This discussion of procedural tactics and disputes in the Senate is intended to demonstrate a simple fact: the Senate could be a much more majoritarian chamber than it is. Presumably, as in the House, the majority party would be the primary beneficiary of pro-majority reforms. But Senators have been reluctant to make major reforms, even when they are members of the majority party and their party's agenda is being thwarted by Senate minorities. They have, however, imposed new interpretations on Senate rules that advantage the majority party (for examples, see Koger 2002, chap. 9).

Why doesn't the majority party impose parliamentary "reinterpretations" that suppress filibustering? The nuclear-option showdown provides one answer to this question. It may be that Senate majorities rarely restrict obstruction because the minority refrains from pursuing filibusters that would provoke drastic reform. In the case of the Gang of 14, a bipartisan group of senators agreed to allow controversial judges to pass as long as the majority abandoned its reform plan.

This outcome ties into a second explanation for the persistence of Senate filibustering. In another work (Koger 2006), I find support for a classic argument that senators make against cloture reform, particularly cloture by majority vote. In a legislative setting, majority rule invites domination by party leaders, presidents, and interest groups who buy or coerce enough votes to win. Drastic reform would not necessarily benefit the members of the majority party because it would invite increased pressure to toe the party line and to ignore personal or constituent preferences. It seems that in 2005, moderates of both parties successfully averted a transformation of the Senate and preserved their own critical role in Senate politics.

Notes

1. "Filibuster" is defined as the use of delaying tactics to prevent a decision by a legislative chamber for strategic gain. For this chapter, I use the term "obstruction" as a synonym for filibustering.

2. Indeed, in 1968 the nomination of Abe Fortas for chief justice was blocked by a filibuster (Koger n.d.).

3. The Senate had no cloture rule before 1917; see Koger 2007 and Wawro and Schickler 2007 on the adoption of the Senate cloture rule. From 1949 to 1959, Rule 22 did not apply to resolutions to amend Senate rules.

4. Article 1, section 5 of the U.S. Constitution states, "Each House may determine the Rules of its Proceedings." In *United States v. Ballin*, 144 U.S. 1, 5, 12 S. Ct. 507, 509, the Court said: "Neither do the advantages or disadvantages, the wisdom or folly, of . . . a rule present any matters for judicial consideration. With the courts the question is only one of power. The constitution empowers each house to determine its rules of proceedings. It may not by its rules ignore constitutional restraints or violate fundamental rights, and there should be a reasonable relation between the mode or method of proceeding established by the rule and the result which is sought to be attained. But within these limitations all matters of method are open to the determination of the house, and it is no impeachment of the rule to say that some other way would be better, more accurate, or even more just." Each chamber thus has great discretion to choose and interpret its own rules. The Supreme Court has rendered decisions, however, on the interpretation of congressional rules as they pertain to the legitimacy of executive appointments (*United States v. Smith*, 286 U.S. 6 [1932]) and the investigatory powers of standing committees (*Chrisoffel v. United States*, 338 U.S. 84 [1949], *Yellin v. United States*, 374 U.S. 109 [1963], *Wheeldin v. Wheeler*, 373 U.S. 647 [1963] 373 U.S. 647), but the Supreme Court clearly recognizes that internal legislative rules are not cognizable by the courts.

5. See Koger 2006 and Wawro and Schickler 2006 for more examples.

6. "A Filibuster Ends, but Not the Gas War," *Time*, October 17, 1977, http://www.time.com, accessed December 6, 2006.

7. I describe such a case in the Rhode Island Senate in 1924, when a Republican majority attempted to outlast a Democratic lieutenant governor (Koger n.d.).

8. This difference is significant at the .01 level using a paired t-test.

9. This difference is significant at the .001 level using a paired t-test.

10. Republican staffers on the Judiciary Committee accessed these memos from the computer system they shared with Democratic committee staffers. The Senate sergeant at arms and the Justice Department subsequently investigated this infiltration.

11. Specifically, Democrats wanted to maintain a policy whereby each senator is sent a "blue slip" for a nomination to a position in his or her state and the nomination is vetoed if a senator returns a negative blue slip. See Binder 2007 on the origins of this practice.

12. The Republicans refer to their threatened gambit as the "constitutional" option, ignoring a general rule of political rhetoric: the label with fewer syllables wins.

13. "Senate GOP Preps to Confront 'Obstruction,'" *CongressDaily*, April 1, 2004.

14. As discussed below, this "marathon" session did not constitute an effort to win by attrition.

15. "Frist to Democrats: Stop Blocking Judges," *Washington Post*, November 12, 2004, A4.

16. Earle 2005b; "Frist Set to Offer Compromise on Judicial Nominees to Avoid 'Nuclear Option,'" *CQ Today*, May 18, 2005, 3.

17. "GOP May Target Use of Filibuster," *Washington Post*, December 13, 2004, A1.

18. The question was, "U.S. Senate rules allow 41 senators to mount a filibuster—refusing to end debate and agree to vote—to block judicial nominees. In the past, this tactic has been used by both Democrats and Republicans to prevent certain judicial nominees from being confirmed. Senate Republican leaders—whose party is now in the majority—want to take away this tactic by changing the rules to require only 51 votes, instead of 60, to break a filibuster. Would you approve or disapprove of changing Senate rules to take away the filibuster and allow all of George W. Bush's judicial nominees to get voted on by the Senate?" http://www.pollingreport.com/congress .htm, accessed April 12, 2005; $N = 1,012$; margin of error is plus or minus 3 percent.

19. The question was, "Senate Democratic leaders have threatened to slow down or stop almost all but the most essential legislative business if Republicans take away their ability to use the filibuster to stop judicial nominees they consider to be conservative extremists. Would you approve or disapprove of the Democrats responding in this way if the Republicans take away the filibuster?"

20. Outside groups also pressured senators to toe the line. After Senate Republican whip Mitch McConnell (R-KY) expressed reservations about "going nuclear," he was criticized by conservative radio host Rush Limbaugh, and the Family Research Council threatened to run television ads in Kentucky urging McConnell to change his position (Bolton 2005b).

21. On the broader network of links between interest groups and formal party organizations, see Koger, Masket, and Noel 2005.

22. Specifically, $\text{Pr(Gang of 14)} = 1.008(.568)\# + .016(.039)[\text{Seniority}] + -.111(.332)[\text{Reelection}] + -6.194(1.404)^{***}[\text{Extremism}]$; $N = 100$, pseudo-$R^2 = .3321$, and Wald $\chi^2(3) = 21.47^{***}$. In alternate specifications, the results were unchanged when "retiring" and "running for reelection" were estimated as separate dichotomous variables. If we use "distance from own party median" as the ideological variable, it is statistically significant, but the relationship is weaker and substantively questionable—no ultraliberal Democrats or ultraconservative Republicans were in the Gang of 14.

23. I find (in Koger 2006) that from 1918 to 1925, support for majority cloture increased with proximity to the party median. The key difference between this chapter and Koger 2006 is that the latter utilizes data sets in which most senators expressed some preference on a question. In this case, senators self-selected (for the most part) into the Gang of 14. The implication of Koger 2006 is that in the event of a roll-call vote on the nuclear option, support for that option would have been low among moderates

(as shown), liberal senators (no surprise), and staunch conservatives, who would fear the long-term consequences of centralizing power in the Senate, particularly if senators voted sincerely.

24. On the general claim that threats of reform can deter legislators from obstructing, see Koger 2004, n.d.; and Wawro and Schickler 2006.

PART III

10

Minority-Party Power in the Senate and House of Representatives

SEAN GAILMARD AND JEFFERY A. JENKINS

Over the past decade and a half, the study of party power has dominated the scholarly literature on the U.S. Congress. After a long period in which party decline, partisan demobilization, and strategic individualism defined the research agenda on American politics, and especially Congress, scholars began to revive the notion that political parties were important analytical units in structuring congressional behavior and legislative organization more generally. A set of "strong-party theories" emerged, notably the conditional party government theory (Rohde 1991; Aldrich 1995b) and the party cartel theory (Cox and McCubbins 1993, 2005), to challenge the conventional view of weak parties of the previous decades. Critiques of these new party theories soon followed, led by Krehbiel (1993b, 1998), and the subsequent period has been spent refining party and nonparty theories and developing appropriate methodologies to identify and test for party effects.

While the strides made by congressional scholars in pursuit of a general understanding of party power have indeed been significant, we have still only begun to scratch the surface. Two clear limitations exist in the literature, as studies of party power in Congress have focused almost exclusively on (*a*) the House of Representatives and (*b*) within that domain, the *majority* party. This has reinforced scholars' implicit assumption that party power—to the degree that it exists—resides within the majority, because of its ability to control the legislative agenda (in either a positive or a negative way). And the mechanisms for such agenda control are considered to be stronger in the House, wherein a formal set of institutional arrangements—such as the speakership and the Rules Committee—have long been established. Thus, our knowledge of *minority-party* power is quite limited, and those few studies that have examined it specifically have done so solely within the confines of the House (see, e.g., Aldrich and Rohde 2000a; Krehbiel and Meirowitz 2002; Evans and Renjilian 2004; and Jenkins, Crespin, and Carson 2005).

When considering minority-party power across the Senate and House, the conventional wisdom has been that the minority is considerably stronger in the Senate. This follows from the same premise that implies majority-party weakness in the Senate: formal authority to initiate as well as block legislative proposals is much more decentralized in the Senate than in the House. Thus, the institutional deck is stacked against majority-party agenda control and in favor of obstruction by minority coalitions, including the minority party. For example, any minority coalition, should it include at least forty-one members in the post-1975 period, can filibuster the majority's attempts to alter status quos.[1] Moreover, should the majority's legislative proposal make it to the Senate floor, the minority can introduce any number of nongermane amendments to raise issues that it wants considered, with the intent of either killing the majority's bill or altering the bill's content (which could potentially roll the majority or produce legislation that is consensual). Informal procedures also exist in the Senate, such as the "hold," which allows a single member to object to the content of a legislative proposal (Evans and Lipinski 2005). As a result of these various formal and informal institutional arrangements, scholars typically view the Senate as an arena in which leaders of the majority and minority parties negotiate a legislative agenda in advance, which results in a considerable amount of business being transacted via unanimous consent agreements (Sinclair 2000; Oleszek 2004; Smith 2005; Smith, Roberts, and Vander Wielen 2006).

In this chapter we explore this conventional wisdom. If the Senate's institutional arrangements do confer more power on the minority party as compared to the House's institutional arrangements, then standard measures of party power should reflect that reality. Recently, we investigated the parallel conventional wisdom for the majority party and uncovered little empirical support for it, finding no significant difference in a type of agenda power exhibited by the Senate majority relative to the House majority (see Gailmard and Jenkins 2007). Thus, conventional wisdom as it relates to party power across the legislative chambers cannot be taken for granted, especially for the minority party, as it has been largely ignored in the scholarly literature. We also go a step further and examine several determinants of party power in the Senate and compare them to those in the House.

Our first broader goal in this chapter is to continue making strides toward a deeper theoretical understanding of the institutional foundations of party power in Congress. Such an understanding, we believe, requires moving beyond insular, chamber-specific analyses to search for patterns of party power that transcend the individual institutional features of the Senate or House. Our prior article suggests that the dominant explanation for the perceived wisdom that the House majority is more powerful than the Senate majority—specifically, that the institutional features of the House confer more agenda-setting power on the majority—is at best only part of the story. That is, the similarity in success achieved by the House and Senate majorities in restricting agenda access suggests that some additional feature, perhaps common to both chambers, is necessary to include in any explanation of party power. Here, we examine whether the conventional wisdom associated with minority-party power across the Senate and House also gives way, thereby providing additional evidence that the traditional chamber-specific explanations and theories must be augmented in some capacity.

A second broader goal in this chapter is to spur methodological advances in the study of Congress by further emphasizing the Senate and House as comparisons and benchmarks for each other. Notably, Gregory Koger and Bruce I. Oppenheimer and Marc J. Hetherington adopt a similar comparative strategy in their contributions to this volume. Koger uses it to parse out the relevant differences between House and Senate, amid a sea of similarities, that are candidates in principle to explain salient differences in their majority-party organization and structures. Oppenheimer and Hetherington point to differences in the coalition-building process across chambers in their analysis of why the Senate majority party has been less able than the House to govern from the party rather than the chamber center. This type of comparison has been underemphasized in a literature that has tended to focus on each chamber in isolation, and disproportionately on the House. In aggregate, a significant portion of this volume, as well as our prior research (Gailmard and Jenkins 2007), suggests that scholars of Congress have much to learn from such comparisons. The chambers have adopted or evolved structures for handling internal chamber business that in some cases are very similar (e.g., standing committees) but in other cases are strikingly different in form, if not always in effect (e.g., agenda restrictions available to party leaders). The extent and effects of these differences have a great deal to say about the role of these institutions in congressional representation and the policy process.

In the next section, we discuss the data and measures that we rely on to explore minority-party power in the Senate, and we provide preliminary evidence of such power across three different legislative vehicles: Senate-originated bills, confirmation votes, and conference-committee reports. In doing so, we also make explicit comparisons between minority-party power in the Senate and the House. Following this, we examine the determinants of minority-party power in the Senate for the three legislative vehicles in question and then compare these determinants to those associated with minority-party power in the House on similar legislative vehicles.

Minority-Party Power: Concept, Measurement, and Preliminary Evidence

In examining minority-party power, we focus our attention on *negative agenda control*, or the minority's ability to keep bills opposed by a majority of its members from receiving floor consideration. This is a key feature of party power in the cartel theory espoused by Cox and McCubbins (2002, 2005; see also Campbell, Cox, and McCubbins 2002).[2] As mentioned, the conventional wisdom is that the Senate minority party wields substantial negative agenda control, considerably more than the House minority party, thanks to the minority-friendly institutional structure in the Senate. The filibuster allows a large enough minority to obstruct on both substantive and procedural matters, thereby thwarting the majority. In addition, the minority possesses the ability to offer nongermane amendments (or riders) to bills that do gain floor consideration, which, if successful, can stymie the majority's intent and cause said bills to fail. Thus, the filibuster and nongermane amendments provide the minority with significant blocking power. As Smith (2005, 256) states, "The absence of general limits on debate and amendments [in the Senate] limits the value of majority status and having a strong majority leader." The House minority party is not provided with these institutional allowances—no filibuster exists, and nongermane amendments are prohibited—which, according to the conventional wisdom, severely limits its negative agenda power.

To explore negative agenda power, we adopt party "roll rates" as our measure (Cox and McCubbins 2002, 2005). When a party majority opposes a bill on the floor but it nonetheless passes, the party is said to have been "rolled." A party roll rate in a Congress is then just the ratio of party rolls to final-passage votes. Roll rates can thus be thought of as an empirical marker of negative agenda control, in that rolls are observed failures of the party to stop measures that its membership opposes. If a party is able to block potential agenda items at the pre-floor stage—or, alternatively, to prevent pre-floor decisions from being compromised via some floor-based mechanism—then rolls should be less frequent than if a party does not possess these abilities. Greater negative agenda power is thus associated with (and is indicated by) lower party roll rates.[3]

The empirical expectations, then, are straightforward. Given that the Senate minority party possesses meaningful blocking instruments, such as the filibuster, the hold, and the ability to offer nongermane amendments, while the House minority party does not, Senate minority-party roll rates should be lower than House minority-party roll rates, all else equal.

To evaluate these expectations, we collect minority-party roll-rate data on all final-passage votes that elicited a roll call in the Senate and House from the 45th through 106th Congresses (1877–2000).[4] This interval is suitable because it begins shortly before the rise of floor leadership in each chamber (Campbell, Cox, and McCubbins 2002; Cox and McCubbins 2005) and covers the post-Reconstruction era in congressional history, wherein the same two-party system has operated and politics have been regular (or reasonably so) across the entire period. We examine roll rates on three different legislative vehicles: chamber-originated bills (S bills in the Senate, HR bills in the House), conference-committee reports, and confirmations of executive nominees. These three categories provide important variation with regard to negative agenda power, which we discuss at length in the next section.

Senate minority-party roll rates, along with House minority-party roll rates on similar legislative vehicles (where applicable), are presented in table 10.1.[5] The "per-Congress average" treats every Congress as an equally weighted observation regardless of the number of final-passage votes that took place in it. The "series average" is the ratio of rolls to final-passage votes on each vehicle, aggregating over the entire time span for both the numerator and denominator without regard to the Congress in which the vote occurred.

Looking first at the numbers in the top half of the table, we find that the minority is rolled relatively frequently across chambers and across legislative instruments in comparison to the majority party, which is almost exclusively in the single digits (see Gailmard and Jenkins 2007).[6] At the same time, there is substantial minority-party variation, from a series-average low of 19.6 percent on S bills in the Senate to a per-Congress average high of 36.2 percent on conference reports in the House. The observed Senate minority-party roll rates are lower than the observed House minority-party roll rates on all comparable legislative instruments (chamber-originated bills and conference reports), regardless of whether per-Congress averages or series averages are used.

TABLE 10.1. Minority-party roll rates, 45th through 106th Congresses (1877–2000)

Unconditional means, Senate and House

Roll rate (%)	Senate			House	
	S bills	Conference reports	Confirmation votes	HR bills	Conference reports
Per-Congress average	24.4	34.7	21.6	34.4	36.2
Series average	19.6	26.7	25.9	28.1	28.9
Number of Congresses	62	61	52	62	62
Number of final-passage votes	1,209	774	707	3,804	1,417

Comparison of comparable legislative instruments across chambers

Roll rate (%)	Chamber-originated bills			Conference reports		
	Senate	House	t-/z-test (p-value)	Senate	House	t-/z-test (p-value)
Per-Congress average	24.4	34.4	−2.87 (0.048)	34.7	36.2	−0.30 (0.768)
Series average	19.6	28.1	5.85 (0.0001)	26.7	28.9	1.06 (0.292)
Number of Congresses	62	62		61	62	
Number of final-passage votes	1,209	3,804		774	1,417	

Note: Two-tailed *t*-tests for per-Congress average comparisons; two-tailed *z*-tests for series-average comparisons.

In the bottom half of the table, we compare House and Senate minority-party roll rates on comparable legislative instruments in a more systematic way. We examine differences in unconditional roll rates, to determine whether they are significantly different from zero.[7] We find that the Senate–House differences on chamber-originated bills are indeed significant, regardless of whether we focus on per-Congress averages ($p = 0.048$) or series averages ($p = 0.0001$). Thus, the Senate minority party is rolled significantly less often than the House minority party, a result that is consistent with the aforementioned notion that the Senate minority party possesses a greater array of institutional weapons to ward off the majority party's advances. A different story emerges for votes on conference reports, however, as Senate–House differences prove *not* to be significant in both per-Congress ($p = 0.768$) and series-average ($p = 0.292$) comparisons. On conference reports, then, the Senate and House minority parties are rolled at statistically indistinguishable rates, a finding that is at odds with the conventional wisdom regarding the Senate minority party's greater institutional advantages.

Minority Negative Agenda Control in the Senate

The previous section compares minority roll rates across legislative vehicles and chambers unconditionally, without regard for the political circumstances in which they were generated. However, these unconditional levels of minority roll rates can be broken down into two parts: (1) the political context and conditions in the chamber that the party leadership faces in attempting to exercise control; and (2) the party's ability to translate any particular set of conditions into a favorable outcome—in the case of roll rates, stopping the consideration of measures that its members generally oppose but can win in a floor vote. While the average figures in table 10.1 blend these two components, the extent of party power has more to do with (2) than with (1). The issue is not so much what conditions the party leadership inherits, but rather what it does to secure the party's desired outcome in the face of those conditions. Put differently, the party leadership can be viewed abstractly as a function. It maps conditions it faces into observed levels of party roll rates or other measures of party achievement. What is of interest in assessing party power is the function, not the domain values it acts upon.

In concrete terms, to assess the degree to which the Senate minority party exhibits meaningful negative agenda control, exogenous factors that may affect the legislative environment also need to be considered. Such factors would include whether (*a*) the Senate and House or (*b*) the Senate and president are controlled by the same or different parties. If these outside actors— the House majority or the president—can influence the Senate's agenda and the choice of bills that are considered on the floor, then this will affect the Senate's raw roll-rate averages. For example, if the minority party in the Senate is the *majority* party in the House—that is, if there is divided congressional government—this may limit the number of Senate bills proposed by the Senate majority that will roll the minority. Such bills will likely not pass muster in the House, given the difference in partisan control. Thus, under divided congressional government, more-consensual legislation—bills that will be favored by both the majority and the minority—may be chosen. This will likely have the greatest effect on conference reports, legislation that is constructed largely by majority-party conferees from *each* chamber. Likewise, if the Senate majority and the president are divided, which would mean that the Senate minority and the president are of the *same* party, this may lead to the Senate minority's being rolled at a lower rate. The threat of a presidential veto may limit the ability of the Senate majority to select leg-islation that would roll the minority. In addition, under divided Senate–presidential control, executive nominations would likely be very amenable to the preferences of the minority. In short, to determine the degree to which the Senate minority party can influence its roll rate, salient factors both inside and outside the chamber that potentially affect its roll rate must be taken into account.

To this end, we analyze variation in Senate minority-party roll rates, and their conditional expectations given covariates, on Senate-originated bills (S bills), conference-committee reports, and confirmations of execu-tive nominees. This allows us to explore outside-actor effects on the Sen-ate minority party's negative agenda control across different legislative vehicles. The unit of analysis in these models is a single Congress, and the data incorporate all Congresses between the 45th and 106th (1877–2000). We estimate the conditional mean of the Senate minority-party roll rate for each legislative vehicle as a function of Senate majority-party disagree-ment with the House and president. These disagreements are captured by dummy variables: one if divided-party control of each set of institutions, zero if unified-party control. We also include a continuous variable to ac-count for the size of the minority-party "roll zone," which is measured as the absolute difference between the first-dimension DW-NOMINATE scores of the median member of the minority party and the overall Senate median (see Cox and McCubbins 2002, 2005).[8] A larger roll zone should be associated with a higher roll rate. In addition, we examine one aspect of the aforementioned conventional wisdom directly, by incorporating a dummy variable to indicate when the minority party controlled a filibuster pivot.[9] Such control should reduce the minority party's roll rate, as the filibuster should block out a portion of the minority's roll zone. Finally, to avoid spurious associations due to trends, we also included a linear time trend.[10]

The results are based on ordinary least squares estimation; to avoid in-ference problems due to heteroskedasticity or serial correlation,[11] we used Newey-West (heteroskedasticity-autocorrelation consistent) standard er-rors. The OLS parameter estimates are presented in table 10.2, with Newey-West standard errors in parentheses.

Looking first at S bills (column 1 of table 10.2), we find that divided gov-ernment, whether in terms of House–Senate differences or Senate–president differences, does not reduce minority-party roll rates. Substantively, this sug-gests that external actors do not significantly influence whether the minority party opposes Senate-originated legislation that passes in the chamber. In

TABLE 10.2. Regression results, minority-party roll rates in the Senate, by legislative vehicle, 45th through 106th Congresses (1877–2000)

Explanatory variable	S bills	Confirmation votes	Conference reports
Minority-party median–floor median absolute distance	41.45** (15.73)	47.30*** (15.65)	44.06* (26.34)
Senate–House divided government	-5.51 (4.99)	-11.67** (5.46)	-21.09** (10.33)
Senate–president divided government	-2.84 (4.82)	-35.89*** (3.81)	5.23 (7.44)
Minority control of a filibuster pivot	-7.94 (11.66)	4.29 (5.95)	-13.33 (11.49)
Time trend	-0.15 (0.16)	-0.13 (0.13)	-0.55** (0.22)
Constant	18.57 (16.27)	19.40 (11.91)	45.04** (20.56)
F-statistic (number of observations)	4.08*** (62)	33.28*** (52)	6.69*** (61)

Note: Each column is a separate model of the Senate majority-party roll rate. Entries are OLS estimates with Newey-West standard errors in parentheses.

* denotes significance at $\alpha = 0.10$ or less; ** denotes 0.05 or less; *** denotes 0.01 or less.

addition, since the coefficient on minority control of the filibuster pivot is not significantly different from zero, there is little evidence of Senate minority negative agenda control. In contrast, the roll-zone variable, the distance between the floor and minority-party medians, is positive and significant, as expected.

The results for the confirmation-vote and conference-report regressions indicate more interesting influences from outside the Senate. In the confirmation-vote model, the divided Senate–president variable is negative and significant, as expected, indicating that minority-party roll rates decline when the president and the minority are of the same party. In the conference-report model, the divided House–Senate variable is negative and significant, as expected, indicating that minority-party roll rates decline when conference reports are generated by a cross-chamber committee that is divided by party. In both models, the roll-zone variable is positive and significant, as in the S bill model. Finally, just as in the S bill model, the coefficient on minority control of the filibuster pivot in both models is not significantly different from zero. Thus, these regressions provide little evidence to suggest that the Senate minority party successfully deploys the filibuster to reduce its roll rate. However, the trend variable in the conference-report model is negative and significant, indicating that the minority is more successful over time at blocking unfavorable legislation. This constitutes some indirect evidence for minority-party negative agenda control on one legislative vehicle. (More will be said about indirect evidence in the next section.)

It is instructive to compare the parameter estimates for each variable across models. Such a comparison addresses, for example, where external actors have their greatest influence on the minority party's ability to keep unwanted proposals off the agenda, and whether internal chamber conflict has a greater effect on minority agenda control for some legislative vehicles than for others. As we pointed out in our work on majority-party negative agenda control (Gailmard and Jenkins 2007), an adequate comparison across models requires a hypothesis test, because the coefficients are realizations of random variables. Wald (χ^2) tests provide one way to make the desired comparisons. For these tests, which essentially compare entries across rows of table 10.2, the null hypothesis is that the coefficient on a given variable is identical across models, and the alternative hypothesis is two-sided. The test informs a judgment of whether the effect of a given variable is systematically greater on one legislative vehicle than on another.[12]

In table 10.3, we compare coefficients across the three models in this way. The chief result is that divided partisan control affects the legislative instrument over which it has the most natural substantive relationship. The divided Senate–president coefficient on confirmation votes is significantly different from the divided Senate–president coefficients in the other two models. The divided House–Senate coefficient in the conference-report regression is significantly different from the House–Senate coefficient in the S bill regression. Also interesting is that the relationship between the size of the minority-party roll zone and the minority roll rate does not differ across the three legislative vehicles. Finally, the time trend in the conference-report regression is significantly different from the time trend in the other regressions; thus, the minority party is more successful at lowering its roll rate across time on conference reports than on confirmation votes or S bills.

These findings, by themselves, offer little to suggest that the Senate minority party wields significant negative agenda control. There is no direct evidence, based on minority control of the filibuster pivot, and there is only mild indirect evidence, based on the time-trend variable and the significant, negative effect it exhibits in the conference-report regression. This is actually somewhat at odds with conventional wisdom about the Senate,

TABLE 10.3. Tests for differences in effects across Senate models

Explanatory variable	S bills–conference reports	S bills–confirmation votes	Confirmation votes–conference reports
Minority-party median–floor median absolute distance	0.01 (0.90)	0.07 (0.80)	0.01 (0.91)
Senate–House divided government	3.03* (0.08)	0.85 (0.36)	0.63 (0.43)
Senate–president divided government	1.50 (0.22)	26.29*** (0.001)	19.86*** (0.001)
Minority control of a filibuster pivot	1.29 (0.26)	1.07 (0.30)	2.39 (0.12)
Time trend	5.99** (0.01)	0.01 (0.90)	3.24* (0.07)
Constant	4.25** (0.04)	0.001 (0.97)	1.45 (0.23)

Note: Entries are Wald (χ^2) test statistics for difference in parameter estimates across regression models from table 10.2, with p-values in parentheses.

* denotes significance at $\alpha = 0.10$ or less; ** denotes 0.05 or less; *** denotes 0.01 or less.

which holds that minority coalitions in general, and the minority party in particular, have potent weapons to block chamber business. But negative agenda control may be difficult to assess in one chamber in isolation, because there is no natural benchmark of what counts as a "large" or "small" degree of it. To determine whether the Senate minority party exercises significant negative agenda control, a benchmark that exhibits weak channels of party strength and negative agenda control is useful. A natural candidate for such a benchmark, based on conventional wisdom, is the House minority party. Thus, we set out to determine how strong the Senate minority party's negative agenda control is in a relative sense through a set of cross-chamber roll-rate regressions and parameter-estimate comparisons.

Minority Negative Agenda Power in the Senate and House

A slight reinterpretation of conventional wisdom about the Senate minority party is that whatever its absolute level of negative agenda power, it possesses substantially more of it than its counterpart in the House. This is because the Senate is a consensual body with significant blocking power held by minority coalitions in general, and the minority party in particular, while the House is a rigidly majoritarian body.

TABLE 10.4. Regression results, minority-party roll rates in the Senate and House, by legislative vehicle, 45th through 106th Congresses (1877–2000)

Explanatory variable	S bills	HR bills	Wald test statistic (p-value)	Senate conference reports	House conference reports	Wald test statistic (p-value)
Minority party– chamber median distance	41.45** (15.73)	79.88*** (11.72)	3.25* (0.07)	44.06* (26.34)	52.03*** (14.77)	0.08 (0.78)
Senate–House divided government	–5.51 (4.99)	–1.98 (6.50)	0.20 (0.65)	–21.09** (10.33)	–5.61 (9.76)	1.01 (0.32)
Chamber–president divided government	–2.84 (4.82)	–5.31 (3.25)	0.25 (0.62)	5.23 (7.44)	–4.21 (7.35)	1.34 (0.25)
Minority control of filibuster pivot	–7.94 (11.66)	—	—	–13.33 (11.49)	—	—
Time trend	–0.15 (0.16)	0.23** (0.11)	6.07** (0.01)	–0.55** (0.22)	–0.12 (0.21)	2.46 (0.12)
Constant	18.57 (16.27)	–12.64 (8.79)	3.81** (0.05)	45.04** (20.56)	14.91 (12.11)	2.11 (0.15)
F-statistic (number of observations)	4.08*** (62)	12.64*** (62)		6.69*** (61)	4.98*** (62)	

Note: Columns are separate models of the Senate or House majority-party roll rate. Entries are OLS estimates with Newey-West standard errors in parentheses. For tests that individual coefficients are different from 0, * denotes significance at $\alpha = 0.10$ or less; ** denotes 0.05 or less; *** denotes 0.01 or less. Wald (χ^2) statistics are from tests for difference in model coefficients across columns, with two-tailed p-values (not standard errors) in parentheses.

We apply the same distinction from the previous section—between a function itself and the underlying domain values on which it operates—to assess this conventional wisdom. We compare regression models for the Senate and the House that specify minority roll rates on two legislative vehicles, chamber-originated bills and conference reports, as a function of conditions in the chamber and other institutions in the lawmaking process. The results are presented in table 10.4. The columns for S bills, HR bills, Senate conference reports, and House conference reports all present a model for minority roll rates on that legislative vehicle in that chamber. The Senate models are recapitulations of the results from table 10.2. The House models are new estimates for table 10.4.

The results across the two legislative vehicles are mixed. On chamber-originated bills, the House minority roll rate is significantly more sensitive to the distance between the minority-party median and the chamber median than is the Senate minority roll rate. On the other hand, the intercept term in the House model is significantly *lower* than in the Senate model: for any given set of conditions, the House minority has a baseline ability to protect the chamber agenda that the Senate minority does not have. The passage of time has seen significant erosion of the House minority's negative agenda control, but not that of the Senate minority. On conference reports, *none* of the covariates specifying political conditions has a significantly different effect in the House than in the Senate.

These comparisons allow us to further probe the degree of Senate minority-party power. While our most explicit measure of formal negative power for the Senate minority—a filibuster pivot that is a member of the minority party—indicates no evidence of such power, other measures may suggest indirect evidence. For example, in the models for chamber-originated bills, the difference in the trend variable across the chambers suggests that the House minority finds its roll rate increasing over time, while the Senate minority is able to maintain its status quo roll rate. In addition, the effect of the size of the minority roll zone (as captured by the distance between the minority-party median and the chamber median) and the minority roll rate is significantly larger in the House than in the Senate. These two differences may indicate that the Senate minority party uses its nonfilibuster institutional advantages to (partially) ward off the advances of the majority. For example, by exploiting the Senate's relatively open amendment process, the minority party may be able to offer amendments, germane or nongermane, that make a bill it opposes more to its liking. This is not authority to unconditionally block agenda access for undesired initiatives, but rather authority to make proposals on the agenda more desirable on the margins to the minority party. The overall effect is nevertheless that the minority party does not have to take undesirable agenda items as given. Because the House minority possesses no such advantages, it cannot withstand majority incursions onto the agenda, which leads to an increasing roll rate over time (a positive and significant trend variable, which is significantly different from the negative trend for the Senate minority) and a higher roll rate for every marginal increase in the size of the roll zone (79.88, versus 41.45 for the Senate minority).

A different picture emerges in the conference-report models, however, as the cross-chamber differences in all coefficients are statistically insignificant. At first blush, these nondifferences seem to reflect that the Senate minority party is no more advantaged than the House minority party when considering conference reports. As discussed previously, outside of the filibuster, the Senate minority's chief procedural weapon is its ability to offer nongermane amendments, which can change the substance of legislation and potentially sidetrack the majority's legislative intent. But as Oleszek (2004, 280) notes, "Both chambers require conference reports to be accepted or rejected in their entirety; they are not open to amendment." Thus, the nongermane-amendment weapon is removed from the Senate minority's arsenal during consideration of conference reports. The ability for the Senate minority (or a single member of the Senate minority) to sidetrack unanimous consent, via a hold, for example, also has little bite with respect to conference reports. This is because conference reports are privileged; in response to an objection to unanimous consent, "the majority leader can offer a nondebatable motion to take up the conference report" (Oleszek 2004, 280). Thus, other than possession of the filibuster—which does not appear to be a significant weapon for the Senate minority on conference reports, or any other legislative vehicle, for that matter—the Senate and House minorities are quite similar in their ability to wield negative agenda control on conference-report votes.

The difficulty that our results present for this explanation is that the Senate minority roll rate is no more responsive to the size of the chamber roll zone on conference reports than on S bills (cf. table 10.3). We do not find that Senate minority power erodes on conference reports relative to S bills, despite the foreclosure of some agenda-control tactics on conference reports, as described above. Rather, we find that the House minority is *less* responsive to its own internal roll zone on conference reports than on HR bills. As its procedural tools of negative agenda control are no weaker on conference reports than HR bills (and are weak in both cases), the nature of this change in the fate of the House minority is not particularly well aligned with conventional wisdom. In other words, while conventional wisdom might predict our finding that the House and Senate minorities are more similar on conference reports than on chamber bills, the prediction is at best right for the wrong reasons. The specific reason for the increased similarity across chambers on conference reports is not anticipated by the conventional wisdom.

Overall, then, the results in table 10.4 offer some evidence consistent with the conventional wisdom about House and Senate minority-party agenda control, but they offer other evidence—in particular, the reason for the increased similarity across chambers for conference reports—that is not consistent with it. To put these findings in context, compare them to the results on majority negative agenda control across the Senate and House in Gailmard and Jenkins (2007). There we found only *one* significant difference in parameter estimates (including intercept terms and time trends) across chambers: on divided congressional government on chamber-specific legislation. While the majority-party results reveal a striking similarity across chambers, given the mismatch of institutional tools of agenda control that the chamber majorities each possess, the minority-party results reveal a similarity that is present but less pronounced.

Conclusion

Our goal in the chapter has been to investigate minority-party power in the Senate and the House, specifically, negative agenda control as measured by roll rates. The minority party has often been ignored in studies of party power in Congress, and when it has been considered, it is typically within a study of the House exclusively. Therefore, focusing on the minority party can help achieve the broader goal of understanding the institutional foundations of party power in Congress.

Our results show that the Senate minority party does not enjoy a lower roll rate, on average, when the filibuster pivot (on the minority side of the median) is a member of the minority party. This is somewhat at odds with conventional wisdom on the Senate minority and its procedural tools, because the filibuster is perhaps the most conspicuous procedural instrument for negative agenda control in the Senate. On the other hand, the Senate minority party's roll rate on chamber-originated bills is less sensitive to conflict with the chamber median than is the House minority's roll rate on HR bills. This is more consistent with the conventional wisdom that Senate minority coalitions, including the minority party, have greater institutional advantages in preventing undesired agenda items from receiving successful consideration in the chamber. Our results provide only circumstantial evidence that one such advantage is the more open amendment process in the Senate, and further research is necessary to establish the effect of this factor directly.

Between the results in this chapter and our earlier work on majority negative agenda control in the Senate and House (Gailmard and Jenkins 2007), a set of empirical conclusions begins to emerge. Here, we find mixed evidence that the Senate minority possesses greater ability to restrict its chamber's agenda than does the House minority. In our previous work, we found consistent evidence that the Senate and House majorities have about the same ability to resist agenda incursions from outside political actors. Together, these findings are consistent with the contention that blocking power and negative agenda control in the Senate are broadly distributed.

On the other hand, negative agenda control in the House is concentrated in the hands of any coalition larger than a majority that is willing, for whatever reason, to vote together. A coalition of any size has an easier time "gumming up the works" in the Senate than in the House; this translates into greater minority blocking power in the Senate than in the House (cf. the chapter by Oppenheimer and Hetherington in this volume for a demonstration of the effects of this power on coalition formation and hence the content of legislation), and majority blocking power in the Senate that matches that in the House without the strictly majoritarian procedural tools to sustain it.

Notes

We thank Andrea Campbell, Mathew McCubbins, Nathan Monroe, and David Rohde for access to various Senate and House data sets used in this analysis, and Jason Roberts and conference participants for helpful comments.

1. Since 1975, the majority needs at least sixty votes to invoke cloture (i.e., to break a filibuster, or cut off debate). Between 1917 and 1975, the majority needed at least two-thirds of the members present and voting to invoke cloture.

2. *Positive agenda power*, or a party's ability to ensure floor consideration for bills supported by a majority of its members, is more in line with the conditional party government theory espoused by Rohde (1991) and Aldrich (1995b), among others.

3. For a critique of roll rates as a measure of majority-party agenda power, see Krehbiel 2007. We acknowledge that roll rates may not be an ideally perfect measure, but for our purposes of comparing the chambers, it is not necessary for roll rates to be isomorphic to negative agenda control. Problems with the measure in general should affect its application to either chamber, so that comparing across chambers is still valid. It is crucial that roll rates be defined consistently across legislative vehicles and chambers and at least correlated with negative agenda control. These conditions are plausible even though, as Krehbiel points out, roll rates may be "small" even if parties have no power.

4. Final-passage votes can change policy, and thus they directly affect a member's utility, position taking, and reelection chances. Thus, following Cox and McCubbins, we use these votes to define roll rates. Final-passage votes that require a supermajority for passage are excluded from the analysis.

5. There is no counterpart in the House to Senate confirmation votes.

6. The one exception is the per-Congress majority-party roll rate of 10.2 percent on confirmation votes (Gailmard and Jenkins 2007).

7. Difference-in-means tests are used for per-Congress average comparisons, while difference-in-proportions tests are used for series-average comparisons.

8. For a description and discussion of NOMINATE scores, see Poole and Rosenthal (1997, 2007).

9. We assume that the minority party controlled a filibuster pivot if (*a*) since 1975, it maintained at least forty-one members in the chamber; (*b*) between 1917 and 1975, it maintained at least one-third plus one members in the chamber; and (*c*) before 1917, it maintained at least one member in the chamber. Thus, before 1917, we assume that the minority always controlled a filibuster pivot, since there was no formal cloture rule in place.

10. Based on Dickey-Fuller tests, the time series of the dependent variable is difference stationary, but not trend stationary. Therefore, we include a time trend in the regressions and do not pursue first differencing or transformations appropriate for an integrated series.

11. We allowed for second-order autocorrelation in the error term—for example, in case of an election-year effect. But first versus second order did not greatly affect the results.

12. Gelman and Stern (2006) make a similar point more generally and explore problems of comparing significance levels.

11

Catch-22: Cloture, Energy Policy, and the Limits of Conditional Party Government

BRUCE I. OPPENHEIMER AND MARC J. HETHERINGTON

This chapter analyzes and contrasts the congressional struggle over energy legislation in the 1970s with the one of 2001–5. In doing so, it serves as a vehicle for evaluating the impact of changes that have occurred in U.S. governing parties as they have gone from relatively weak, ideologically diverse, noncohesive, overlapping organizing structures that granted their leaders limited powers to stronger, relatively ideologically homogeneous, highly cohesive (by historical standards) and polarized ones, willing to grant their leaders far greater authority and resources with which to mobilize their members. Among the questions we will try to answer in the course of this analysis are the following: (1) In what ways has the move to what has been labeled "conditional party government" affected the nature of coalition building in Congress? (2) Have the effects been different in the Senate than in the House? (3) What has been the impact on the nature of public policy? Does conditional party government result in the passage of legislation at median party positions, as opposed to at median chamber positions?

Our findings will suggest that while coalition building has changed significantly in both chambers, the effect of stronger parties and leaders remains substantially muted in the Senate compared to the House, in part because of the relative powers granted to the party leaders in the two institutions and the effectiveness of those powers in dealing with party members; and in part because of the cloture rule in the Senate and the need to produce supermajorities on controversial legislation. In addition, we will argue that while the process of dealing with energy legislation closely fits with the expectations of conditional party government, the end policy results resemble median chamber positions of the 1970s more closely than they do the non-incremental outcomes that one might expect under party government. Importantly, the Senate has been the primary brake in translating party governing strategies into median-party-position legislative outputs.

Moreover, it appears that only anomalous circumstances will allow the Senate to produce results consistent with conditional party government, even when voting in the chamber is obviously characterized by it. We will argue that cloture creates a catch-22 for party leaders. When Senate parties with fewer than sixty in their caucus pursue more ideologically extreme policy results, they increase the probability of a filibuster from the other side. If, alternatively, they manage to elect enough members to make the majority filibuster-proof, they almost inevitably include more members in the caucus who are either more moderate themselves or represent constituencies that are. In either case, policy outputs will, as a result, tend to drift from the median party position toward the median chamber position.

In chapter 8 of this volume, Chris Den Hartog and Nathan W. Monroe find that the majority party in the Senate has a real advantage over the minority in exerting blocking power through the use of motions to table. By contrast, we are concerned with the constraints that institutional arrangements of the Senate place on the majority party's ability to pass major items on its legislative agenda, even when the prerequisites of conditional party government exist.

It is not our intent to enter the debate over, or test competing theories about, the impact of parties in Congress (Aldrich 1995b; Cox and McCubbins 1993; Krehbiel 1998; Rohde 1991; Schickler 2000). We prefer to leave that to others. Instead, we assume that parties and the strength of parties in Congress have consequences for governing. Our concern is with whether the stronger governing parties have a different impact on the workings of the Senate than on those of the House and whether various features of the Senate mute the policy consequences of conditional party government. It is worth noting that most of the previous research on conditional party government has focused on the House.

The Quest for Party Government

For nearly a century, political scientists bemoaned the state of American political parties. From Woodrow Wilson (1885) to E. E. Schattschneider (1942) to James MacGregor Burns (1963), dissatisfaction with the ability of the American political party system to even approach a model of responsible party government echoed through the discipline and among political journalists. Weak American parties had little control over candidate selection. Candidates increasingly ran campaigns detached from national party positions, especially when those positions were in conflict with constituency preference. Voters were urged to make election choices based on candidate qualities rather than party and party positions. Once in office, winning candidates were not beholden to their parties or to national party platforms or issue positions. The party leadership had few resources available in the form of either rewards or sanctions to promote party cohesion. And voters frequently viewed the parties as indistinguishable. Because American parties were weak, they could rarely deliver on the policy positions they advocated during election campaigns, lacked the incentives to behave responsibly, and could escape accountability. Structural features of American government and politics, including different terms of office for House members, senators, and the president, the growth of primary elections as a candidate-selection vehicle, and a seniority system in Congress, among other things, exacerbated the situation. Only after major electoral upheavals that granted one party a supermajority in Congress as well as control of the presidency (following the 1896, 1932, and 1964 elections) was non-incremental policy change likely to occur.

In the 1980s, this began to change. As Rohde (1991) first demonstrated, congressional parties became increasingly cohesive on roll-call votes, and voting cleavages increasingly split House and Senate members along party lines. The Republican Party became a more uniformly conservative party, and the Democratic Party a more uniformly liberal one. The polarizing nature of the Reagan presidency contributed to the cementing of partisan cleavage lines in Congress. Conservative Democrats and liberal Republicans disappeared from the political landscape on Capitol Hill first, and then more gradually in the electorate. With increasingly polarized and cohesive governing parties in Congress, the prerequisites for something approaching responsible party government were in place by the 1990s, best described by Aldrich and Rohde (2000b) as "conditional party government." They contend that with polarized and cohesive congressional parties, House members and senators are willing to give their party leaders sufficient resources and powers to hold their members behind median party positions on legislation rather than building winning coalitions by moving to median chamber positions.

If one accepts that there has been a marked transformation of the congressional parties since the early 1980s to something consistent with a conditional party government model, the question remains whether that has resulted in the enactment of legislation at the median party position of the majority party. This capability is, after all, the linchpin of conditional party government. Its ability to produce legislation in line with party issue positions is what provides party members the basis on which to win reelection.

To address this question, we will compare the efforts to pass major energy legislation in the 94th through 96th Congresses with those of the 107th through 109th Congresses. Fortunately, many of the energy-policy issues that Congress faced in the 1970s are ones that are again at the forefront in the early twenty-first century—increased dependence on foreign energy sources, rapidly rising and unstable energy prices, the efficacy of production-oriented solutions as opposed to conservation-oriented solutions, environmental concerns, and the development and price competitiveness of new energy technologies. Of course, one may be appropriately skeptical of generalizing about the process and policy effects that have resulted from alterations of the congressional parties on the basis of a single policy area. (We will turn to the question of generalizability at the end of the chapter.) At the very least, however, we expect that the insights drawn from examining the impact of party change on energy legislation will offer some useful qualifications concerning the effect of party strength on legislative outcomes.

The Changed Nature of Coalition Building

One important way in which the struggle to enact energy legislation in the 2000s differs from that in the 1970s is in the means that proponents have selected to build the support necessary to pass bills. With weak congressional parties whose members granted their leaders limited powers, a concerted effort to hold party members to median party positions and build majorities composed almost exclusively of members of the majority party was not feasible, even in the 94th and 95th Congresses, when the Democrats had a two-to-one majority in the House and sixty-one senators.[1] Not only were the members of each party more diverse in ideological terms, but they also tended to be more responsive to constituency pressures when these were in conflict with party positions. When it came to issues like energy policy, Democrats had a sizable number of members representing both energy-producing constituencies and energy-consuming constituencies. And the same was true of congressional Republicans as well, albeit not to as great an extent.

The strategy party leaders employed in the 1970s on energy policy was one of trying to build a coalition around the middle and outward (Behringer, Evans, and Materese 2006; Oppenheimer 1980, 1981). The major problem they faced in the enactment of energy legislation was the capacity of the extremes to defeat compromises formulated by the middle.[2] Efforts to forge a variety of compromises (the gradual price decontrol of oil linked to a windfall-profits tax, the extension of price regulation to intrastate natural gas with the phasing out of natural-gas price regulation, a mix of production and conservation incentives) found regular opposition from House members and senators from energy-producing constituencies (who opposed windfall-profits taxes and who wanted immediate price decontrols on oil and gas as incentives for increased production) and also those representing strong consumer/conservation constituencies (who argued that prices were already high enough to encourage production and favored conservation approaches and the development of alternatives to fossil fuels for energy supply).

Through the 94th Congress, the extremes coalesced not just to defeat compromise positions but also to prevent compromise positions from being considered on the floor, especially taking advantage of the divided committee jurisdiction for energy legislation in the House. Neither the Ford administration nor the Democratic congressional leadership had the capacity to hold enough members of each party together to overcome opposition from the extremes. The problem is best exemplified by what occurred in 1975 in the House. With energy-tax issues under the jurisdiction of the Ways and Means Committee and price-control issues under the jurisdiction of the Interstate and Foreign Commerce Committee, opponents from both extremes used jurisdictional conflicts to prevent the House from considering oil-price decontrol and a windfall-profits tax simultaneously. In the Ways and Means Committee, opponents from both sides attacked the energy-tax bill of the committee chair, Al Ullman (D-OR). A proposed gasoline tax of forty cents per gallon eroded to three cents. An excise tax on "gas-guzzler" automobiles was weakened, and a tax credit for efficient ones was defeated. Most importantly, any action on a windfall-profits tax was deferred until after Congress resolved the oil-price decontrol issue. Not only were these efforts the work of members favoring production approaches, but those favoring conservation approaches joined them. The latter knew that without substantial energy-tax provisions in place, they could defeat efforts at oil-price decontrol.

When the Commerce Committee began work on its energy bill, HR 7014, debate centered on an amendment to link decontrol of oil prices to the enactment of a windfall-profits tax. Opponents of the linking on the Ways and Means Committee imposed on Ullman to fight this effort. In the immediate aftermath of Democratic Caucus reforms that had resulted in the defeat of three incumbent committee chairs and the divesting of a range of committee-chair powers, committee chairs felt compelled to protect the jurisdiction of their committees. Ullman was no exception, and he wound up undermining the compromise that he favored. In referring to the Commerce Committee debate, Ullman charged: "What we are doing here is, in effect, voting out a tax bill without having hearings, without having tax experts from the joint committee look at all the ramifications, without having the Ways and Means Committee look at the whole gamut of options" (Arrandale 1975, 1016). Moreover, House Democratic party leaders lacked the power to do much about the situation. Although the Democratic Caucus had just given Speaker Carl Albert (D-OK) the power of multiple referral and greater control of the Rules Committee membership, he was most reluctant to employ them, except in minimal ways, understanding that a divided party might remove these powers if it did not like the way they were used.

Thus, two pillars of an energy policy ended up being considered separately, and any hope of merger was lost when each was unraveled on the House floor. Despite what at the time was a novel "modified" rule accompanying HR 6860, the energy-tax bill, there were twenty roll-call votes on amendments, the bill was stripped of its key provisions, and it required two weeks to complete floor action. Much the same was true of the Commerce Committee's bill. Extended hearings and markup delayed the bill in committee, and when the House considered it, twenty-three amendments were offered. Delaying the Commerce bill effectively undercut the last opportunity to merge tax, conservation, and price-decontrol provisions.

Although Congress was more successful in enacting energy legislation during the Carter administration, the same strategy of the extremes attacking the middle emerged. This strategy was evident from the introduction of the Carter energy package early in 1977 all the way through to votes on the conference report. Two crucial roll-call votes, one in each chamber, illustrate the unusual nature of the coalitions.[3] In the Senate, Howard Metzenbaum (D-OH) moved to recommit the conference report with instructions to delete almost all of its natural-gas pricing provision. The motion was defeated but had the support of twenty-one Republicans and eighteen Democrats. Included among those voting with Metzenbaum were the Senate's most liberal Democrats (Gaylord Nelson and William Proxmire of Wisconsin, James Abourezk and George McGovern of South Dakota, Paul Sarbanes of Maryland, Donald Riegle of Michigan, and Ted Kennedy of Massachusetts) but also energy-state Democrats (Lloyd Bentsen of Texas and Bennett Johnston and Russell Long of Louisiana). Republican supporters included, among others, Dewey Bartlett and Henry Bellmon of Oklahoma, Clifford Hansen and Malcolm Wallop of Wyoming, Robert Dole of Kansas, and Barry Goldwater of Arizona, but also Lowell Weicker of Connecticut.

A logistic regression analysis of that roll call provides a more precise test for the extremes-against-the-middle hypothesis. The vote on Metzenbaum's recommittal motion is the dependent variable. Independent variables are the senator's party, the senator's DW-NOMINATE score in the 95th Congress, and a measure of state natural-gas production per capita in 1978. Both a linear and curvilinear relationship between the vote and ideology are tested. The linear formulation requires only the inclusion of the member's DW-NOMINATE score on the right-hand side. To test for the curvilinear relationship, the square of the DW-NOMINATE score is also included in the model. Evidence of a curvilinear relationship would be both DW-NOMINATE and its square appearing as statistically significant.[4]

The results appear in table 11.1. Those in the first column suggest that if there is a relationship between voting on Metzenbaum and ideology, it is not linear. DW-NOMINATE alone fails to even approach conventional levels of significance. When the squared term is included, however, the DW-NOMINATE score and the squared score are both significant and carry positive signs, indicating a curvilinear relationship between ideology and the vote on Metzenbaum. This is true even with a control for energy production, which is also significant.

In figure 11.1, which plots the probability of voting for Metzenbaum against the DW-NOMINATE score while holding energy production and

TABLE 11.1. Vote for Metzenbaum as a function of party, ideology, and constituency, 1978: logistic regression estimates

Variable	Linear Parameter estimate (standard error)	Curvilinear Parameter estimate (standard error)
Constant	−0.565	−1.986***
	(0.420)	(0.625)
Party	0.456	0.349
	(0.671)	(0.829)
DW-NOMINATE	1.343	2.690*
	(0.967)	(1.430)
DW-NOMINATE squared	—	12.077***
		(3.029)
Per capita gas production	0.632	1.189*
	(0.540)	(0.583)
Cox and Snell R^2	.12	.32
N	98	98

*$p < .05$; **$p < .01$; ***$p < .001$; one-tailed test

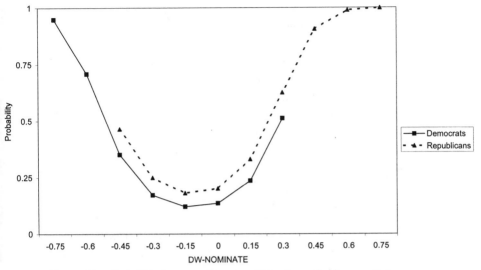

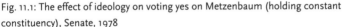

Fig. 11.1: The effect of ideology on voting yes on Metzenbaum (holding constant constituency), Senate, 1978

party constant, the curvilinear effect is clearly in evidence. Those senators at both ideological extremes were the ones most likely to support Metzenbaum. Moreover, the effect is substantively quite large. Among Democrats, the probability of the most liberal members supporting Metzenbaum approaches 1.0. But among those near the party median, the probability drops below .2. For the most conservative Democrats, however, the probability jumps again to above .5.

In the House, a similar coalition formed in opposition to the motion on the previous question made by Richard Bolling (D-MO) on the rule providing that the five separate conference reports that constituted the National Energy Act be considered en bloc, an essential procedural maneuver if the program was to be enacted. The motion was adopted 207–206. Among the seventy-nine Democrats who joined the Republicans in an effort to defeat the rule were seventeen members from the big energy-producing states of Texas, Oklahoma, and Louisiana. But they were joined by House members who were among the most liberal representatives from energy-consuming districts, including six northern Californians, six New Yorkers, five from Minnesota and Wisconsin, and even five from Speaker Thomas P. "Tip" O'Neill's home delegation representing Massachusetts (despite the fact that the Speaker was a major architect of the strategy to pass the legislation).[5]

To analyze the vote more rigorously, we use the same approach as with the Metzenbaum vote, estimating separate models for the different treatments of ideology, linear and curvilinear. The results follow the same pattern. The linear treatment, which appears in the first column in table 11.2, fails to approach conventional levels of statistical significance. Note, however, that in the second column, both the DW-NOMINATE score and the score squared are again statistically significant and with the same sign, thus supporting the curvilinear relationship. In addition, party is negatively signed and statistically significant, suggesting that Republicans, as expected, were less supportive than Democrats. On a procedural vote, where party and party leadership generally have more sway, the strength of party is hardly surprising.

Figure 11.2 presents graphically the results from table 11.2. The y-axis is the probability of voting for the Bolling motion, and the x-axis is the member's ideology. Among Democrats, one can see clearly that as the DW-NOMINATE score increases from −.7 to −.2, the likelihood of a member's voting for the rule increases from less than .2 to over .8. It then declines markedly as the DW-NOMINATE score increases. Even among Republicans, only eight of whom voted for the rule, the curve takes on a similar shape.[6]

Beyond demonstrating how the extremes coalesced in efforts to defeat compromise energy legislation that had the support of the middle, these votes also attest to the limited influence of parties and party leaders over their members. Even with more than 290 Democratic House members, Speaker O'Neill was barely able to deliver a victory to a president of his own party on the most important piece of that president's legislative agenda. Yet

TABLE 11.2. Vote for Bolling as a function of party and ideology, 1978: logistic regression estimates

Variable	Linear Parameter estimate (standard error)	Curvilinear Parameter estimate (standard error)
Constant	0.947*** (0.220)	1.115*** (0.246)
Party	−3.741*** (0.512)	−2.679*** (0.527)
DW-NOMINATE	0.081 (0.608)	−3.322*** (1.139)
DW-NOMINATE squared	—	−9.545*** (2.053)
Cox and Snell R^2	.36	.40
N	414	414

*$p < .05$; **$p < .01$; ***$p < .001$; one-tailed test

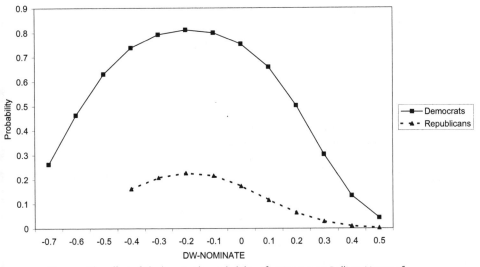

Fig. 11.2: The effect of ideology on the probability of voting yes on Bolling, House of Representatives, 1978

it is crucial to realize that on energy legislation, which was the centerpiece for the new Carter administration, O'Neill was able to exercise leadership powers to a far greater extent than had previously been the case. He used sequential referral to limit the time available to various standing committees to produce their parts of the legislation. He persuaded the membership to consent to the creation of the Ad Hoc Select Committee on Energy, providing the leadership and opportunity for post-standing-committee adjustment to the legislation by a body whose Democratic members he had carefully selected. He had the cooperation of the Democratic members of the Rules Committee in producing an unusually (for its time) complex restrictive rule for considering the legislation on the floor, and later in producing the rule for consideration of the conference-committee report. Although such leadership powers would be commonplace in the era of conditional party government, they were exceptional when used in the 95th Congress.

The narrowness of the margin in passing the Carter energy package also afforded an opportunity for members to act as free agents and hold the legislation hostage. This occurred even among some of those who supported the legislation in the end. Nowhere was this more evident than in the bargaining that occurred among conferees in the spring and summer of 1978, which Oppenheimer (1981, 284–85) detailed in an article from which we quote at length.

By March 1978 it appeared a compromise allowing for deregulation by 1985 had been reached. Five members on each side of the natural gas issue supported the compromise, and the Senate conferees approved it, 10–7. Then, by a slim 13–12 margin, the House conferees accepted the compromise with an amendment. (This indicated a loss of three antideregulation House conferees without any gain from the proderegulation side.) Senator Pete Domenici (R-N.M.), one of the 10 supporting the compromise, threatened to withdraw his support in reaction to the House amendment, and Senator Abourezk, an opponent of the compromise, threatened to filibuster any plan that allowed for deregulation. Once again a compromise unraveled.

In late April a group of House and Senate conferees and Secretary of Energy James Schlesinger seemingly had worked out a new natural gas compromise, but now 2 of the 13 House conferees who had accepted the March compromise, Henry Reuss (D-WI) and James Corman (D-CA), objected to the new agreement. Reuss reportedly felt it was too generous and would assist separate passage of the crude oil equalization tax that he opposed, and Corman wanted to insure a strong crude oil tax if he were to support the new compromise. Obviously, to win Reuss back would mean losing Corman and vice versa. A 13–12 majority in March became a 12–13 minority in April.

This required bargaining with yet another hostage holder, Joe Waggonner (D-LA), who had problems with the extension of price controls to intrastate natural gas. By mid-May a compromise was finally worked out allowing for increases in the ceiling prices for intrastate gas. Waggonner provided the deciding vote among the House conferees, and the Senate conferees accepted the new agreement. All that remained was for the staff to draft the proper language. But when the final language was presented to the conferees in August, three House and two Senate conferees who had supported the May compromise refused to sign the report, again holding the legislation hostage. Although some claimed that the formal language did not reflect what they thought had been agreed to in May, others held out on related issues. For example, Louisianians Senator Johnston and Representative Waggonner, in the interests of a Louisiana pipeline company, became concerned with a Federal Energy Regulatory Commission case involving allocation of natural gas in intrastate markets.

Thirteen votes were reassembled on the House side only after Corman and Charles Rangel (D-N.Y.), who had not agreed to the May compromise, replaced Reuss and Waggonner. President Carter reassured Corman and Rangel that the poor would be given protection from large increases in energy prices. On the Senate side Domenici and James McClure (R-ID) agreed to rejoin those supporting the report, thus providing a majority. Afterwards, however, McClure revealed that his support for the report was gained in return for President Carter softening his position on the breeder nuclear reactor.

It is important to note from the above, however, that there was one clear advantage for coalition builders in constructing majorities from the middle outward. They had the flexibility to move the legislation in either direction in an effort to gain support. Thus, if they were having difficulty picking up support from those on the political left, they could always threaten to negotiate for votes with those on the political right, and vice versa. As we shall see, that is in stark contrast with the bargaining situation party leaders faced in 2001–5.

One would be correct to note that in the 96th Congress, when Congress enacted a windfall-profits tax on oil companies (a condition that President Carter set in order for him to end oil-price control gradually), the key issues and votes no longer pitted the extremes against the middle. That was largely because it was generally assumed that some form of windfall-profits tax would be enacted and that Carter was committed to following through with his side of the bargain. Carter's proposal had effectively split the opposition. Once that bargain was struck, there was nothing to be gained from those opposed to windfall-profits taxes coalescing with those opposed to price de-control. Thus, the issues to be resolved instead were ones about the size of the tax, how long it would last, and how the revenues from it would be used. On those issues, members generally divided along energy-producing versus energy-consuming constituency lines.

Throughout the 1970s, resolving energy legislative issues involved efforts to move policy solutions toward the middle and to reach compromises that allowed that middle to expand to produce winning coalitions. Where that resolution point was varied in terms of which party controlled the presidency and the composition of the House and Senate. The struggle was largely one of facing those who preferred the status quo on energy policy to the available alternatives that a compromise position might produce.

Energy-Policy Coalitions, 2001–5

By contrast, the struggle to enact energy legislation since 2001 has been quite different strategically. Unlike the efforts in the 1970s, legislation was not be-ing formulated around the preferred position of the middle members of the House and Senate on the issue. Instead, it was pitched to changing the status quo energy policies by enacting legislation that reflected the median posi-tion of congressional Republicans and relied on resources that Republican House members and senators had given to their party leaders to hold party members to that position. Passing an energy bill at the median party posi-tion has been far easier to achieve in the House than in the Senate, in large part because the cloture rule in the Senate has allowed the Democrats, as the minority party except for eighteen months of the 107th Congress, to block efforts at cloture. In addition, as we will discuss, Senate leaders have fewer resources available than their House counterparts, and those resources are less effective in getting members to adhere to median party positions.

Over the course of the 2001–5 period, the passage of energy legislation hinged on how Republican congressional leaders and the Bush administration weighed competing costs and benefits in the options available to them. What were the costs and benefits of adhering to median party positions and having energy legislation defeated, as opposed to those of moving toward median chamber positions to build coalitions large enough to pass the legislation? In the 107th and 108th Congresses, the cost-benefit calculation resulted in the failure to enact energy legislation. But by 2005, media attention and the saliency of energy issues to the public rose sufficiently that Republicans were willing to move away from median party positions to ensure that the Senate would pass a bill.

To illustrate and better comprehend the changed nature of coalition building, it is useful first to examine the House floor voting on the amendment offered by Edward Markey (D-MA) to strike provisions allowing for oil and gas exploration in the Arctic National Wildlife Refuge (ANWR) and on the motion by Lois Capps (D-CA) to strike the MTBE (methyl tertiary butyl ether) liability provision during the consideration of HR 6 in April 2005. On both of these votes, but particularly on the latter, there were only a limited number of Democrats who voted against these amendments—thirty on Markey and fourteen on Capps—and most of them were from energy-producing states. Of the Democrats who voted against Capps, eleven were from Texas, Louisiana, and Oklahoma. And they are an overwhelming majority of the current Democratic House members from those states, who numbered only fourteen in the 109th Congress. By comparison, in the 95th Congress there were thirty-two Democratic House members from those states.

The decline in the number of Democratic House members representing energy-producing states and districts has meant that the cleavages on energy legislation were more reinforcing in the 2001–5 period than they were in the 1970s. Republican House members more heavily represented energy-producing districts than they did in the 1970s, and Democrats more heavily represented consuming districts. This undercut the tendencies toward moderation in developing energy-policy options in the House. With few Democratic House members from producing constituencies, there was little voice within the Democratic caucus to moderate in favor of more producer-oriented solutions. And with members from energy-producing constituencies more dominant with the Republican House membership, producer-oriented solutions were the mainstay of the party's energy legislation. Constituency-based cleavages that were more reinforcing of party cleavages (as opposed to crosscutting) have certainly contributed to a higher level of party polarization. Further, it has meant that members are less likely to be exposed to contrary points of view from among their fellow caucus members.

Because they were the majority party, House Republicans could afford to lose some consuming-district party members from the Northeast and upper Midwest on key energy votes. With the help of the declining number of energy-state Democrats, they still could get party-backed energy bills through the House largely intact.

Because of the cloture rule in the Senate, however, the ability to hold to party positions in producing energy legislation has proved far less tenable in passing legislation in that chamber. It is one thing to build a majority around a median party position, and another to garner the votes of sixty senators for cloture. Again, the effects of party, ideology, and constituency factors illustrate why the calculus in the Senate differs. This can be seen in an analysis of the 2002 cloture vote on the Murkowski amendment, which would have allowed oil and gas development in ANWR (and was generally consistent with the energy bill Republicans had passed in the House), and of the 2003 cloture vote on the conference report on HR 6.[7]

In analyzing each vote, we again used logistic regression with the same approach in mind, first estimating a model with a linear term for ideology and then a second model with a curvilinear treatment of ideology. We expect, of course, that the linear expectation will be borne out in the contemporary period. In each instance, the vote of the senator for or against cloture is the dependent variable. In the case of the cloture vote on the Murkowski substitute in 2002, we also included a measure of energy production per capita in the senator's state as an independent variable.[8]

As the results in table 11.3 show, our expectations are borne out, suggesting the changing nature of coalition building. Whereas in the previous period coalitions were constructed outward from the chamber median, this is no longer the case. As evidence, note the negative results in the second column test for the curvilinear relationship. The squared DW-NOMINATE score is not statistically significant and carries a sign opposite of that of the unsquared score, indicating that there is no support for a curvilinear relationship. Instead, only the linear term is significant, indicating that coalitions are built outward in one direction from the *party* median. In addition, energy production is statistically significant. The more conservative

TABLE 11.3. Vote for Murkowski as a function of party, ideology, and constituency, 2002: logistic regression estimates

Variable	Linear Parameter estimate (standard error)	Curvilinear Parameter estimate (standard error)
Constant	−0.553	−0.215
	(0.935)	(1.139)
Party	−0.530	−0.743
	(1.502)	(1.556)
DW-NOMINATE	7.339***	7.846***
	(2.317)	(2.571)
DW-NOMINATE squared	—	−2.502
		(4.583)
Per capita BTU production	1.023*	1.023*
	(0.576)	(0.559)
Cox and Snell R^2	.56	.56
N	100	100

$*p < .05; **p < .01; ***p < .001$; one-tailed test

the senator and the more energy production in the state, the more likely the senator was to have voted for cloture. It is also worth noting that the same set of variables in the contemporary period explain much more variance than they did in the 1970s, with the Cox and Snell R-square increasing from .32 in the earlier period to .56 in the later one.

To understand the relative impact of these variables on the likelihood of a senator's voting for cloture, one can examine the curves in figure 11.3, which show the probability of voting for the Murkowski cloture motion as a function of member ideology and state energy production. Several things are apparent. First, the effect of energy production and ideology on the probability of voting for cloture is evident among both Democrats and Republicans. Second, the effect of both state energy production and ideology is most marked among those closest to the chamber median. Specifically, it is among the least liberal Democratic senators from the highest energy-producing states that we see the biggest increase in the likelihood of voting for cloture (compared to those at the party median on ideology and at a median level of state energy production). Among Republicans, it is among the least conservative from the lowest energy-producing states that we find the least likelihood of voting for cloture.

Third, because half the senators of each party would fall beyond the respective lines for the party medians in figure 11.3, there were relatively few

Democratic senators that the model would predict to have a .25 or greater probability of voting for cloture or Republican senators who would have a .25 or greater probability of voting against cloture. And only for Democratic senators at the extreme on both measures does the model predict a probability of greater than 50–50 of voting with an overwhelming majority of the other party. Thus, ironically, although ideology and constituency (as measured by state energy production) are statistically significant in the model, and party is not, they had limited substantive implications for the outcome of this cloture vote, which was 46–54.[9] Unable to produce even a Senate majority and far short of the votes needed for cloture, Senate Republicans had to either alter their strategy or accept the continued defeat of energy legislation.

Although Senate Republicans recognized the need to produce a bill capable of winning sixty votes in the Senate in 2003, the final bill was written "entirely by Republicans," consistent with efforts to hold party members together behind party positions (Anselmo 2003). Unlike the energy package in the 95th Congress, the conference negotiations in 2003 involved only Republicans. House Republican leaders and conferees were reluctant to move away from the median party positions in their version of the bill. Senate Republican conferees, however, citing the need for sixty votes in the Senate, insisted on dropping the House provisions allowing for oil and

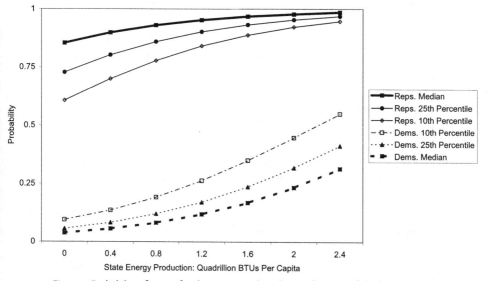

Fig. 11.3: Probability of voting for cloture on Murkowski, as a function of ideology and energy production, 2002

gas drilling in ANWR. (Earlier in 2003, the Senate had removed an ANWR provision from the budget resolution on a 52–48 vote. Hence, Senate conferees were in a strong position in arguing that it would be impossible to get cloture on an energy bill that allowed for drilling in ANWR.)

The Senate Republican conferees also sustained the Senate position to double consumption of ethanol by 2012. That appeared to be the best vehicle for attracting the support of enough farm-state Senate Democrats to reach the sixty-vote level. Although these two changes clearly moved the legislation away from the preferred position of House Republicans and the Bush administration (as we shall discuss later, this is probably not an unreasonable estimate of the median Republican party position in the Senate as well), the former insisted on preserving a liability waiver for MTBE producers that was a critical provision for Energy and Commerce Committee chair Billy Tauzin (R-LA) and for House Majority Leader Tom DeLay (R-TX).

The corn sweetener and the removal of ANWR exploration had the predicted effect, as thirteen Democrats voted for cloture on HR 6, as opposed to only five in 2002. But those concessions proved insufficient, as the MTBE issue became more salient. Again, a logistic regression analysis of the vote provides more exact estimates of the effect of ideology and constituency factors on the cloture vote. In addition to the ideology, party, and energy-production variables that we employed for the analysis of the 2002 vote, we included another constituency variable, the level of state corn production in bushels per capita.[10]

The results appear in table 11.4. Again, both ideology and constituency variables have a statistically significant effect on the probability of voting for cloture in the linear model. The probability of voting for cloture increases as member conservatism, state energy production, and state corn production increase. As in the 2002 cloture vote (and in contrast with the key votes from the 1970s), the test for a curvilinear model yields a statistically insignificant relationship for the squared DW-NOMINATE score with a sign opposite that of the unsquared variable.

Despite the significance of constituency variables on the probability of senators' voting for cloture, corn and energy production in their states had relatively little impact for most Republican senators. As can be seen in figure 11.4, only among the least conservative Republicans and those who represent states with little or no corn production does the probability of voting against cloture drop below .5. Even for Republicans with DW-NOMINATE scores in the twenty-fifth percentile or above, the likelihood of voting for cloture was at least .75. But with the very narrow defeat of cloture, on a 57–40 vote, these very moderate Republican senators were critical.[11] Despite getting the

TABLE 11.4. Vote for cloture on HR 6 as a function of party, ideology, and constituency, 2003: logistic regression estimates

Variable	Linear Parameter estimate (standard error)	Curvilinear Parameter estimate (standard error)
Constant	0.852	2.473
	(1.358)	(1.944)
Party	−3.013	−4.390
	(2.151)	(2.646)
DW-NOMINATE	11.692***	14.526***
	(3.415)	(4.651)
DW-NOMINATE squared	—	−11.848
		(8.148)
Per capita BTU production	1.187*	1.220
	(0.701)	(0.832)
Per capita corn production	0.031**	0.047**
	(0.011)	(0.018)
Cox and Snell R^2	.61	.62
N	98	98

$*p < .05$; $**p < .01$; $***p < .001$; one-tailed test

conference to move away from the median party positions on ANWR and ethanol that were contained in the House bill, Senate Republican party leaders were not able to win the support of any of the five Republicans from the low corn- and energy-production states of New England on the cloture vote, three of whom were among the four least conservative Republicans in the Senate. After one accounts for the vote of Majority Leader Bill Frist (R-TN) against cloture, to allow for him to move for reconsideration, Republicans still remained two votes short. And although he claimed that he would pursue the additional votes needed during the second session, Frist was unable to do so.

For Democratic senators, the effect of constituency factors on the likelihood of voting for cloture was far greater. The ethanol provision clearly was effective in attracting the support of corn-state Democrats. As one can see in figure 11.4, there is a very steep increase in the probability of voting for cloture among Democratic senators if their state exceeds fifty bushels per capita in corn production. Seven of the eight Democratic senators representing states with corn production in excess of one hundred bushels per capita voted for cloture in 2003. None of them had done so in 2002. Indeed, the effect of corn production dwarfs that of ideology in explaining the

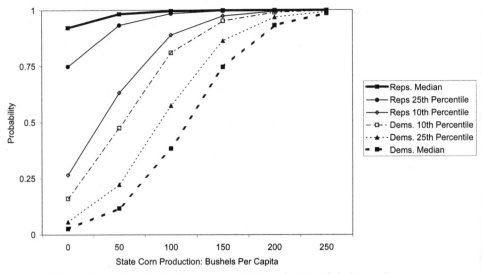

Fig. 11.4: Probability of voting for cloture on HR 6 as a function of ideology and corn production (holding constant energy production), 2003

likelihood that Democratic senators voted for cloture. Moving away from Republican median party positions on the energy-bill conference report proved far more effective in drawing the support of Democrats away from their median party position than in holding on to moderate and energy-consuming-state Republican senators. In fact, Tom Daschle (D-SD), the minority leader, was one of the Democrats who voted for cloture. And one could argue that this was the result of a movement away from the Republican median party position on the energy bill in the dropping of ANWR drilling and the addition of the more generous ethanol provision. Constituency factors, especially state corn production, had a big independent effect on the vote decision.

From this analysis, one is tempted to conclude that adding the ethanol provision to the bill, even if it was viewed as either tangential or opposed to Republican party and Bush administration energy-policy goals, was very effective in adding votes of Democratic senators for cloture on the energy legislation while preserving the overall production thrust of the bill (absent ANWR). This conclusion, however, requires a significant caveat regarding whether these farm-state Democratic senators cast sincere votes. Knowing that their votes would not be enough to invoke cloture, they were free to vote for it. In doing so, they could please pro-ethanol constituencies without undermining their party's position of being opposed to the bill.

Clearly, part of the reason that Republicans in the Senate were unable to produce an energy bill at what approximated the median party position when their House counterparts could is the cloture rule of the Senate. Recognizing that they would need sixty votes to pass an energy bill, Republican conferees had to move away from median party positions on some energy-legislation provisions in the 108th Congress and did so on ANWR and ethanol. But that was still insufficient, because Republican party leaders lacked the power to hold enough Republican senators. House Republican leaders would not relent on MTBE liability protection. Without that change, Frist could not garner the support of New England Republican senators. In the end, the costs for House Republicans of moving farther from the median party position on energy legislation in order to pick up the additional votes needed for cloture outweighed the benefits of enacting legislation. They preferred to wait for the outcome of the 2004 elections and hope that seat gains might make additional concessions unnecessary.

The 109th Congress

Given the outcome of the 2004 election, one might think that the stalemate on energy legislation would have been resolved at closer to the median party position that House Republicans favored. The party's net gain of four Senate seats would seemingly mean that there were enough votes to invoke cloture. Despite the gains in the Senate, it is unclear whether the Republican leadership was any closer to producing the sixty votes needed for cloture. Three of the six new Republican senators replaced Democrats who had voted for cloture in 2003. A fourth, Mel Martinez (R-FL), represented an environmentally sensitive state with concerns about the bill's inclusion of provisions potentially opening the eastern Gulf of Mexico to offshore drilling.[12] And the gains for cloture with the replacement of Democrats John Edwards and Ernest Hollings by Republicans Richard Burr and Jim DeMint in the Carolinas would be offset with Democratic wins in open seats that Republicans had held in Colorado and Illinois. Because of a sizable energy-producing constituency in the former, first-term Democrat Ken Salazar (D-CO) might be persuadable to vote for cloture. That was far from certain, however, and would still leave the Senate Republican leadership a vote short on cloture.

House Republicans continued to operate in much the same fashion as they had in 2003. The bill that reached the floor again provided for drilling in ANWR, for liability protection for MTBE manufacturers, for extensive tax benefits for fossil fuels, few incentives for renewable sources, and modest provisions regarding ethanol. The rule for considering the bill on the House floor did make a large number of amendments in order but with very limited time allowed for debate on each.[13] The few amendments that were adopted were relatively minor in terms of substantive impact. Consideration of this major bill occupied the House floor for a total of less than fourteen hours over two days.

By comparison, the Senate efforts actively involved Democrats in the formulation of the bill. Energy and Natural Resources Committee chair Pete Domenici (R-NM), strongly committed to enacting legislation, worked closely with his same-state colleague and ranking minority member on the committee, Jeff Bingaman. In the end, that committee's part of the legislative package was reported out following markup on a 21–1 vote. The Senate Finance Committee took a similar approach with the tax aspects of the legislation. The bill that reached the Senate floor had no provision for drilling in ANWR[14] and no liability protection for MTBE producers. It did, however, contain more generous ethanol and renewable-energy provisions and less-favorable tax treatment of fossil fuels than did the House bill. On the floor, Democrats unsuccessfully offered amendments increasing CAFE (corporate average fuel economy) standards and on global warming (a sense of the Senate amendment acknowledging the link between emissions and climate change was agreed to), consistent with what might be the median position for that party. Unlike in the House, the most tightly contested votes were on issues of more localized concern, with Florida's senators trying to remove a provision in the bill allowing for the Interior Department to do an inventory of offshore energy reserves in the eastern Gulf of Mexico and Louisiana's senators succeeding in improving their state's royalty payments (Hunter and Evans 2005). Cloture was invoked on a 92–4 vote, and the bill passed 85–12.

It took conferees less than a month following the Senate passage of HR 6 to reach an agreement, despite major substantive differences between the House and Senate versions of the legislation.[15] Unlike in 2003, Democrats were included in conference negotiations in exchange for their agreeing to cooperate during the conference deliberations. House Energy and Commerce Committee chair Joe Barton (R-TX), a strong supporter of the median party positions in the House bill, especially the MTBE liability provision, expressed ambivalence about this more inclusive strategy: "It's hard to sit there and negotiate when you know you have the votes. . . . But if you do that, at the end when it comes to the floor, everybody has a stake in it" (Adams 2005). In the end, however, House conferees acceded or moved closer to the Senate bill on most of the areas of disagreement, ensuring that cloture would not pose a problem in approval of the conference report, as it had in 2003.

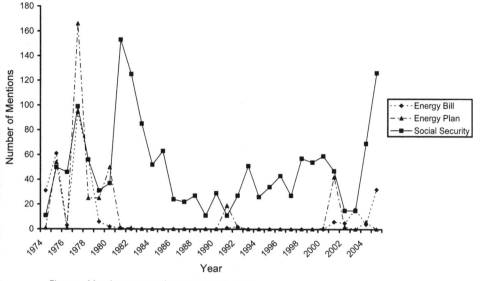

Fig. 11.5: Mentions on evening news, 1974–2005

The conference report included nothing on ANWR or on MTBE liability (beyond keeping lawsuits in federal court). The ethanol requirement of 7.5 billion gallons by 2012 was far closer to the 8 billion gallons in the Senate bill than the 5 billion in the House bill. And provisions on tax incentives for fossil fuels and for renewable energy sources were also closer to the figures in the Senate bill. Unlike in 2003, the conference report did not require a cloture vote in the Senate and was adopted 74–26, with the support of all but six Republicans and a majority of Democrats.

Why were House Republicans and the Bush administration willing to move even farther from median party positions on energy legislation in 2005 than they had been a year earlier? In the aftermath of Bush's reelection, as well as seat gains in both chambers, one might have expected that they would have moved back closer to median party positions. But, as mentioned above, despite the Senate seat gains, the Republican leadership was no closer to cloture, nor did it possess the appropriate resources to hold outlier Republican senators closer to the median party positions. Accordingly, they were again faced with the option of moving closer to chamber median positions or the defeat of energy legislation for the third Congress in a row. The costs of producing no legislation, however, had changed.

An indicator of this change is the level of media attention that energy legislation was receiving. Figure 11.5 displays data from the Vanderbilt News Data Archive on the number of times the terms "energy bill" and "energy plan" were mentioned during the nightly national newscasts from 1974 to 2005. In 2005, the frequency of mentions of "energy bill" started to approach that of the mid- to late 1970s. Since that time, the only year when there were more than a couple of mentions had been 2003, and even then it was only half the number for 2005. Although not nearly as frequent as the mention of Social Security on the evening news, the jump in the mentions of energy suggests a growing concern on the part of both the media and the public, as energy prices rose in an increasing volatile environment. In that context, the cost of holding closer to a median party position on energy legislation and producing no legislation was no longer acceptable.

Assumptions about Median Party Positions

Throughout this chapter, and most notably in the analysis of the struggle to pass an energy bill in the 2001–5 period, we have made some assumptions about the substantive content of energy legislation relative to the median position of House and Senate Republicans. Some may argue that these assumptions are incorrect and that the energy bill enacted in 2005 really approximated the median party position of congressional Republicans in both houses and in the Bush administration. To maintain this perspective, however, requires that one contend that the announced administration position and the House-passed bill were simply bargaining positions that were more extreme than the median party position. We find little that would support that interpretation, for the following reasons.

First, if the bill that passed in 2005 really was at the median party position and not close to a median chamber position, then why wouldn't House Republicans have agreed to compromise in 2003 on MTBE? In other respects, the 2003 bill was more favorable to their position than the 2005 bill. In 2005 the subsidies for alternative energy sources and the requirements for ethanol use were higher, and the support for fossil fuels was lower. And Republicans relented on the MTBE liability-waiver provision.

Second, in 2005 Democratic House members were included in the formulation of the Senate bill and in the conference-committee negotiations. Committee chair Pete Domenici worked closely with the ranking minority member, Jeff Bingaman, to produce a bipartisan bill in the Senate. And Representative Joe Barton (R-TX) consented, with some reluctance, to Democrats' playing a full role in the conference deliberations. This was a clear departure from the more partisan strategy Republicans employed in 2001 and 2003. In 2001, the respective Senate and House Republican energy-committee leaders, Frank Murkowski (R-AK) and Billy Tauzin (R-LA), had kept Democrats from participating in markup and in the conference and had, according to *CQ Weekly*, "tried to force the legislation through by brute strength" (Adams 2005).

Third, in 2005 the Senate bill passed with overwhelming support from both parties at the committee level, on final passage, and on adoption of the conference-committee report. That did not occur in 2003. Yet it is clear that Senate Republicans were able to defeat Democratic floor amendments that would have moved the bill closer to a median Democratic party position. In the House, where the bill contained an ANWR exploration provision, liability protection for MTBE producers, higher fossil-fuel support, lower support for alternative energy, and low ethanol requirements, 80 percent of Democrats voted against it and 90 percent of Republicans supported it. As noted above, on most of the crucial issues, the conference report moved the legislation far closer to the Senate bill provisions. And even House Democratic support for the conference report, while not a majority, was nearly twice what it had been on final passage for the original bill.

Thus, we feel confident in claiming that the energy bill that was enacted in 2005 was substantively close to what one would describe as a median chamber position. At the very least, it was far closer to that position than were the bills that failed in the two previous Congresses, or any of the three bills that passed the House—all of which were closer to, or at, median party positions.

The Senate as a Limiting Force on Conditional Party Government

One lesson from this research is that there is a difference between the process of conditional party government and the production of policy outputs consistent with it. In the 2001–5 period, all the necessary ingredients for conditional party government were seemingly present on energy legislation. The parties continued to be polarized on their policy preferences. Their members were largely cohesive on the issue. The party leaders, especially in the House, had the resources with which to hold their members to median party positions. And at the start of the 109th Congress, even the Republican leadership in the Senate had gained increasing power in committee assignments and in influencing the selection of term-limited committee chairs.[16] Moreover, following the 2004 elections, Republicans again reached their high-water mark in both chambers in terms of seats held (232 in the House and 55 in the Senate) during their period of majority control that began in 1995. They also had the resources of a Republican White

House. Yet in 2005, after four years of failure to produce an energy bill, the Republican leadership moved away from a conditional party government position and enacted legislation that was closer to median chamber positions on the issue.

The need for a sixty-vote majority to impose cloture in the Senate was at the center of this decision. The House was continually able to produce an energy bill at something that approximated the median party position, and except for the brief period when Democrats held majority control of the Senate, that position, or something close to it, enjoyed the support of a Senate majority. But under conditional party government, as Republicans discovered, median party positions on major legislation will frequently provoke a cohesive minority-party filibuster. Without sixty votes, the choice is then one of moving away from the median party position toward the median chamber position or continuing with the policy status quo. And even some movement toward the median chamber position, such as the concessions House Republicans made to their Senate colleagues in the 2003 conference, may still prove insufficient.

Of course, the majority party can and does try to win sufficient seats in the next election to produce the needed sixty votes in the Senate. But the cloture rule still challenges even seemingly sizable party majorities in their efforts to achieve conditional party government outcomes. After all, as a party expands the size of its chamber majority, it inevitably starts winning seats in states that are less secure for its party's candidates. Those additional senators either (1) are likely to hold policy positions that are more moderate than the median party positions, or (2) will feel constrained to moderate for reelection purposes. Thus, the added majority-party senators may undermine the party cohesion that is essential to conditional party government and may be less willing to allow party leaders the resources with which to hold the membership to median party positions. To give leaders such resources means that these senators will be forced to cast votes that will endanger them in their bids for reelection.

Thus, the cloture rule in the Senate presented the Republicans with a series of catch-22s. They could pass energy legislation with a simple majority as long as they produced a bill close to the median chamber position. Under conditional party government, however, Republicans did not want that bill. They wanted a bill that was at the median party position. But to pass a bill at the median party position required sixty votes for cloture. The only way to produce sixty votes was to move toward the median chamber position. The choice then was between a bill they did not want and one that they could not have.

Having won control of the Senate in the 2006 elections, the Democrats face an even more difficult task of turning conditional party government as process into legislative outcomes. The apportionment basis of the Senate now favors the Republicans, because there are roughly ten more so-called red states than blue states. For Democrats to produce sixty votes for cloture, accordingly, means relying on an even larger number of senators from states where the partisan balance is more unfavorable than it was for Republicans when they were in a similar position. Moreover, it is highly unlikely that Democrats could win this number of Senate seats in the polarized but evenly divided setting of contemporary American politics.

More Than Cloture

The cloture rule is surely the major constraint on conditional party government. But it is not the constraint of a cloture pivot alone that is undermining conditional party government in the Senate. Although there is substantial evidence that, like the House, the Senate has a historically high level of party polarization and party cohesiveness on a fairly broad range of issues and has given its party leaders greater power and resources to hold senators to median party positions, Senate party leaders lack many of the tools that their House counterparts possess. Following the lead of Republican House reformers, for example, Senate Republicans moved to a three-Congress limit for committee chairs in 1995 and to a procedure that no longer guaranteed adherence to seniority in selecting them. In the House, this has meant active involvement by the party leadership in selecting committee chairs, frequent selection of chairs in violation of seniority, getting commitments of cooperation from those bidding for chair positions, and passing over members not thought to be sufficiently committed to median party positions.

In the Senate, however, no violations of seniority have occurred in the selection of committee chairs, although in two instances there were threats to either remove or deny a chairmanship because the senator differed with the party on a key substantive issue.[17] The party leadership in the Senate has less influence over the selection of committee chairs and less ability to reward or sanction members in that process compared to their House counterparts. Similarly, House leaders have more influence over committee assignments. Only at the start of the 109th Congress did the Senate Republican Conference stipulate that in the future, the majority leader would have the authority to fill half the party's vacancies on A-level committees on a basis other than seniority. The increasing leeway of majority leaders in the Senate to formulate complex unanimous consent agreements and to decide whether to honor holds pales in comparison to the scheduling prerogatives that recent House Speakers enjoyed while working with a co-operative Republican Rules Committee majority. So while it is clear that in both chambers majority-party members have given their leadership greater powers with which to hold members to median party positions, senators have not been willing to go as far as House members. Senate individualism is still substantially preserved (Sinclair 1989, 2005).[18]

From an electoral perspective, senators have less incentive to yield as much power to their party leaders as House members do. Representing more diverse and more competitive constituencies than House members, senators are more reluctant to give leaders the discretion to hold them to median party positions. They may fear that having to adhere to such positions will increase their electoral vulnerability.

More speculatively, even if Senate leaders were given powers commensurate with those of House leaders, it is doubtful that those powers would be as effective in holding senators to median party positions as they are with House members. Senators get their political influence largely from being senators, rather than from the positions they hold in the Senate. Committee-chair and subcommittee-chair positions and assignments on prestigious committees may enhance a senator's clout somewhat, but there are other avenues to influence. In the House, however, chair positions, committee assignments, and party leadership positions largely define one's status and influence in the institution. Moreover, the prerogatives of individual senators are simply greater in an institution with a more permeable and less important committee structure, a less strict set of rules and procedures, and reliance on unanimous consent for conducting routine business than they are for House members.

With this formidable range of constraints on conditional party government policy outcomes firmly in place in the Senate, we suggest that the analysis of energy policy presented here is likely generalizable to other policy domains. In the 104th Congress, many of the items in the Republican Contract with America and other legislative goals that passed the House quickly received a far less favorable reception in the Senate, including a number of cases where filibusters or threats to use them sidetracked the legislation. With rare exceptions, it has been the Senate that has proven to be the stumbling block, rather than the House (Sinclair 2005, 17). It is true that congressional Republicans, in concert with President Bush, have more recently had great success implementing non-incremental change in tax policy and, since 2001, in the execution of foreign affairs; but beyond cutting taxes (something that constituencies are unlikely to argue vociferously against) and foreign policy (an area in which Congress traditionally defers to the president), the Bush years have not been marked by a rush of non-incremental policy changes, despite remarkably high levels of party discipline. Indeed, some of the major innovations may have a more liberal than conservative lean to them, including big-government programs such as the No Child Left Behind Act and a prescription-drug benefit for senior citizens.

Indeed, Bush and the Republican leadership in Congress enjoyed no success at all on Social Security privatization, the president's signature second-term domestic-policy initiative. The fact that the plan never had much support among voters was much more important to congressional leaders than the cohesive majorities that they regularly mustered in both the House and the Senate. It is worth noting as well that outcomes were similar in 1993–94, when Democrats held the presidency and both houses of Congress. Clinton got what he wanted on budget cuts and tax increases because these are immune to the filibuster in the Senate. Leaders in both houses were able to deliver, at great electoral cost, bare majorities. But they were either unwilling or unable to deliver on Clinton's signature first-term issue, health-care reform. The compromise result, devised in the Senate by Edward Kennedy (D-MA) and Nancy Kassenbaum (R-KS), was a severely watered down initiative.

Our findings, especially those involving the cloture rule, seem at first glance to be contrary to those of Sean Gailmard and Jeffery A. Jenkins in their chapter in this volume comparing minority-party power in the Senate and the House. One should note, however, that their analysis aggregates data from Congresses over nearly 125 years, a period during which party strength varied considerably and which also includes nearly a century when use of the filibuster was rare. It may well be that over that span, the filibuster does not appear to be a vehicle of negative agenda control. By contrast, we argue that the use and effectiveness of the filibuster vary with party strength. In periods of conditional party government, when the majority party tries to pass legislation at median party positions, a cohesive minority party is likely to employ or threaten to employ a filibuster and force the majority to choose between no bill or one that approximates the median chamber position.

Conclusions

We have demonstrated that in trying to build a winning coalition to enact energy legislation in recent years, Republicans in Congress have clearly pursued a more party-based strategy more consistent with the expectation of conditional party government than was evident in the coalition building of the 1970s. In the 1970s, with party, ideology, and constituency factors more crosscutting, winning coalitions on energy policy were built outward from the chamber medians in the House and the Senate. Often, this led to opposition from the extremes. Because of the diversity of the membership in each party, House members and senators were reluctant to yield power to their respective party leaders to hold members to party positions.

With the increase in interparty polarization and intraparty cohesiveness since the 1980s and the granting of greater powers to the party leadership, pursuit of more party-based coalition building occurred on energy policy in the 2001–5 period. That has meant building coalitions using the majority-party median position as the starting point. But this strategy was far more effective in the House than in the Senate. With the cloture rule, with Senate party leaders having fewer resources, and with senators holding more independent bases of influence, building winning coalitions in the Senate has necessitated moving away from the party median toward the median chamber position. For much of the period, House Republicans and the Bush administration resisted this movement, with the result that legislation was defeated in the Senate. In 2005, however, with public attention to energy issues renewed, the administration and House Republicans were forced to settle for a bill that appeared closer to the median chamber position than to the median Republican party position.

Our findings suggest that while the nature of building winning coalitions in Congress has changed since an era when parties were far weaker than they are recently, the policy results are comparable. Although many of the same changes have occurred to parties in both institutions, the Senate's rules and institutional constraints and the strategic preferences of its members mean that the Senate may not be able to produce outcomes consistent with conditional party government expectations. That has put the Bush administration and House Republicans in the position of either accepting policy outcomes closer to median chamber positions or seeing legislation fail to be enacted.

One of the ironies of what has occurred as parties in Congress have approached the model that many prominent political scientists have advocated for more than a century is that this shift has not resulted in the types of policy outcomes that those critics of weak American parties anticipated. Parties may win office and be cohesive but still be frequently unable to enact the policies on which they campaigned.

Notes

1. In the House during the 95th Congress, the DW-NOMINATE scores for Democratic members ranged from −.763 to .9, with a mean of −.288 and a standard deviation of .212. For House Republicans, the range was from −.268 to .76, with a mean of .264 and a standard deviation of .171.

2. In this sense, roll calls on energy legislation in the 1970s are not typical. Many roll calls of the period fit a linear relationship, with the likelihood of voting for the legislation being directly related to member ideology. We do not believe, however, that this affects the implications of our findings as they relate to the existence of—or, in the 1970s, the absence of—conditional party government. As we shall see, the nonlinearity of the energy votes in the 1970s precludes a conditional party government interpretation.

3. Although one might argue in favor of analyzing other energy roll calls, these were the two energy votes that Congressional Quarterly selected for inclusion in its Key Votes in 1978.

4. We estimated models using the DW-NOMINATE scores' second dimension as well, just to make certain that the constituency effects that we find are robust to a specification including this measure of constituency on racial matters. The results were consistent. Since the second dimension taps racial policy and not energy policy, we use the first-dimension scores alone.

5. It is not our claim that O'Neill did not make efforts to get wavering House Democrats to support the rule or that he was unsuccessful in doing so. In fact, his efforts were crucial in the late stages of the voting on the Bolling motion. Our point is that the Democratic leadership could not prevent so large a number of its members from voting against the rule.

6. The curves in figure 11.2 are plotted for the DW-NOMINATE ranges for which there are members in the respective parties. But one should realize that only around 8 percent of Democratic House members have positive scores, and slightly less than 8 percent of Republicans have negative scores.

7. In both the 107th and 108th Congresses, the energy bill received the same bill number, HR 6, in the House.

8. The energy-production measure is total state energy production in 2000 in terms of quadrillion BTUs per capita as obtained from Department of Energy figures. We use a different energy-production measure than we used for our analysis of the 1970s votes because that legislation was more heavily focused on natural gas.

9. In part, the low effect of state energy production among Democrats is due to the fact that the highest energy production for a state represented by a Democratic senator was 2.088 quadrillion BTUs per capita, whereas among Republican senators, the highest was 14.28 quadrillion BTUs per capita.

10. The data on corn production are for the year 2002 and come from the U.S. Department of Agriculture, National Agricultural Statistics Survey.

11. For the purposes of the statistical analysis, Majority Leader Bill Frist (R-TN) was coded as voting for cloture, because the reason he changed his vote was to preserve his ability to move for reconsideration.

12. In the end, Martinez and all but three members of the Florida congressional delegation voted against the conference report.

13. The rule limited all but three amendments to ten minutes of debate. It allowed twenty minutes on one dealing with electricity- and gas-marketing fraud, thirty minutes on ANWR, and thirty minutes on a Democratic alternative to the bill.

14. Because an ANWR provision had been included in the budget resolution and it was anticipated that it would be part of the reconciliation package, there was less pressure to include it within the energy bill than previously. The strategic advantage of including ANWR in budget legislation was that such legislation is immune from filibusters. In 2003, an effort to include ANWR in the budget resolution was defeated in the Senate, but the provision narrowly survived in 2005. In the end, however, ANWR drilling did not survive negotiations over the reconciliation package, and the attempts by Senator Ted Stevens (R-AK) to include it as a rider on a must-pass appropriations bill also failed.

15. House Republicans continued to give the bill the same number when it was introduced at the start of each Congress.

16. The Senate Republican Conference gave the majority leader the power to make half the appointments to A-level committees on a basis other than seniority. In addition, with the first wave of Republican Senate committee chairs having to step down because of term limits, conservative Senate Republicans, with the tacit approval of the leadership, threatened the assumption of the Judiciary Committee chair by Arlen Specter (R-PA).

17. In the 104th Congress, concern focused on the vote by Mark Hatfield (R-OR) against a balanced-budget constitutional amendment, and in the 109th on Arlen Specter's pro-choice position as it might affect judicial nominations.

18. Sinclair (2005, 1) discusses the growing tension in the Senate between "fairly cohesive party contingents that aggressively exploit Senate rules to pursue partisan advantage" and "the persistence of the Senate individualism."

12

Distributive and Partisan Politics in the U.S. Senate: An Exploration of Earmarks

MICHAEL H. CRESPIN AND CHARLES J. FINOCCHIARO

In recent years, members of Congress have engaged in a rapidly accelerating drive to garner particularistic benefits for their constituents, much to the dismay of many observers and budget hawks. While critics, most of whom watch from the outside (Senator John McCain being a notable exception), decry the annual practice of inserting into appropriations legislation line items that fund projects back home, members realize the value of their efforts in this regard. As Mayhew (1974) observed, such activities reap electoral rewards in the form of credit-claiming opportunities. Thus, it is no surprise that the practice continues largely uninhibited despite both popular and elite-level criticisms.

With the ubiquity of pork-barrel spending being a hallmark of the modern Congress, scholars have sought to explain the distributional mechanisms that allocate funds across states and districts. Most of these accounts focus on certain types of programs or categories of earmarks (funds designated for a specific purpose). Our aim in this chapter is to consider more fully the potential for party effects in the distribution of pork in the upper chamber of the U.S. Congress across a wide spectrum of policy areas.

At first glance, the Senate, with its more collegial leadership style and distribution of power, is perhaps not a strong candidate for exploring questions related to majority-party advantage. However, it occupies a position in the sequence of the appropriations process that offers unique opportunities to add to or undo actions taken in the lower chamber (Fenno 1966), and the must-pass nature of appropriations legislation likely makes it an appealing vehicle for partisan advantage. To the degree that senators find particularistic policies an attractive means of gaining electoral advantage for themselves and their party, there is reason to expect the majority party to profit from pork.

If majority status matters, the effect of changes in party control is likely to manifest itself in pork-barrel politics. Indeed, as the Democrats returned to majority status following the Jeffords switch in 2001, parties stood to gain or lose significant resources even in the area of pork-barrel spending based on their majority or minority status. News coverage of the appropriations process following James Jeffords's switch in party caucus indicated that Senate Democrats, upon assuming the reins of the Appropriations Committee, initiated a dramatic shift in spending that saw their constituents benefit at a very high rate, while their Republican counterparts in many cases witnessed a steep decline in project funding.[1]

While the Jeffords switch illustrates the importance of majority control, this chapter systematically examines the extent to which the majority party in the Senate is advantaged in the accrual of pork. If the party in control of the Senate has an advantage, we would expect it to garner a disproportionate share of the pork dollars to be distributed.

We begin with a review of the literature on distributive and partisan theories before turning to more recent efforts at explaining congressional earmarks. We then describe the data and methods employed in our analysis, and present descriptive and then multiple regression results accounting for the role of parties, institutional status, and other factors in the allocation of pork. The final section concludes and offers some extensions for future research.

Distributive and Partisan Theories of Politics

Where does the "politics of pork" fit when we think about the major theories of congressional organization? One school of thought, distributive theories of lawmaking, would argue that pork-barrel projects should be evenly distributed among representatives in order to facilitate the lawmaking process. Conversely, theories that argue that party plays a consequential role in deciding legislative outcomes might suggest that the majority party should receive the greatest share of pork dollars. Below, we will argue that when it comes to the Senate and its unique set of rules, there should be enough pork for everyone to take a share, but members in the majority party, as well as those holding key leadership positions, should bring home more bacon than members of the minority party. Although the Senate is generally considered more collegial than the House, the majority party maintains enough of an institutional advantage that it can win this spending game.

Distributive Politics

Distributive (or gains-from-exchange) theories were developed by Weingast (1979), Weingast and Marshall (1988), Shepsle and Weingast (1987), Fiorina (1977), Ferejohn (1986), and Mayhew (1974). In short, they posit that the internal operations of Congress are designed to promote the distribution of policy benefits to electorally important constituencies.

These theories suggest a state of the world where the committee system exists in order to facilitate logrolling across issue dimensions and helps to solve the collective-action problems inherent in a legislative body where members want to vote with their districts in order to get reelected (Mayhew 1974; Arnold 1990). If members are placed onto (or select) committees that best represent their constituents' interests and then report bills to the floor dealing with that specific jurisdiction, then other non–committee members will vote with that committee since it does not harm them (or their reelection chances) because of the multidimensionality of issues. For example, members from the Agriculture Committee will support the opening of military bases as long as it does not harm agricultural interests, and vice versa. Further, in an important addition to distributive theories, Weingast and Marshall (1988) argue that since committees have gatekeeping power over their specific policy area and members have control over their committee seats via the seniority rule, logrolling will be institutionally supported.[2]

Shepsle and Weingast (1981a) develop a formal model to explain the universalism inherent in distributional politics that results from members' uncertainty over who will be part of future winning coalitions. Their model tries to resolve the difference between the minimal-winning-coalition arguments made by Buchanan and Tullock (1962) and Riker (1962) and the empirical reality of universalism common in various issue areas such as rivers and harbors (Ferejohn 1974), tax loopholes (Manley 1970), private bills (Froman 1967), and categorical grants-in-aid (Mayhew 1974).

Shepsle and Weingast (1981a) predict universalism, and they argue that it still applies in a partisan world. If parties are strong and members are certain of remaining in the majority in the future, then universalism should be spread across all members of the majority party, not just a minimal winning coalition within the party. However, if members are uncertain about remaining in the majority party over the course of their careers, or parties cannot enforce discipline, they may prefer a more universalistic mode of distributing benefits.[3] This may be the case in the Senate, where party leaders do not have the powers present in the House. Although many policy areas are supported by small, intense coalitions (Stein and Bickers 1995), they need the support of a majority (or in the case of the Senate, a super-majority), so the universalism approach may still hold.

Partisan Politics

In contrast to the distributional theories of lawmaking, Cox and McCub-bins's cartel model (1993, 2005) and the conditional party government theory of Rohde (1991) and Aldrich and Rohde (1998, 2000b, 2001) posit a partisan theory of lawmaking in the U.S. House.[4] Cartel theory tells us that the key to legislative success in Congress lies in controlling the agenda. Parties act as procedural cartels by exercising negative agenda control to assure that no legislation reaches the floor that could possibly split the party or move the status quo in ways that are unfavorable to the party. To make certain that such legislation does not receive a floor vote, rank-and-file members are expected to support the party on procedural votes in exchange for the possibility of securing a more powerful position in the institution and increasing the probability of maintaining (or achieving) majority status.

Conditional party government argues that party strength is conditional on internal party homogeneity and external heterogeneity between the two parties. When both conditions hold, rank-and-file members cede power to the leadership so the party can "encourage" members to act in ways to fur-ther the party's goals. One way to stay in favor with the leadership is to vote with the party when needed on important legislation. If sending money to districts, or states, improves the chances of winning reelection (Mayhew 1974) and hence remaining in the majority, then parties will have reason to make sure the bulk of the goods go to their districts.

Balla et al. (2002) try to bring together the two broad classes of legislative organization theory and find that the *likelihood* of receiving a pork-barrel project is distributed evenly between the majority and minority parties but that the majority enjoys an advantage in the *dollar amount* of earmarks. This finding does help to reconcile the universal theories of distributive politics with the results of majority-party advantage put forth by others (Levitt and Snyder 1995; Carsey and Rundquist 1999; Lee and Oppenheimer 1999; Lee 2000). The results are consistent with the theory that the major-ity party can insulate itself from being blamed for a lack of fiscal restraint if both parties are guilty of spending money on local concerns. Yet the majority maintains an advantage by spending more on their constituents than the minority.

Interestingly, Balla et al. find that partisan advantage appeared to be associated only with the lower chamber, not the Senate. This finding of no party influence in the Senate, the authors argue, is consistent with the literature that describes a weak party system in the Senate (Ripley 1969; Sinclair 1989; Smith 1989). Since the authors caution that their test is limited to one type of pork in a single policy area—academic earmarks—we feel it is important to revisit the null finding in the Senate and look across a broader set of pork-barrel projects for majority advantage.

Majority Advantage in the Senate Appropriations Process

We build upon the work of Balla et al. (2002) to develop our theory and hypotheses with regard to the distribution of pork in the Senate, and, like them, we take as our starting point two competing sets of theories. The first set, which will stand as our null hypothesis, suggests that legislators should receive pork in a universalistic fashion, with something for everyone. Members of Congress will logroll across the various subsets of policies in order to assure funding for their specific set of preferred projects. In contrast, other theories assume a role for political parties in the distributive-politics game. If the reelection rates for elected officials who bring home more goods for their district are higher, then the majority party has an incentive to make sure its members obtain, on average, more than the minority party. In short, we use the distribution of pork-barrel spending as a test of majority-party strength. If parties are "strong," then more pork dollars should be allocated to members of the majority party.

How does the majority maintain its advantage in the Senate? The search for party effects is more complicated in the upper chamber (Campbell, Cox, and McCubbins 2002). Unlike in the House, where the majority can use the Rules Committee to dictate outcomes (Cox and McCubbins 2005), the Senate majority party must turn to other tools and procedures to achieve the desired results, such as the motion to table (see chapter 8 in this volume, by Chris Den Hartog and Nathan W. Monroe). At each stage of the appropriations process, we argue, the majority party is able to keep more of the pork dollars for its own members because of various procedural maneuvers.

First and foremost, the appropriations bills are must-pass legislation, since failure to pass the bills would cause a government shutdown.[5] Efforts by the minority to filibuster the appropriations bills would therefore not be desirable, since the minority would likely be portrayed by the majority as obstructionist.[6] In fact, the bills usually pass by large margins in both chambers.

At the initial subcommittee and committee markup stages, where pork projects could be added, the majority party, by definition, has a majority of the votes, so it should be able to shape the legislation largely as it sees fit. Majority members have the power of the gavel at both levels, so they have an advantage when it comes to calling witnesses and scheduling times for markup. Although this may appear minor, the ability to schedule votes or markups at the discretion of the chair makes it difficult to catch the majority off guard in the hope of winning an occasional vote.

If minority committee members do prove difficult, they could easily be bought off with their own pork projects.[7] Once members of the subcommittees and full committees are content with legislation, then working the bill through the floor should be easier, since a winning coalition should exist between the majority party and the minority-party members who serve on the Appropriations Committee. If this is indeed the case, we should expect to find that members who serve on the Appropriations Committee from either party should receive more pork compared to their colleagues. However, members from the majority party on the committee should obtain more than minority-party members.

During the next stage of the process, legislating on the floor, the majority continues to hold an advantage. Although any member can offer amendments on the floor, the majority has the use of the motion to table in order to kill any amendments offered by the minority. This motion is not open to debate, so it becomes useful for the majority in stifling minority attempts to add additional earmarks. As Crespin and Monroe (2005) have demonstrated, the majority party is nearly always successful in the use of the motion to table. If necessary, the majority leader can also use the right of first recognition to fill the amendment tree (see Schiller 2000b). Given the majority party's advantage at each stage of the process, we expect it to receive a disproportionate share of pork dollars.

Data and Method

To examine the influence of partisan, institutional, and electoral factors on the allocation of distributive outlays in the Senate, we employ a compilation of pork projects identified by the nonprofit, nonpartisan organization Citizens Against Government Waste (CAGW). Since 1991, CAGW has released an annual report of the pork-barrel projects contained in the (typically) thirteen appropriations bills that fund the various activities of the federal government. According to CAGW's definition, "a 'pork' project is a line-item in an appropriations bill that designates tax dollars for a specific purpose

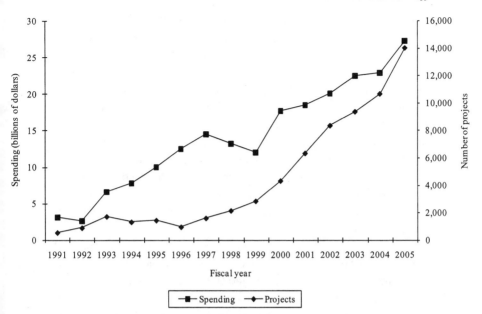

Fig. 12.1: Spending on pork projects and number of projects, 1991–2005

in circumvention of established budgetary procedures." In order to be included in the annual report, a project must meet at least two of the following criteria: it must be requested by only one chamber of Congress, not specifically authorized, not competitively awarded, not requested by the president, far in excess of the president's budget request or the previous year's funding, not the subject of congressional hearings, or serving only a local or special interest.[8] In practice, every project identified by CAGW meets the last criterion, so that what distinguishes the various projects is the way in which they are added outside of the conventional appropriations process.[9] CAGW is careful to note that theirs is not a comprehensive list of earmarks, as earmarks, which designate funds for a specific beneficiary or locality, may or may not be included via established budgetary procedures. Only earmarks that are inserted outside the established rules are categorized as pork.

Numerous observers have described the significant growth over recent years in the number and scope of pork projects. This trend is clearly borne out in the data compiled by CAGW. Figure 12.1 depicts the annual trend in the number of projects and the total dollar value for fiscal years 1991 through 2005, both of which exhibit high rates of growth during the period.

Each project identified is coded according to its status in the legislative process—more specifically, whether it was inserted into the legislation at the request of only the House or the Senate, whether there was a budget request for the project by the administration, whether the project was inserted at the conference-committee stage, or some combination of these. A unique aspect of this data and our analysis, then, is our ability to parse out chamber-specific effects. While previous studies have examined the overall distribution of pork, we are able to investigate the effects of Senate-specific factors in the allocation of pork to states within the Senate appropriations process exclusive of what occurs in the House or in conference. For each fiscal year, we created a summary measure of pork at the state level: the total dollar value of all pork projects inserted via Senate action. This continuous measure will serve as our dependent variable in the ordinary least squares (OLS) regression analysis to follow, although we will present some other data descriptively as well.

Additionally, we estimate models of total pork added in the Senate via the various appropriations bills. In describing the typically appellate role played by Senate appropriators, Fenno (1966) notes the more accommodating nature of the process in the upper chamber, and the attempt to help members with particular funding requests. Subcommittee chairs are also afforded substantial leeway. As Kiewiet and McCubbins (1991) argue, even in what scholars used to consider the bastion of the "guardianship" model—the House Appropriations Committee—there is evidence that committee and subcommittee party contingents represent their broader caucus. This is not to say that the politics of the Senate Appropriations Committee is a purely universalistic or partisan process, however. It may well be the case that evidence of partisan deck-stacking will be more pronounced in certain issue areas than others—perhaps along the lines of how much pork is available for distribution. As Marshall and Prins (1999) observed, conflict and partisanship vary across the appropriations subcommittees.

Descriptive Measure of Pork

For figures 12.2 to 12.5, we divide the states into five categories of ten states each and display measures of pork over our period of study, 1995–2005. The first two figures contain all pork-barrel projects, while the second pair show only pork added in the Senate. The darkest states are those that received the most pork (either total or per capita), with gradations down to the states that received the least amount.

Figure 12.2 presents the total amount of pork per state over the entire time period. As one might expect, large states such as California, Florida,

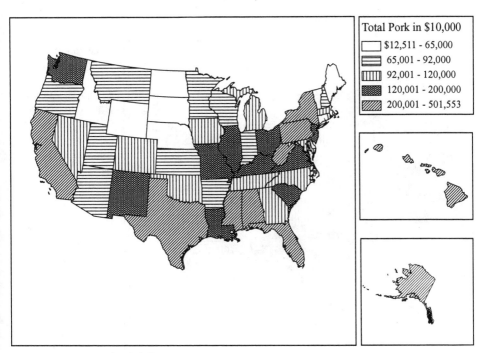

Fig. 12.2: Total pork dollars, 1995–2005

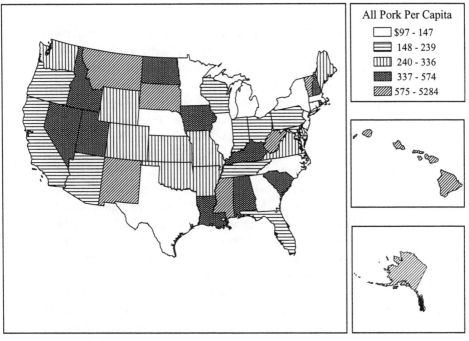

Fig. 12.3: Total pork per capita, 1995–2005

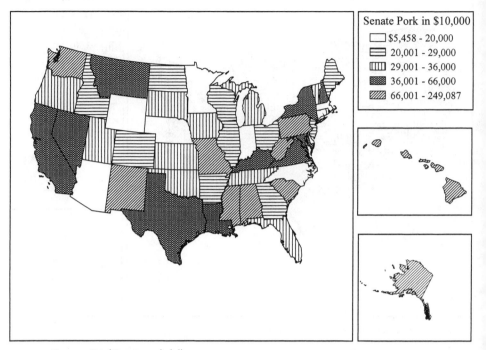

Fig. 12.4: Total Senate pork dollars, 1995–2005

Texas, New York, and Pennsylvania receive a substantial amount of pork-project money. In contrast, small states such as North and South Dakota, Vermont, Maine, and Wyoming fall on the other end of the scale. Some states may seem out of place in the rankings, though. Mississippi's sizable share of pork can potentially be attributed to Senate Majority Leader Trent Lott (R-MS), who likely collaborated with fellow Mississippian and senior Republican appropriator Thad Cochran. Also, Alabama, Alaska, and Hawaii received a great deal of pork. Much of Alaska's money was probably due to Republican senator Ted Stevens's chairmanship or ranking position on the full Senate Appropriations Committee, along with Alaska Republican Don Young's position as chair of the House Transportation Committee. Finally, Hawaii received a great deal of pork, especially defense dollars, probably because of the large number of military establishments in the state and because Daniel Inouye (D–HI) was the senior Democrat on the Senate Defense Appropriations Subcommittee.

A small-state advantage is better displayed in figure 12.3, which shows per capita pork for each state. Alaska, Mississippi, and Hawaii remain in the top group and are joined by Montana, South Dakota, West Virginia,

New Hampshire, New Mexico, and Vermont. Of these new states in the top category, all but New Mexico and West Virginia were in the bottom two groups of states for the previous category. Further, California, Florida, New York, Pennsylvania, and Texas have now shifted from the top category to the bottom two groups. Alaska is the winner in the per capita pork game. During our period of study, more than $5,200 per person found its way back to the northernmost state. Michigan is the biggest loser in the per capita pork battle, receiving less pork per person than any other state, a sparse $97. Since small states tend to be in the top categories and larger states in the lower groups, there is some evidence to suggest that small states are advantaged in the distribution of pork-barrel projects.[10]

When we look at total pork that is added in the Senate only (see figure 12.4), the results are similar, but not identical, to those in figure 12.2. Alabama, Alaska, Hawaii, Mississippi, Pennsylvania, and West Virginia are in the top group of pork-receiving states. West Virginia is the home state of the Senate Appropriations Committee's most senior Democrat, Robert Byrd. However, California, Florida, New York, and Texas are no longer in the top quintile and are replaced by Missouri, New Mexico, South Carolina, and

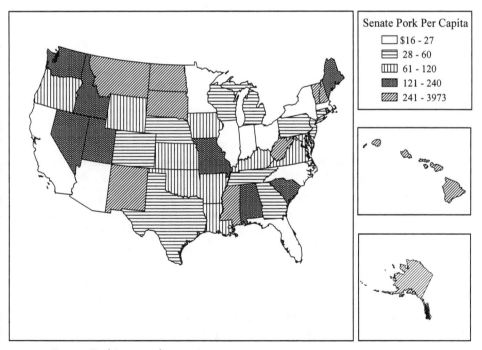

Senate Pork Per Capita
- $16 - 27
- 28 - 60
- 61 - 120
- 121 - 240
- 241 - 3973

Fig. 12.5: Total Senate pork per capita, 1995–2005

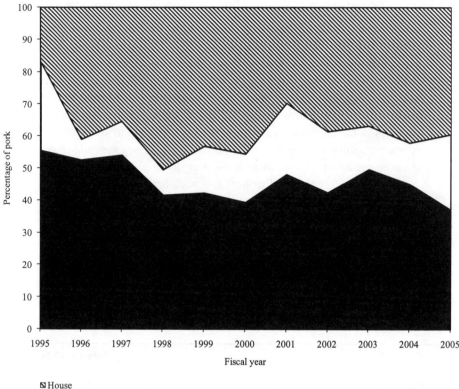

House
Conference
Senate
Fig. 12.6: Chamber differences in pork distribution

Washington. In the bottom quintile, we still see smaller states such as Wyoming and Rhode Island, but also medium-size states such as Massachusetts, Minnesota, and Indiana.

Finally, figure 12.5 displays the per capita pork added in the Senate. From this figure, the clear small-state advantage persists, as the single-district states of Alaska, Montana, North Dakota, South Dakota, and Vermont are all in the top category. Meanwhile, California, Florida, New York, and Texas, the four largest states, are all in the bottom two groups.

Next, figure 12.6 displays the distribution of pork dollars based on where they were added in the appropriations process—in the House, the Senate, or conference. Over the entire period, the bulk of the pork dollars came from projects added before the conference committee, with 46 and 38 percent of the dollars added in the Senate and House, respectively, and only

16 percent at the conference stage. In some years, more dollars were added in the House than in the Senate; but in only one year, 1995, did pork dollars added in conference outpace either of the two chambers. This suggests that if members are being bought off with projects, fewer are getting their pork at the end of the process.

Figure 12.7 shows the distribution of dollars by delegation type for only those projects that senators added for their states. The upper portion of the figure represents states that had two minority senators in the delegation, the middle portion represents states with a split delegation, and the lower portion represents states with two senators serving in the majority party.[11] For every fiscal year except 1997, states with a majority-party delegation received a plurality of pork dollars. On average, states with a majority delegation received 21 percentage points more pork than states with a minority-party

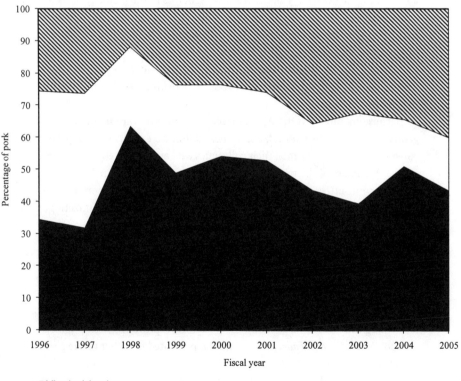

Minority delegation
Split delegation
Majority delegation
Fig. 12.7: Senate delegation differences in pork distribution

delegation. This difference was greatest in 1998, with 64 percent of pork going to states with two majority-party members and only 12 percent of pork dollars being spent in states represented by the minority party only. This figure suggests there may be a majority-party advantage in the Senate.

Systematic Results

Having presented a descriptive picture of some of the dynamics of pork distribution in the Senate, we turn next to a more systematic analysis. Based on the expectations described earlier, our models include measures capturing a number of factors predicted to influence the amount of pork obtained by a state. Of primary interest are the variables relating to majority-party status. To measure the degree to which the majority party receives a disproportionate share of pork, we examine the status of the Senate majority party within a state using two variables. States with two senators in the majority party are classified as *Majority-Party Delegation*, while those with only one majority-party member are labeled *Split Party Delegation*. The baseline category is made up of those states with two minority-party senators.[12] To the degree that there is a general benefit for the majority party, we should expect states with a majority-party delegation to produce a positive and significant effect in pork production.

Because members of the Appropriations Committee are in an advantageous position to steer pork back to their states, we expect them to garner considerably more pork than their colleagues who are not seated on the committee. Members of the majority party who chair the full committee or one of its subcommittees should fare better than ranking minority members and backbenchers, respectively, to the degree that partisan and organizational accounts explain pork allocation. In light of this, we measure the effect of holding certain positions with the following variables: *Appropriations Chair, Appropriations Subcommittee Chair, Appropriations Ranking Member, Appropriations Subcommittee Ranking Member, and Appropriations Member.*[13]

Similarly, party leaders are likely to accrue benefits from the pork-barrel process. In the cartel perspective, this benefit may be an inducement for internalizing the costs of organizing the party. To capture leadership effects, we code *Senate Party Leader* as 1 for states represented by either of the party leaders or party whips.

In addition to the partisan and institutional variables, we consider the potential role of the electoral cycle. One might expect a senator who is up for reelection to be more active in the quest for credit-claiming opportunities. The variable *Up for Reelection* is a dichotomous indicator for a state in which a Senate seat will be contested in the next election. This measure is interacted with a majority-status indicator in order to capture whether there is a majority-party senator up for reelection in the next cycle: *Up for Reelection (Majority)*. Additionally, because some have predicted that the majority party will be more likely to exclude the minority from the benefits of pork as the majority's margin increases and it feels more secure in its majority status, we control for *Majority Party Size*, which is simply the number of seats held by the party in power. The *State Population* measure accounts for the potential for pork distribution based on variation in state size. Finally, the models include year fixed effects to control for any year-to-year changes.

The first column of table 12.1 presents the results of our OLS analysis of total funding at the state level for pork projects inserted via the Senate appropriations process, across all subcommittees. The variables of primary interest relate to the majority-party status of the state delegation as well as the partisan nature of key positions of institutional power. We find support for the hypothesis that majority-party members fare better than their minority counterparts. In particular, states with two majority-party senators receive about $14.7 million more in pork than states with two minority-party senators (the baseline category). Split delegations are not statistically distinguishable from minority-party delegations.

Continuing with partisan factors relating to committee status, the home state of the Appropriations Committee chair garners approximately $157.5 million more in project funds than its non-committee majority-party counterparts, while states represented by the ranking member of the full committee bring home approximately $61.2 million more than states without a seat on the committee. The difference in favor of the chair relative to the ranking member is in this case statistically significant at $p = 0.054$. Finally, states with a senator who chaired one of the Appropriations subcommittees or sat as the minority ranking member accrued $49.8 million and $35.4 million more, respectively, than states that lacked membership on the committee. This amount for subcommittee chairs is on top of the extra money they receive for being a member of the majority party.

States with a senator in the party leadership also received an additional bonus of approximately $44.2 million. The variables measuring electoral effects (e.g., whether a senator from the state was up for reelection) do not obtain significance at conventional levels, nor does state population.[14] However, there is a systematic relationship between the size of the majority party and the amount of pork that gets distributed among the states. For instance, an increase of two seats in the majority party's margin carries with it an increase of about $30 million in pork per state.

TABLE 12.1. Fiscal distribution of pork projects among the states, by subcommittee, 1996–2005

Variable	All	Agriculture	Commerce
Majority-Party Delegation	1468.92*	15.93	136.18
	(704.88)	(26.74)	(104.10)
Split Party Delegation	−466.21	13.47	−.70
	(576.73)	(28.83)	(67.80)
Appropriations Chair	15747.37*	−74.84	759.15
	(3958.56)	(206.73)	(1137.16)
Appropriations Ranking	6117.34*	−596.22	−2742.42
Member	(3046.08)	(372.97)	(2018.53)
Appropriations Member	—	46.97*	179.11*
		(17.71)	(89.00)
Subcommittee Member	—	114.88*	52.98
		(44.78)	(140.43)
Subcommittee Chair	4978.99*	356.95*	2142.85*
	(843.00)	(96.85)	(497.17)
Subcommittee Ranking	3539.17*	513.74*	1967.24*
Member	(620.39)	(264.54)	(619.85)
Senate Party Leader	4420.74*	144.68*	70.62
	(2398.49)	(75.18)	(93.54)
Up for Reelection	−493.36	−13.23	−6.18
	(748.44)	(27.32)	(90.76)
Up for Reelection (Majority)	−1186.72	−19.69	−198.72*
	(805.70)	(27.01)	(102.87)
Majority Party Size	3003.22*	−23.46	351.36*
	(700.98)	(18.14)	(63.27)
State Population	5.18e-06	−4.44e-06*	6.93e-06
	(.000033)	(1.42e-06)	(5.47e-06)
Constant	−160652*	1341.03	−18913.64*
	(37294.8)	(977.02)	(3411.85)
N	500	500	500
R^2	0.327	0.321	0.393
F-statistic	12.42*	8.48*	8.71*

Until now, we have largely focused on all of the pork projects for a fiscal year together. However, as discussed previously, there may be differences across the various subcommittee bills in terms of the amount of pork dollars. This fact is made clear in figure 12.8, which displays the total amount of pork coming from thirteen of the fourteen Appropriations subcommittee bills that can be credited to a particular state from 1995 to 2005.[15] The Transportation Subcommittee distributes the greatest share of pork dollars, followed by Defense and

TABLE 12.1. *continued*

Defense	Energy	Interior	Labor/HHS
1009.87*	211.13	107.45*	−13.95
(583.36)	(204.16)	(45.57)	(44.61)
53.83	221.21	127.74	84.00*
(223.2512)	(235.49)	(77.71)	(46.15)
−2404.67	1042.01	1451.48*	311.91
(3192.18)	(1048.37)	(850.15)	(436.14)
−3709.96	−767.28	−292.37	−245.24
(3696.90)	(1830.30)	(1179.06)	(728.83)
81.10	44.81	83.69*	25.75
(178.51)	(92.42)	(49.94)	(24.42)
1572.73*	555.39*	216.38*	116.16*
(596.67)	(304.30)	(48.69)	(54.95)
8210.18*	292.39	610.12	64.99
(3509.49)	(417.13)	(439.91)	(127.78)
13422.79*	2273.08	−345.72	279.31
(4424.43)	(1703.64)	(496.58)	(328.82)
3656.12	−57.75	98.21	−46.36
(2265.03)	(218.81)	(60.47)	(32.453)
−174.65	124.90	−88.81	−8.67
(528.28)	(188.90)	(70.42)	(38.35)
−373.65	−89.53	−100.62	9.77
(591.62)	(170.82)	(71.12)	(41.90)
989.58*	252.11*	213.85*	223.44*
(489.17)	(65.22)	(46.03)	(41.56)
−.000015	.0000185*	9.14e-06	3.87e-06
(.000012)	(6.64e-06)	(5.86e-06)	(2.56e-06)
−53652.45*	−13872.4*	−11575.5*	−11891.2*
(26079.22)	(3476.30)	(2484.87)	(2209.20)
500	500	500	500
0.241	0.189	0.361	0.296
2.28*	4.73*	8.33*	6.38*

Military Construction. There is almost no pork in the Foreign Operations, Legislative Branch, and Homeland Security bills, and the other subcommittees fall somewhere in between. Although there tend to be many Agriculture pork projects, they are relatively inexpensive compared to defense-related projects.

Since there appear to be differences in the amount of pork coming from each of the bills, we turn next to an exploration of the majority-party advantage inherent in each of the subcommittees. Our working assumption

TABLE 12.1. *continued*

Variable	Legislative	Military Construction	Foreign Operations
Majority-Party Delegation	.86	217.17*	1.18
	(1.21)	(88.61)	(1.31)
Split Party Delegation	−.78	50.37	−.71
	(.78)	(78.63)	(1.07)
Appropriations Chair	21.28	1450.33*	−2.39
	(23.57)	(879.80)	(2.98)
Appropriations Ranking Member	45.82	405.07	−1.97
	(50.92)	(1409.37)	(4.94)
Appropriations Member	−2.21	53.08	.08
	(2.47)	(66.00)	(.24)
Subcommittee Member	−1.17	386.71*	1.02
	(1.29)	(119.37)	(1.47)
Subcommittee Chair	−.73	1294.63*	20.56
	(1.94)	(255.16)	(20.42)
Subcommittee Ranking Member	2.03	1396.10*	−.75
	(2.92)	(249.84)	(1.30)
Senate Party Leader	.12	755.09*	−4.18
	(.60)	(125.57)	(3.59)
Up for Reelection	−.57	−40.03	.71
	(.52)	(76.88)	(.86)
Up for Reelection (Majority)	6.19	−128.24	.33
	(6.10)	(99.13)	(1.94)
Majority Party Size	.25	270.53*	1.99
	(.39)	(93.03)	(1.87)
State Population	9.29e-08	−4.14e-06	−2.98e-08
	(7.39e-08)	(5.02e-06)	(2.95e-08)
Constant	−13.75	−14043.39*	−106.20
	(20.78)	(4977.37)	(98.74)
N	500	500	500
R^2	0.038	0.367	0.087
F-statistic	0.12	11.22*	0.11

is that the majority party will take more of the pork for itself when there is more pork to divide. In certain cases, the jurisdiction of the subcommittee does not lend itself particularly well to large earmarks. For instance, we consider agriculture to be a prototypical distributive issue area, yet much of the distribution that occurs in this area is through programmatic subsidies and does not appear to show up in sizable earmarks.

In order to estimate the majority party's advantage when it comes to the individual appropriations bills, we employed nearly the same regression

TABLE 12.1. *continued*

Transportation	Treasury	VA/HUD	Homeland Security
452.64*	18.46	180.48*	−3.03
(148.63)	(60.73)	(50.99)	(4.71)
177.87	13.38	84.37*	27.56
(115.70)	(34.48)	(39.77)	(18.05)
−1610.21	−313.13	−2824.30*	−128.42
(1604.98)	(372.23)	(444.10)	(86.89)
−8694.30*	−743.10	−6741.33*	−237.69
(2345.85)	(712.41)	(785.01)	(167.86)
518.03*	36.56	356.95*	10.58
(113.67)	(34.89)	(38.46)	(7.98)
223.33	72.80	139.11*	19.65
(161.89)	(127.08)	(51.67)	(19.70)
2085.53*	−43.06	1071.94*	−23.36
(1173.63)	(125.44)	(339.03)	(19.83)
1636.81*	−12.58	462.15*	—
(691.33)	(184.10)	(174.85)	
31.46	−43.04*	178.80*	−7.98
(143.64)	(23.33)	(80.56)	(8.98)
−70.78	−9.81	−39.23	14.79
(122.54)	(37.73)	(36.75)	(9.81)
−139.40	−32.14	−41.35	−8.84
(180.20)	(44.95)	(55.95)	(9.82)
355.56*	24.77	360.00*	—
(87.52)	(36.39)	(40.78)	
.00004*	1.49e-06	1.36e-06	3.47e-07
(.00001)	(1.93e-06)	(2.10e-06)	(3.37e-07)
−19411.12*	−1259.56	−19423.22*	−11.65
(4732.53)	(1901.69)	(2189.82)	(8.36)
500	400	500	100
0.533	0.044	0.587	0.141
13.78*	1.26	32.34*	0.27

* $p < 0.05$; one-tailed test. Year fixed effects are not reported. Estimates are OLS coefficients, with robust standard errors in parentheses. Dependent variable is dollars awarded (in tens of thousands of dollars).

specification presented in the first column of table 12.1. The model includes measures for committee and leadership status, reelection, majority size in the chamber, and population. We also control for state representation with *Appropriations Member* and *Subcommittee Member* for the particular panel being estimated in the model. As with the preceding results, the model is estimated with year fixed effects and robust standard errors. Because the main variable of interest has to do with the majority-party status of state Senate delegations, we chose to present the coefficient estimates, along with the 90 percent confidence intervals, in a figure as well as alongside the full results that appear in the table.

As figure 12.9 demonstrates, those committees distributing the largest share of pork projects also tend to be the ones most impacted by the partisanship of state delegations. The four bills with the largest amount of pork dollars—Transportation, Defense, Military Construction, and VA/HUD—all reveal a partisan tenor in the allocation of pork dollars among the states. We also found significant majority-party advantage for the Interior bill. In two instances, Labor/HHS and VA/HUD, we find that split delegations have an advantage over minority delegations, too. In no instance do states represented by a minority delegation do better than those with one or both majority-party senators.

These results also enable us to see that the Appropriations chair takes earmarks out of the Interior and Military Construction bills but actually

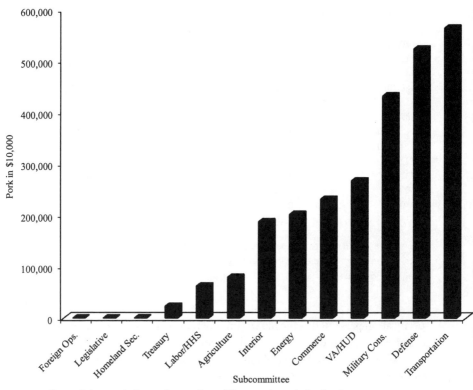

Fig. 12.8: Appropriations subcommittee differences in pork distribution

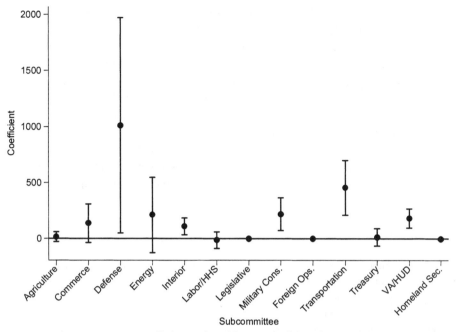

Fig. 12.9: Majority-party coefficients and confidence intervals by subcommittee

does much worse on the VA/HUD bill. This finding is probably a result of particular state concerns, rather than partisan politics. Although states represented by the Appropriations ranking member get more pork overall, it does not appear to be coming from any particular bill. We find, too, that in many cases, subcommittee chairs, along with ranking members, do particularly well, as we would expect. States with a senator who serves on the relevant subcommittee also do well in terms of earmarks.

Conclusion

In this chapter, we began with the notion that the majority party should have an advantage when it comes to the distribution of pork. Since bringing home bigger projects should help members get reelected, the majority party should receive a disproportionate share of pork dollars. Because the majority party possesses certain institutional advantages, it ought to be able to ensure that pork is distributed more or less how it sees fit.

Employing a data set that measures where pork was added in the legislative process, we were able to test these hypotheses and found results consistent with our theory. The majority party maintains an advantage when it comes to pork dollars. While previous research was not able to uncover evidence of partisan advantage in the Senate, by looking across a broader range of pork-barrel projects, we demonstrated that majority-party advantages are present not just where previous studies have found them (in the House), but also in the Senate. This result is important because it is not specific to any particular policy area. While we do not find the advantage on each of the appropriations bills, the majority party on average does better, and in no case does the minority party have an advantage.

In the future, we hope to explore in greater detail the process by which pork is added to appropriations bills. We also think it would be useful to better understand the link between earmarking and election results.

Notes

The authors gratefully acknowledge the able research assistance of Thom Hierl and helpful comments from the conference participants.

1. See, e.g., Alexander Bolton, "Senate Dems Wield Power, Feast on Pork," *The Hill,* September 5, 2001.
2. The seniority rule is no longer sacrosanct in the House, but it is still strong in the Senate. Krehbiel (1991) argued that the discharge petition could be used to overcome committee gatekeeping powers. However, it is rarely successful.
3. See Wawro and Schickler (2004) for a test of universalism in the Senate.
4. Of course, partisan theories are not without their critics; see, e.g., Krehbiel (1993b, 1998, 1999).
5. In theory, the Congress could pass a series of continuing resolutions to keep the government running, but this is not a feasible long-term solution. Of course, the separate bills may be combined into omnibus legislation if so desired.
6. In the budget battles between Congress and President Clinton, this was not the case.
7. In a search for votes at this stage, we found only a handful of recorded votes, indicating that most bills passed by voice vote with a high degree of consensus.
8. This and much additional information is available from CAGW's Web site, http://www.cagw.org.
9. Something generally ignored in the study of distributive politics and pork projects (including this one) is the process of obtaining the projects. In the House and Senate, members formally submit requests to the different subcommittees, assigning a rank to each project. House members are limited in the number of requests they can make, but not senators. While we might imagine the earmark-request process as ad hoc, it is actually rather formal. Since members rank projects, there is likely a strategic element to the requests. We hope to explore this dynamic in future work.
10. In an alternative analysis, we tested the effect of state size on per capita dollars. The results indicate that as the state's population increases, it receives fewer per capita

dollars in pork projects. This result is consistent with Lee (2000) and Lee and Oppenheimer (1999), who argue that small states should be advantaged in distributive politics because they are cheaper to buy off than larger states.

11. One dynamic we plan to explore in future analysis is the relationship between same-state senators in the appropriations process, an issue touched upon by Schiller (2000a).

12. Our data do not allow us to disentangle which senator obtained a pork project. Since both of the senators from a state can claim credit for delivering pork, this coding scheme seemed appropriate. For our purposes, we are interested in exploring differences across delegation types, and we do not have a theoretical expectation that the payoff is proportional for each additional majority-party senator from a particular state—an assumption that would be necessary if we had one variable coded to measure the three delegation types. In fact, it may be the case that states with split delegations do worse than those with two minority members, as the minority members may work together to earn pork for their state better than would a split delegation.

13. In the model that includes all subcommittees, we do not include a separate indicator for simple membership on the committee, because nearly every member either chairs or sits as ranking member of a subcommittee. In an alternative model, we included the additional control variable of committee membership. This variable was not significant and exhibited classic signs of multicollinearity. However, for the subcommittee models, we do include a general Appropriations Committee membership variable.

14. We performed joint significance tests on the two reelection variables and failed to find evidence of a joint effect.

15. There was no pork added on the Senate side for the DC appropriations bill during the period of our analysis. The Homeland Security Appropriations Subcommittee was added in 2003, and in order to maintain the same number of subcommittees, the nonsecurity components of the Transportation Subcommittee were rolled into the Treasury Subcommittee's jurisdiction to form the new Transportation, Treasury, and General Government Subcommittee (see Paul Kane, "Stevens Relents on Homeland," *Roll Call,* February 26, 2003). For ease of presentation, and because the transportation bill encompasses much more pork than that of Treasury, we classified this committee under Transportation for the 108th Congress (fiscal years 2004–5).

References

Abramowitz, Alan. 1988. "Explaining Senate Election Outcomes." *American Political Science Review* 82:385–403.

Abramowitz, Alan I., and Jeffrey A. Segal. 1992. *Senate Elections.* Ann Arbor: University of Michigan Press.

Abramson, Paul R., John H. Aldrich, and David W. Rohde. 2003. *Change and Continuity in the 2000 and 2002 Elections.* Washington, DC: CQ Press.

———. 2007. *Change and Continuity in the 2004 and 2006 Elections.* Washington, DC: CQ Press.

Adams, Rebecca. 2005. "Hard-Fought Energy Bill Clears." *CQ Weekly*, July 29, 2108.

Adler, E. Scott. 2002. *Why Congressional Reforms Fail: Reelection and the House Committee System.* Chicago: University of Chicago Press.

———. n.d. "Congressional District Data File, 87th–105th Congress." University of Colorado, Boulder.

Adler, E. Scott, and John S. Lapinski. 1997. "Demand-Side Theory and Congressional Committee Composition: A Constituency Characteristics Approach." *American Journal of Political Science* 41:895–918.

Ainsworth, Scott, and Marcus Flathman. 1995. "Unanimous Consent Agreements as Leadership Tools." *Legislative Studies Quarterly* 20:177–95.

Aldrich, John H. 1995a. "A Model of a Legislature with Two Parties and a Committee System." In *Positive Theories of Congressional Institutions*, ed. Kenneth A. Shepsle and Barry W. Weingast, 173–99. Ann Arbor: University of Michigan Press.

———. 1995b. *Why Parties? The Origin and Transformation of Political Parties in America.* Chicago: University of Chicago Press.

Aldrich, John, Michael Brady, Scott de Marchi, Ian McDonald, Brendan Nyhan, David Rohde, and Michael Tofias. 2006. "The Dynamics of Partisan Behavior: CPG in the House and in the Districts, 1982–2000." Paper prepared for the annual meeting of the Southern Political Science Association, Atlanta.

Aldrich, John H., and David W. Rohde. 1998. "The Transition to Republican Rule in the House: Implications for Theories of Congressional Politics." *Political Science Quarterly* 112:541–67.

———. 2000a. "The Consequences of Party Organization in the House: The Role of the Majority and Minority Parties in Conditional Party Government." In *Polarized Politics: Congress and the President in a Partisan Era*, ed. Jon R. Bond and Richard Fleisher, 31–72. Washington, DC: CQ Press.

———. 2000b. "The Republican Revolution and the House Appropriations Committee." *Journal of Politics* 62:1–33.

———. 2001. "The Logic of Conditional Party Government: Revisiting the Electoral Connection." In *Congress Reconsidered*, 7th ed., ed. Lawrence C. Dodd and Bruce I. Oppenheimer, 269–92. Washington, DC: CQ Press.

———. 2005. "Congressional Committees in a Partisan Era." In *Congress Reconsidered*, 8th ed., ed. Lawrence C. Dodd and Bruce I. Oppenheimer, 249–70. Washington, DC: CQ Press.

Allen, Mike, and Amy Goldstein. 2002. "Bush Has Plan to Speed Judicial Confirmations." *Washington Post*, October 31.

Anselmo, Joseph C. 2003. "Omnibus Energy Conference Finally Yields Results." *CQ Weekly*, November 15, 2840.

Ansolabehere, Stephen, James M. Snyder, and Charles Stewart III. 2001a. "Candidate Positioning in U.S. House Elections." *American Journal of Political Science* 45:136–59.

———. 2001b. "The Effects of Party and Preferences on Congressional Roll-Call Voting." *Legislative Studies Quarterly* 26:533–72.

Arnold, R. Douglas. 1990. *The Logic of Congressional Action*. New Haven, CT: Yale University Press.

Arrandale, Tom. 1975. "Divided Panel Reports Energy Tax Bill." *CQ Weekly Report*, May 17, 1016–20.

Babington, Charles. 2005a. "Frist Likely to Push for Ban on Filibusters." *Washington Post*, April 15.

———. 2005b. "Frist Urges End to Nominee Filibusters." *Washington Post*, April 25.

Bagehot, Walter. [1867] 1963. *The English Constitution*. Reprint. London: Collins.

Bailey, Michael, and David W. Brady. 1998. "Heterogeneity and Representation: The Senate and Free Trade." *American Journal of Political Science* 42:524–45.

Baker, Ross K. 1989. *The New Fat Cats: Members of Congress as Political Benefactors*. New York: Priority Press.

Balla, Steven J., Eric D. Lawrence, Forrest Maltzman, and Lee Sigelman. 2002. "Partisanship, Blame Avoidance, and the Distribution of Legislative Pork." *American Journal of Political Science* 46:515–25.

Bargen, Andrew. 2003. "Senators, Status Quos, and Agenda-Setting: A Spatial Story of Policy Making in the U.S. Senate, 1953–1996." Paper presented at the annual meeting of the American Political Science Association, Philadelphia.

Beer, Samuel H. 1982. *Britain against Itself: The Political Contradictions of Collectivism*. New York: W. W. Norton.

Behringer, Courtney L., C. Lawrence Evans, and Elizabeth R. Materese. 2006. "Parties, Preferences and the House Whip Process." Paper presented at the annual meeting of the Southern Political Science Association, Atlanta.

Bell, Lauren Cohen. 2002. *Warring Factions: Interest Groups, Money, and the New Politics of Senate Confirmation*. Columbus: Ohio State University Press.

Bell, Lauren C., and Jason M. Roberts. 2005. "Keeping Score: Parties, Interest Groups, and Roll Call Voting in the U.S. House of Representatives." Paper presented at the annual meeting of the American Political Science Association, Washington, DC.

Berinsky, Adam. 2005. "Assuming the Costs of War: Events, Elites and American Public Support for Military Conflict." http://web.mit.edu/berinsky/www.war.pdf.

Beth, Richard S. 1993. *The Motion to Proceed to Consider a Measure in the Senate, 1979–1992*. Washington, DC: Congressional Research Service.

———. 1997a. *The Discharge Rule in the House: Principal Features and Uses*. CRS Report for Congress, Order Code 97-552 GOV.

———. 1997b. *The Discharge Rule in the House: Recent Use in Historical Perspective*. CRS Report for Congress, Order Code 97-856 GOV.

Bettelheim, Adriel. 2004. "Senate Seniority System Helps Specter Stay the Course." *CQ Weekly*, November 31, 2686.

Binder, Sarah A. 1997. *Minority Rights, Majority Rule: Partisanship and the Development of Congress*. New York: Cambridge University Press.

———. 2007. "Where Do Institutions Come From? Exploring the Origins of the Senate Blue Slip." *Studies in American Political Development* 21:1–15.

Binder, Sarah A., Eric D. Lawrence, and Forrest Maltzman. 1999. "Uncovering the Hidden Effect of Party." *Journal of Politics* 61:815–31.

Binder, Sarah A., and Steven S. Smith. 1997. *Politics or Principle? Filibustering in the United States Senate*. Washington, DC: Brookings Institution.

Bishin, Benjamin G. 2000. "Constituency Influence in Congress: Does Subconstituency Matter?" *Legislative Studies Quarterly* 25:389–415.

Bishin, Benjamin G., Jay K. Dow, and James Adams. 2006. "Does Democracy 'Suffer' From Diversity? Issue Representation and Diversity in Senate Elections." *Public Choice* 129:201–15.

Bolton, Alexander. 2003a. "GOP Splits over Tough Tactics on Bush Judges." *The Hill*, May 14.

———. 2003b. "How Ted Cemented Filibuster." *The Hill*, November 19.

———. 2004. "Frist Finger on 'Nuclear' Button." *The Hill*, May 13.

———. 2005a. "Frist Begins to Squeeze the Trigger." *The Hill*, May 4.

———. 2005b. "Nelson: Let's Make a Deal." *The Hill*, April 13.

———. 2005c. "On Judges, Conservatives and Liberals Agree: No Deal." *The Hill*, April 27.

———. 2005d. "Santorum: Frist Will Go Nuclear." *The Hill*, April 7.

———. 2005e. "Santorum Reads Nuke Polls, Applies the Brakes." *The Hill*, April 21.

Bolton, Alexander, and Geoff Earle. 2003. "Hatch Group May Go 'Nuclear' on Judges." *The Hill*, May 7.

Bond, Jon R. 1983. "The Influence of Constituency Diversity on Electoral Competition in Voting for Congress, 1974–1978." *Legislative Studies Quarterly* 8:201–17.

Bovitz, Gregory L., and Jamie L. Carson. 2006. "Position Taking and Electoral Accountability in the U.S. House of Representatives." *Political Research Quarterly* 59: 297–312.

Brady, David W., Hahrie Han, and Jeremy C. Pope. 2007. "Primary Elections and Candidate Ideology." *Legislative Studies Quarterly* 32:79–106.

Brambor, Thomas, William Clark, and Matt Golder. 2006. "Understanding Interaction Models: Improving Empirical Analyses." *Political Analysis* 14:63–82.

Buchanan, James M., and Gordon Tullock. 1962. *The Calculus of Consent.* Ann Arbor: University of Michigan Press.

Bullock, Charles S. III, and John Sprague. 1969. "A Research Note on the Committee Reassignments of Southern Democratic Congressmen." *Journal of Politics* 31: 493–512.

Burden, Barry D., and Tammy M. Frisby. 2004. "Preferences, Partisanship, and Whip Activity in the House of Representatives." *Legislative Studies Quarterly* 29:569–90.

Burdette, Franklin L. 1940. *Filibustering in the Senate.* Princeton, NJ: Princeton University Press.

Burnham, Walter Dean. 1975. "Insulation and Responsiveness in Congressional Elections." *Political Science Quarterly* 90:411–35.

Burns, James MacGregor. 1963. *The Deadlock of Democracy.* Englewood Cliffs, NJ: Prentice-Hall.

Calmes, Jacqueline. 1987. "Byrd Struggles to Lead Deeply Divided Senate." *CQ Weekly Report,* July 4, 1419.

Campbell, Andrea C. 2004. "Fighting Fire with Fire: Strategic Amending in the 105th Senate." Paper presented at the annual meeting of the American Political Science Association, Chicago.

Campbell, Andrea C., Gary W. Cox, and Mathew D. McCubbins. 2002. "Agenda Power in the US Senate, 1877–1986." In *Party, Process, and Political Change in Congress,* ed. David Brady and Mathew D. McCubbins, 146–65. Stanford, CA: Stanford University Press.

Canes-Wrone, Brandice, David W. Brady, and John F. Cogan. 2002. "Out of Step, Out of Office: Electoral Accountability and House Members' Voting." *American Political Science Review* 96:127–40.

Canon, David T., and Charles Stewart III. 2002. "Parties and Hierarchies in Senate Committees, 1789–1946." In *U.S. Senate Exceptionalism,* ed. Bruce I. Oppenheimer, 157–81. Columbus: Ohio State University Press.

Carmines, Edward G., and James A. Stimson. 1989. *Issue Evolution: Race and the Transformation of American Politics.* Princeton, NJ: Princeton University Press.

Caro, Robert A. 2002. *Master of the Senate: The Years of Lyndon Johnson.* New York: Knopf.

Carsey, Thomas M., and Barry Rundquist. 1999. "Party and Committee in Distributive Politics: Evidence from Defense Spending." *Journal of Politics* 61:1156–69.

Carson, Jamie L. 2005. "Strategy, Selection, and Candidate Competition in U.S. House and Senate Elections." *Journal of Politics* 67:1–28.

Carson, Jamie L., Gregory L. Koger, and Matthew Lebo. 2006. "The Electoral Consequences of Party Loyalty in Congress." Paper presented at the annual meeting of the Midwest Political Science Association, Chicago.

Cassata, Donna. 1995. "GOP Retreats on Hatfield, but War Far from Over." *CQ Weekly*, March 11, 729–31.

Center for Responsive Politics. 2004. "Leadership PACs: PAC Contributions to Federal Candidates, 1987–2004." http://www.opensecrets.org/pacs.

Clausen, Aage. 1973. *How Congressmen Decide: A Policy Focus.* New York: St. Martin's Press.

Cochran, John. 2003. "Interest Groups Make Sure Lawmakers Know the 'Score.'" *CQ Weekly*, April 19, 924.

Collie, Melissa P. 1986. "New Directions in Congressional Research." *Legislative Studies Section Newsletter* 10 (November–December): 90–92.

Congressional Directory, 80th–108th Congresses. Washington, DC: U.S. Government Printing Office.

Cooper, Joseph, and David W. Brady. 1981. "Institutional Context and Leadership Style: The House from Cannon to Rayburn." *American Political Science Review* 75:411–25.

Cooper, Joseph, and Elizabeth Rybicki. 2002. "Analyzing Institutional Change: Bill Introduction in the Nineteenth-Century Senate." In *U.S. Senate Exceptionalism*, ed. Bruce I. Oppenheimer, 182–211. Columbus: Ohio State University Press.

Cooper, Joseph, and Garry Young. 2002. "Party and Preference in Congressional Decision Making: Roll Call Voting in the House of Representatives, 1889–1999." In *Party, Process, and Political Change in Congress*, ed. David Brady and Mathew D. McCubbins, 64–106. Stanford, CA: Stanford University Press.

Covington, Cary R. 1987. "Staying Private: Gaining Congressional Support for Unpublicized Presidential Preferences on Roll Call Votes." *Journal of Politics* 49:737–55.

Cox, Gary W., and Mathew D. McCubbins. 1993. *Legislative Leviathan: Party Government in the House.* Berkeley and Los Angeles: University of California Press.

———. 2002. "Agenda Power in the U.S. House of Representatives, 1877–1986." In *Party, Process, and Political Change in Congress*, ed. David Brady and Mathew D. McCubbins, 107–45. Stanford, CA: Stanford University Press.

———. 2005. *Setting the Agenda: Responsible Party Government in the U.S. House of Representatives.* New York: Cambridge University Press.

———. 2007. *Legislative Leviathan: Party Government in the House.* 2nd ed. Berkeley and Los Angeles: University of California Press.

Cox, Gary W., and Keith T. Poole. 2002. "On Measuring Partisanship in Roll Call Voting: The U.S. House of Representatives, 1877–1999." *American Journal of Political Science* 46:477–89.

Crespin, Michael H., and Nathan Monroe. 2005. "Are Partisan Theories of Agenda Control in the Senate Plausible?" Paper presented at the annual meeting of the Midwest Political Science Association, Chicago.

Davidson, Roger H. 1985. "Senate Leaders: Janitors for an Untidy Chamber?" In *Congress Reconsidered*, 3rd ed., ed. Lawrence C. Dodd and Bruce I. Oppenheimer, 225–52. Washington, DC: CQ Press.

———. 1989. "The Senate: If Everyone Leads, Who Follows?" In *Congress Reconsidered*, 4th ed., ed. Lawrence C. Dodd and Bruce I. Oppenheimer, 275–306. Washington, DC: CQ Press.

Deering, Christopher J. 2001. "Principle or Party? Foreign and National Security Policymaking in the Senate." In *The Contentious Senate*, ed. Colton C. Campbell and Nicol Rae, 43–64. Lanham, MD: Rowman and Littlefield.

———. 2005. "Foreign Affairs and War." In *The Legislative Branch*, ed. Paul J. Quirk and Sarah A. Binder, chap. 12. New York: Oxford University Press.

Deering, Christopher J., and Steven S. Smith. 1997. *Committees in Congress*. 3rd ed. Washington, DC: CQ Press.

Den Hartog, Chris. 2005. "The Powers and Limits of Parties in the U.S. Senate." Paper presented at the annual meeting of the American Political Science Association, Washington, DC.

Den Hartog, Chris, and Nathan W. Monroe. 2007. "Majority Party Influence in the Senate: An Asymmetric-Costs Theory of Agenda Setting." Paper presented at the annual meeting of the Midwest Political Science Association, Chicago.

———. Forthcoming. "The Value of Majority Status: The Effect of Jeffords's Switch on Asset Prices of Republican and Democratic Firms." *Legislative Studies Quarterly*, February 2008.

Desposato, Scott W., and John R. Petrocik. 2003. "The Variable Incumbency Advantage: New Voters, Redistricting, and the Personal Vote." *American Journal of Political Science* 47:18–32.

Dewar, Helen, and Mike Allen. 2003. "Frist Seeks to End Nominees Impasse." *Washington Post*, May 9.

Dewar, Helen, and William Branigin. 2003. "Senate Readying Itself for All-Night Talkathon on Judges." *Washington Post*, November 12.

Dewar, Helen, and Spencer S. Hsu. 2004. "Warner Bucks GOP Right on Probe of Prison Abuse." *Washington Post*, May 28.

Dion, Douglas, and John Huber. 1996. "Procedural Choice and the House Committee on Rules." *Journal of Politics* 58:25–53.

Dlouhy, Jennifer. 2003. "Liberals, Conservatives Both Bracing for a Supreme Court Vacancy." *CQ Weekly Report*, May 31, 1329.

Dodd, Lawrence C. 1978. "The Expanded Roles of the House Democratic Whip System: The 93rd and 94th Congresses." *Congressional Studies* 7:27–56.

Dodd, Lawrence C., and Terry Sullivan. 1981. "Majority Party Leadership and Partisan Vote Gathering: The House Democratic Whip System." In *Understanding Congressional Leadership*, ed. Frank H. Mackaman, 227–60. Washington, DC: CQ Press.

Dominguez, Casey Byrne Knudsen. 2005. "Before the Primary: Party Elite Involvement in Congressional Nominations." Ph.D. diss., University of California, Berkeley.

Donnelly, John M. 2006. "Detainee Treatment Fractures GOP." *CQ Weekly Report*, September 18, 2458.

Donovan, Beth. 1994. "Power in the Twilight." *CQ Weekly Report*, March 12, 578.

Earle, Geoff. 2005a. "Dems Exploit 'Nuclear Option' in a New Fundraising Appeal." *The Hill*, March 2.

———. 2005b. "Frist-Reid Talks Touch on 'Nuclear Option,' Other Issues." *The Hill*, February 17.

Eilperin, Juliet. 1999. "DeLay Enlists His Deputies as Fund-Raisers." *Washington Post*, March 25.

Eisele, Albert. 2001. "Senate Dems Threaten to Block Judges." *The Hill*, April 25.

Erikson, Robert S. 1971. "The Electoral Impact of Congressional Roll Call Voting." *American Political Science Review* 65:1018–32.

Erikson, Robert S., and Gerald C. Wright. 2001. "Voters, Candidates, and Issues in Congressional Elections." In *Congress Reconsidered*, 7th ed., ed. Lawrence C. Dodd and Bruce I. Oppenheimer, 67–95. Washington, DC: CQ Press.

Evans, C. Lawrence. 1991. *Leadership in Committee: A Comparative Analysis of Leadership Behavior in the U.S. Senate*. Ann Arbor: University of Michigan Press.

———. 2001. "Committees, Leaders, and Message Politics." In *Congress Reconsidered*, 7th ed., ed. Lawrence C. Dodd and Bruce I. Oppenheimer, 217–43. Washington, DC: CQ Press.

———. 2004. "The House Whip System and Party Theories of Congress." NSF Proposal (SES-0417759), http://clevan.people.wm.edu/whip.htm.

Evans, C. Lawrence, and Daniel Lipinski. 2005. "Obstruction and Leadership in the U.S. Senate." In *Congress Reconsidered*, 8th ed., ed. Lawrence C. Dodd and Bruce I. Oppenheimer, 227–48. Washington, DC: CQ Press.

Evans, C. Lawrence, and Walter J. Oleszek. 1997. *Congress under Fire: Reform Politics and the Republican Majority*. Boston: Houghton Mifflin.

———. 2000. "The Procedural Context of Senate Deliberation." In *Esteemed Colleagues: Civility and Deliberation in the U.S. Senate*, ed. Burdett A. Loomis, 79–104. Washington, DC: Brookings Institution Press.

Evans, C. Lawrence, and Christopher B. Renjilian. 2004. "Cracking the Whip in the U.S. House: Majority Dominance or Party Balancing?" Paper presented at the annual meeting of the American Political Science Association, Chicago.

Fenno, Richard F. 1966. *Power of the Purse: Appropriations Politics in Congress*. Boston: Little, Brown.

———. 1973. *Congressmen in Committees*. Boston: Little, Brown.

———. 1978. *Home Style: House Members in Their Districts*. New York: HarperCollins.

Ferejohn, John A. 1974. *Pork Barrel Politics*. Stanford, CA: Stanford University Press.

———. 1986. "Logrolling in an Institutional Context." In *Congress and Policy Change*, ed. Gerald C. Wright, Leroy N. Rieselbach, and Lawrence C. Dodd, 223–53. New York: Agathon Press.

Fiorina, Morris P. 1974. *Representatives, Roll Calls, and Constituencies*. Lexington, MA: Lexington Heath.

———. 1977. *Congress: Keystone of the Washington Establishment.* New Haven, CT: Yale University Press.

Fisher, Louis. 2005. "Deciding on War against Iraq: Institutional Failures." In *The Meaning of American Democracy,* ed. Robert Y. Shapiro, 115–36. New York: Academy of Political Science.

Fleisher, Richard, and Jon R. Bond. 2004. "The Shrinking Middle in the U.S. Congress." *British Journal of Political Science* 34:429–52.

Forgette, Richard, and Brian R. Sala. 1999. "Conditional Party Government and Member Turnout on Senate Recorded Votes, 1873–1935." *Journal of Politics* 61:467–84.

Froman, Lewis. 1967. *The Congressional Process.* Boston: Little, Brown.

Gailmard, Sean, and Jeffery A. Jenkins. 2007. "Negative Agenda Control in the Senate and House: Fingerprints of Majority Party Power." *Journal of Politics* 69:689–700.

Gamm, Gerald, and Steven S. Smith. 2000. "Last among Equals: The Senate's Presiding Officer." In *Esteemed Colleagues: Civility and Deliberation in the U.S. Senate,* ed. Burdett A. Loomis, 105–36. Washington, DC: Brookings Institution Press.

Gartner, Scott Sigmund, and Gary M. Segura. 1998. "War, Casualties and Public Opinion." *Journal of Conflict Resolution* 42:278–300.

Gelman, Andrew, and Hal Stern. 2006. "The Difference between 'Significant' and 'Not Significant' Is Not Itself Statistically Significant." *American Statistician* 60:328–31.

Gerber, Alan. 1998. "Estimating the Effect of Campaign Spending on Senate Election Outcomes Using Instrumental Variables." *American Political Science Review* 92:401–11.

Goff, Brian L., and Kevin B. Grier. 1993. "On the (Mis)Measurement of Legislator Ideology and Shirking." *Public Choice* 76:5–20.

Gold, Martin B. 2004. *Senate Procedure and Practice.* Lanham, MD: Rowman and Littlefield.

Goodliffe, Jay. 2007. "Campaign War Chests and Challenger Quality in Senate Elections." *Legislative Studies Quarterly* 32:135–56.

Green, Donald Philip, and Jonathan S. Krasno. 1988. "Salvation for the Spendthrift Incumbent: Reestimating the Effects of Campaign Spending in House Elections." *American Journal of Political Science* 32:884–907.

Greene, William H. 2003. *Econometric Analysis.* 5th ed. New York: Prentice-Hall.

Grier, Kevin. 1989. "Campaign Spending and Senate Elections, 1978–1984." *Public Choice* 63:201–19.

Griffin, John D. 2006. "Electoral Competition and Democratic Responsiveness: A Defense of the Marginality Hypothesis." *Journal of Politics* 68:911–21.

Gronke, Paul. 2000. *Settings, Campaigns, Institutions, and the Vote: A Unified Approach to House and Senate Elections.* Ann Arbor: University of Michigan Press.

Groseclose, Tim, and Charles Stewart III. 1998. "The Value of Committee Seats in the House, 1947–1991." *American Journal of Political Science* 42:453–74.

Haynes, George H. 1938. *The Senate of the United States: Its History and Practice.* Boston: Houghton Mifflin.

Hinckley, Barbara. 1980. "The American Voter in Congressional Elections." *American Political Science Review* 74:641–50.

Holsti, Ole R. 2004. *Public Opinion and American Foreign Policy.* Rev. ed. Ann Arbor: University of Michigan Press.

Hook, Janet. 1988. "The Byrd Years: Surviving in a Media Age through Details and Diligence." *CQ Weekly Report,* April 16, 976.

Hulse, Carl. 2005. "Senate Leaders Break Off Talks on Judicial Nominees." *New York Times,* May 17.

Hunter, Catherine, and Ben Evans. 2005. "Senate Saves Fireworks for Energy Conference." *CQ Weekly,* June 24, 1744.

Hurley, Patricia, 1989. "Parties and Coalitions in Congress." In *Congressional Politics,* ed. Christopher Deering, 113–34. Chicago: Dorsey Press.

Hurt, Charles. 2003. "Memos of Special Interest on Hill." *Washington Times,* November 15.

———. 2005. "Support Falters for the 'Nuclear Option.'" *Washington Times,* March 23.

ICPSR (Inter-university Consortium for Political and Social Research) and Congressional Quarterly, Inc. 1998. *United States Congressional Roll Call Voting Records, 1789–1996* (ICPSR 0004). Ann Arbor, MI: ICPSR.

Jacobson, Gary C. 1980. *Money in Congressional Elections.* New Haven, CT: Yale University Press.

———. 1985. "Money and Votes Reconsidered: Congressional Elections, 1972–1982." *Public Choice* 47:7–62.

———. 1993. "Deficit-Cutting Politics and Congressional Elections." *Political Science Quarterly* 108:375–402.

———. 2004. *The Politics of Congressional Elections.* 6th ed. New York: Addison Wesley Longman.

Jenkins, Jeffery A., Michael A. Crespin, and Jamie L. Carson. 2005. "Parties as Procedural Coalitions in Congress: An Examination of Differing Career Tracks." *Legislative Studies Quarterly* 30:365–89.

Jentleson, Bruce W. 1992. "The Pretty Prudent Public: Post Post-Vietnam American Opinion and the Use of Military Force." *International Studies Quarterly* 36:49–74.

Jones, Bryan D., and Frank R. Baumgartner. 2005. *The Politics of Attention: How Government Prioritizes Problems.* Chicago: University of Chicago Press. Data at http://www.policyagendas.org/.

Kahn, Kim Fridkin, and Patrick J. Kenney. 1999. *The Spectacle of U.S. Senate Campaigns.* Princeton, NJ: Princeton University Press.

Kalt, Joseph P., and Mark A. Zupan. 1984. "Capture and Ideology in the Economic Theory of Politics." *American Economic Review* 74:279–300.

Kane, Paul. 2002. "Pitches Invoke Judges." *Roll Call,* July 8.

Karol, David, and Edward Miguel. 2007. "The Electoral Cost of War: Iraq Casualties and the 2004 U.S. Presidential Election." *Journal of Politics* 69:633–48.

Keller, Bill. 1981. "Small Business Lobby Plays Trick or Treat." *CQ Weekly,* March 21, 509.

Kiewiet, D. Roderick, and Mathew D. McCubbins. 1991. *The Logic of Delegation: Congressional Parties and the Appropriations Process.* Chicago: University of Chicago Press.

King, Gary, Michael Tomz, and Jason Wittenberg. 2000. "Making the Most of Statistical Analyses: Improving Interpretation and Presentation." *American Journal of Political Science* 44:341–55.

Kingdon, John W. 1977. "Models of Legislative Voting." *Journal of Politics* 39:563–95.

———. 1989. *Congressmen's Voting Decisions*. 3rd ed. Ann Arbor: University of Michigan Press.

Klein, Joe. 2006. "Prognosis Looks Grim, Doc." *Time*, April 1.

Koger, Gregory. 2002. "Obstruction in the House and Senate: A Comparative Analysis of Institutional Choice." Ph.D. diss., University of California, Los Angeles.

———. 2003. "The Majoritarian Senate: 'Nuclear Options' in Historical Perspective." Paper presented at the annual meeting of the American Political Science Association, Philadelphia.

———. 2004. "Pivots for Sale: Transaction Costs, Endogenous Rules, and Pivotal Politics." Paper presented at the annual meeting of the American Political Science Association, Chicago.

———. 2006. "Cloture Reform and Party Government in the Senate, 1918–1925." *Journal of Politics* 68:708–19.

———. 2007. "Filibuster Reform in the Senate, 1913–1917." In *Party, Process, and Political Change in Congress*, vol. 2, ed. David W. Brady and Mathew D. McCubbins, 205–25. Stanford, CA: Stanford University Press.

———. n.d. "Going to the Mattresses: Filibustering in Congress, 1789–2004." Manuscript.

Koger, Gregory, Seth Masket, and Hans Noel. 2005. "'We Appreciate Your Support': Information Exchange and Extended Party Networks." Paper prepared for the annual meeting of the American Political Science Association, Washington, DC.

Kolodny, Robin. 1998. *Pursuing Majorities: Congressional Campaign Committees in American Politics*. Norman: University of Oklahoma Press.

Krasno, Jonathan S. 1994. *Challengers, Competition, and Reelection: Comparing Senate and House Elections*. New Haven, CT: Yale University Press.

Krehbiel, Keith. 1986. "Unanimous Consent Agreements: Going Along in the Senate." *Journal of Politics* 48:541–64.

———. 1991. *Information and Legislative Organization*. Ann Arbor: University of Michigan Press.

———. 1993a. "Constituency Characteristics and Legislative Preferences." *Public Choice* 76:21–37.

———. 1993b. "Where's the Party?" *British Journal of Political Science* 23:235–66.

———. 1997. "Restrictive Rules Reconsidered." *American Journal of Political Science* 41:919–44.

———. 1998. *Pivotal Politics: A Theory of U.S. Lawmaking*. Chicago: University of Chicago Press.

———. 1999. "Paradoxes of Parties in Congress." *Legislative Studies Quarterly* 24:31–64.

———. 2000. "Party Discipline and Measures of Partisanship." *American Journal of Political Science* 44:212–27.

———. 2007. "Partisan Roll Rates in a Nonpartisan Legislature." *Journal of Law, Economics and Organization* 23:1–23.

Krehbiel, Keith, and Adam Meirowitz. 2002. "Minority Rights and Majority Power: Theoretical Consequences of the Motion to Recommit." *Legislative Studies Quarterly* 27:191–218.

Krehbiel, Keith, and Jonathan Woon. 2005. "Selection Criteria for Roll Call Votes." Paper presented at the annual meeting of the American Political Science Association, Washington, DC.

Kuklinski, James H., and Lee Sigelman. 1992. "When Objectivity Is Not Objective: Network Television News Coverage of U.S. Senators and the 'Paradox of Objectivity.'" *Journal of Politics* 54:810–33.

Law, R. Brian. 2007. "Committee Prestige in the Senate, 1947–2004." Paper presented at the annual meeting of the Western Political Science Association, Las Vegas.

Lawrence, Eric, Forrest Maltzman, and Steven S. Smith. 2005. "Changing Patterns of Party Effects in Congressional Voting." Paper presented at the annual meeting of the American Political Science Association, Washington, DC.

———. 2006. "Who Wins? Party Effects in Legislative Voting." *Legislative Studies Quarterly* 31:33–70.

Lebo, Matthew, Adam J. McGlynn, and Greg Koger. 2007. "Strategic Party Government: Party Influence in Congress, 1789–2000." *American Journal of Political Science* 51:464–81.

Lee, Frances E. 2000. "Senate Representation and Coalition Building in Distributive Politics." *American Political Science Review* 94:59–72.

———. 2006. "Dividers, Not Uniters: Presidential Leadership and Senate Partisanship, 1981–2004." Paper presented at the Conference on Party Effects in the United States Senate, University of Minnesota, September 29–30.

———. 2008. "Agreeing to Disagree: Agenda Content and Senate Partisanship, 1981–2004." *Legislative Studies Quarterly*, 33:199–222.

Lee, Frances E., and Bruce I. Oppenheimer. 1999. *Sizing Up the Senate: The Unequal Consequences of Equal Representation.* Chicago: University of Chicago Press.

Levitt, Steven D., and James M. Snyder Jr. 1995. "Political Parties and the Distribution of Federal Outlays." *American Journal of Political Science* 39:958–80.

Loewenberg, Gerhard, and Charles O. Jones. 1986. Editors' introduction to *Legislative Studies Quarterly* 11:141–42.

Maltzman, Forrest. 1997. *Competing Principals: Committees, Parties, and the Organization of Congress.* Ann Arbor: University of Michigan Press.

Manley, John. 1970. *The Politics of Finance.* Boston: Little, Brown.

Mann, Thomas E. 1978. *Unsafe at Any Margin: Interpreting Congressional Elections.* Washington, DC: American Enterprise Institute.

Mann, Thomas E., and Norman J. Ornstein. 2006a. *The Broken Branch: How Congress Is Failing America and How to Get It Back on Track.* Oxford: Oxford University Press.

———. 2006b. "When Congress Checks Out." *Foreign Affairs* 85, no. 6, http://foreignaffairs.org.

Mann, Thomas E., and Raymond E. Wolfinger. 1980. "Candidates and Parties in Congressional Elections." *American Political Science Review* 74:617–32.

Marshall, Bryan W., and Brandon C. Prins. 1999. "Issue Domains, Conflict, and Committee Outliers: Evidence from the House and Senate Appropriations Committees." *American Review of Politics* 20:309–28.

Marshall, Bryan W., Brandon C. Prins, and David W. Rohde. 1999. "Fighting Fire with Water: Partisan Procedural Strategies and the Senate Appropriations Committee." *Congress and the Presidency* 26:114–32.

Matthews, Donald R. 1960. *U.S. Senators and Their World.* Chapel Hill: University of North Carolina Press.

Mayhew, David R. 1974. *Congress: The Electoral Connection.* New Haven, CT: Yale University Press.

McCarty, Nolan, Keith T. Poole, and Howard Rosenthal. 1997. *Income Redistribution and the Realignment of American Politics.* Washington, DC: AEI Press.

———. 2001. "The Hunt for Party Discipline in Congress." *American Political Science Review* 95:673–88.

Miller, Warren E., and Donald E. Stokes. 1963. "Constituency Influence in Congress." *American Political Science Review* 57:45–56.

Moore, Michael K., and Sue Thomas. 1991. "Explaining Legislative Success in the U.S. Senate: The Role of the Majority and Minority Parties." *Western Political Quarterly* 44:959–70.

Munger, Michael. 1988. "The Allocation of Desirable Committee Assignments: Extended Queues versus Committee Expansion." *American Journal of Political Science* 32: 317–44.

Nelson, Garrison, with Clark H. Bensen. 1993. *Committees in the U.S. Congress, 1947–1992.* Washington, DC: Congressional Quarterly. Also, "Congressional Committees, 80th–102nd Congresses," data set at http://web.mit.edu/17.251/www/data_page.html.

Oleszek, Walter J. 1971. "Party Whips in the United States Senate." *Journal of Politics* 33:955–79.

———. 2004. *Congressional Procedures and the Policy Process.* 6th ed. Washington, DC: CQ Press.

———. 2007. *Congressional Procedures and the Policy Process.* 7th ed. Washington, DC: CQ Press.

Oppenheimer, Bruce I. 1980. "Policy Effects of U.S. House Reform: Decentralization and the Capacity to Resolve Energy Issues." *Legislative Studies Quarterly* 5:5–30.

———. 1981. "Congress and the New Obstructionism: Developing an Energy Program." In *Congress Reconsidered*, 2nd ed., ed. Lawrence C. Dodd and Bruce I. Oppenheimer, 275–95. Washington, DC: CQ Press.

Ornstein, Norman J., Thomas E. Mann, and Michael J. Malbin. 2002. *Vital Statistics on Congress, 2001–2002.* Washington, DC: AEI.

Ota, Alan K. 2004. "Senate GOP Gives Its Leaders a Powerful New Tool." *CQ Weekly Report*, November 20, 2733.

Overby, L. Marvin, and Lauren C. Bell. 2004. "Rational Behavior or the Norm of Co-operation? Filibustering Behavior among Retiring Senators." *Journal of Politics* 66: 906–24.

Overby, L. Marvin, Beth M. Henschen, Michael H. Walsh, and Julie Strauss. 1992. "Courting Constituents? An Analysis of the Senate Confirmation Vote on Justice Clarence Thomas." *American Political Science Review* 86:997–1003.

Pearson, Kathryn. 2005. "Party Discipline in the Contemporary Congress: Rewarding Loyalty in Theory and in Practice." Ph.D. diss., University of California, Berkeley.

Peltzman, Sam. 1984. "Constituent Interest and Congressional Voting." *Journal of Law and Economics* 27:181–210.

Perine, Keith. 2005. "Fiercest Fight in Partisan War May Be over Supreme Court." *CQ Weekly Report*, January 10, 58.

Petrocik, John R. 1996. "Issue Ownership in Presidential Elections, with a 1980 Case Study" *American Journal of Political Science* 40:825–50.

Pierce, Emily. 2002. "Senate Committees: New Rules for the 'A' Teams?" *CQ Weekly Report*, November 9, 2910.

Poole, Keith T., and Howard Rosenthal. 1991. "Patterns of Congressional Voting." *American Journal of Political Science* 35:228–78.

———. 1997. *Congress: A Political-Economic History of Roll Call Voting.* New York: Oxford University Press.

———. 2006. Voteview data set. http://voteview.com/dwnl.htm.

———. 2007. *Ideology and Congress.* New Brunswick, NJ: Transaction Publishers.

Riddick, Floyd, and Alan Frumin. 1992. *Riddick's Senate Procedure.* Senate Document 101-28. Washington, DC: U.S. Government Printing Office.

Riker, William H. 1962. *The Theory of Political Coalitions.* New Haven, CT: Yale University Press.

Ripley, Randall B. 1964. "The Party Whip Organization in the United States House of Representatives." *American Political Science Review* 58:561–76.

———. 1969. *Power in the Senate.* New York: St. Martin's Press.

Rohde, David W. 1991. *Parties and Leaders in the Postreform House.* Chicago: University of Chicago Press.

———. 1994. "Parties and Committees in the House: Member Motivations, Issues, and Institutional Arrangements." *Legislative Studies Quarterly* 19:341–61.

———. 1995. "Parties and Committees in the House: Members' Motivations, Issues, and Institutional Arrangements." In *Positive Theories of Congressional Institutions,* ed. Kenneth A. Shepsle and Barry W. Weingast, 119–37. Ann Arbor: University of Michigan Press.

———. 2005. "Committees and Policy Formulation." In *The Legislative Branch,* ed. Paul J. Quirk and Sarah A. Binder, 201–24. New York: Oxford University Press.

Rosenbaum, David. 2004. "In the Fulbright Mold, without the Power." *New York Times,* May 3, http://www.nytimes.com/2004/05/03/politics/03TALK.html?.

Rundquist, Barry, and Thomas M. Carsey. 2002. *Congress and Defense Spending.* Norman: University of Oklahoma Press.

Sabato, Larry J., and Bruce Larson. 2002. *The Party's Just Begun: Shaping Political Parties for America's Future.* 2nd ed. New York: Longman.

Schattschneider, E. E. 1942. *Party Government.* New York: Rinehart.

Scherer, Nancy. 2005. *Scoring Points: Politicians, Activists, and the Lower Federal Court Appointment Process.* Stanford, CA: Stanford University Press.

Schickler, Eric. 2000. "Institutional Change in the House of Representatives, 1867–1998." *American Political Science Review* 94:269–88.

———. 2001. *Disjointed Pluralism: Institutional Innovation and the Development of the U.S. Congress.* Princeton, NJ: Princeton University Press.

Schiller, Wendy. 2000a. *Partners and Rivals: Representation in U.S. Senate Delegations.* Princeton, NJ: Princeton University Press.

———. 2000b. "Trent Lott's New Regime: Filling the Amendment Tree to Centralize Power in the U.S. Senate." Paper presented at the annual meeting of the American Political Science Association, Washington, DC.

———. 2002. "Sharing the Same Home Turf: How Senators from the Same State Compete for Geographic Electoral Support." In *U.S. Senate Exceptionalism,* ed. Bruce I. Oppenheimer, 109–31. Columbus: Ohio State University Press.

Schmidt, Amy B., Lawrence W. Kenny, and Rebecca B. Morton. 1996. "Evidence on Electoral Accountability in the U.S. Senate: Are Unfaithful Agents Really Punished?" *Economic Inquiry* 34:545–67.

Schneider, J. 2003. *The Committee Assignment Process in the U.S. Senate: Democratic and Republican Procedures.* Washington, D.C.: U.S. Senate Historian.

Sellers, Patrick J. 2002. "Winning Media Coverage in the U.S. Congress." In *U.S. Senate Exceptionalism,* ed. Bruce I. Oppenheimer, 132–55. Columbus: Ohio State University Press.

Shepsle, Kenneth A., and Barry R. Weingast. 1981a. "Political Preferences of the Pork Barrel? A Generalization." *American Journal of Political Science* 25:96–111.

———. 1981b. "Structure-Induced Equilibrium and Legislative Choice." *Public Choice* 37:503–19.

———. 1987. "The Institutional Foundations of Committee Power." *American Political Science Review* 81:85–104.

Simpson, E. H. 1951. "The Interpretation of Interaction in Contingency Tables." *Journal of the Royal Statistical Society,* series B, 13:238–41.

Sinclair, Barbara. 1989. *The Transformation of the U.S. Senate.* Baltimore: Johns Hopkins University Press.

———. 1992. "The Emergence of Strong Leadership in the 1980s House of Representatives." *Journal of Politics* 54:657–84.

———. 1995. *Legislators, Leaders, and Lawmaking: The U.S. House of Representatives in the Postreform Era.* Baltimore: Johns Hopkins University Press.

———. 1999. "Do Parties Matter?" Paper presented at the History of Congress Conference, Stanford University, Stanford, CA, January 15–16.

———. 2000. *Unorthodox Lawmaking: New Legislative Processes in the U.S. Congress.* 2nd ed. Washington, DC: CQ Press.

———. 2001a. "The New World of U.S. Senators." In *Congress Reconsidered*, 7th ed., ed. Lawrence C. Dodd and Bruce I. Oppenheimer, 1–20. Washington, DC: CQ Press.

———. 2001b. "Patterns and Dynamics of Congressional Change." In *Congress Reconsidered*, 7th ed., ed. Lawrence C. Dodd and Bruce I. Oppenheimer, 1–19. Washington, DC: CQ Press.

———. 2002a. "Do Parties Matter?" In *Party, Process, and Political Change in Congress*, ed. David Brady and Mathew D. McCubbins, 36–63. Stanford, CA: Stanford University Press.

———. 2002b. "The '60-Vote Senate': Strategies, Process and Outcomes." In *U.S. Senate Exceptionalism*, ed. Bruce I. Oppenheimer, 241–61. Columbus: Ohio State University Press.

———. 2005. "The New World of U.S. Senators." In *Congress Reconsidered*, 8th ed., ed. Lawrence C. Dodd and Bruce I. Oppenheimer, 1–22. Washington, DC: CQ Press.

Smith, Steven S. 1989. *Call to Order: Floor Politics in the House and Senate.* Washington, DC: Brookings Institution Press.

———. 2005. "Parties and Leadership in the Senate." In *The Legislative Branch*, ed. Paul J. Quirk and Sarah A. Binder, 255–78. New York, NY: Oxford University Press.

Smith, Steven S., and Marcus Flathman. 1989. "Managing the Senate Floor: Complex Unanimous Consent Agreements since the 1950s." *Legislative Studies Quarterly* 14: 349–74.

Smith, Steven S., and Gerald Gamm. 2001. "The Dynamics of Party Government in Congress." In *Congress Reconsidered*, 7th ed., ed. Lawrence C. Dodd and Bruce I. Oppenheimer, 181–206. Washington, DC: CQ Press.

———. 2002. "Emergence of the Modern Senate: Party Organization, 1937–2002." Paper presented at the annual meeting of the American Political Science Association, Boston.

———. 2005. "The Dynamics of Party Government in Congress." In *Congress Reconsidered*, 8th ed., ed. Lawrence C. Dodd and Bruce I. Oppenheimer, 105–36. Washington, DC: CQ Press.

Smith, Steven S., Jason M. Roberts, and Ryan J. Vander Wielen. 2006. *The American Congress.* 4th ed. New York: Cambridge University Press.

Snyder, James M., and Timothy Groseclose. 2000. "Estimating Party Influence in Congressional Roll Call Voting." *American Journal of Political Science* 44:193–211.

Stein, Robert M., and Kenneth Bickers. 1995. *Perpetuating the Pork Barrel: Policy Subsystem and American Democracy.* New York: Cambridge University Press.

Stevens, Allison. 2004. "More Power to the Senate's Majority Leader?" *CQ Weekly Report*, November 6, 2605.

Stevens, Allison, and Andrew Taylor. 2003. "Frist Faced with Deep Party Rift after Charge of Double Dealing." *CQ Weekly Report*, April 19, 931.

Stewart, Charles III, and Tim Groseclose. 1999. "The Value of Committee Seats in the United States Senate, 1947–1991." *American Journal of Political Science* 43:963–73.

Stewart, Charles III, and Jonathan Woon. 2005. "Congressional Committee Assignments, 103rd to 109th Congresses, 1993–2005." http://web.mit.edu/17.251/www/data_page.html.

Stimson, James A. 2004. *Tides of Consent: How Public Opinion Shapes American Politics.* Cambridge: Cambridge University Press.

Stokes, Donald S., and Warren E. Miller. 1962. "Party Government and the Saliency of Congress." *Public Opinion Quarterly* 26:531–46.

Stratmann, Thomas. 2000. "Congressional Voting over Legislative Careers: Shifting Positions and Changing Constraints." *American Political Science Review* 94:665–76.

Sullivan, Terry. 1990a. "Bargaining with the President: A Simple Game and New Evidence." *American Political Science Review* 84:1167–95.

———. 1990b. "Explaining Why Presidents Count: Signaling and Information." *Journal of Politics* 52:939–62.

Sundquist, James. 1981. *The Decline and Resurgence of Congress.* Washington, DC: Brookings Institution.

Theriault, Sean M. 2007. "Party Polarization in the U.S. Congress." Manuscript, University of Texas at Austin.

Tiefer, Charles. 1989. *Congressional Practice and Procedure: A Reference, Research, and Legislative Guide.* New York: Greenwood Press.

Turner, Julius. 1951. *Party and Constituency: Pressures on Congress.* Baltimore: Johns Hopkins Press.

Uslaner, Eric. 1999. *The Movers and the Shirkers: Downsians and Ideologues in the Senate.* Ann Arbor: University of Michigan Press.

VandeHei, Jim, and Charles Babington. 2005. "From Senator's 2003 Outburst, GOP Hatched 'Nuclear Option.'" *Washington Post,* May 19.

Van Houweling, Robert Parks. 2007. "An Evolving End Game: Partisan Collusion in Conference Committees." In *Party, Process, and Political Change in Congress,* vol. 2, ed. David W. Brady and Mathew D. McCubbins, 309–22. Stanford, CA: Stanford University Press.

Veron, Ilyse J. 1992. "The More Narrow Focus." *CQ Weekly,* May 2, 1136.

Wawro, Gregory J., and Eric Schickler. 2004. "Where's the Pivot? Obstruction and Lawmaking in the Pre-cloture Senate." *American Journal of Political Science* 48: 758–74.

———. 2006. *Filibuster: Obstruction and Lawmaking in the U.S. Senate.* Princeton, NJ: Princeton University Press.

———. 2007. "Cloture Reform Reconsidered." In *Party, Process, and Political Change in Congress,* vol. 2, ed. David W. Brady and Mathew D. McCubbins, 226–48. Stanford, CA: Stanford University Press.

Weingast, Barry R. 1979. "A Rational Choice Perspective on Congressional Norms." *American Journal of Political Science* 23:245–63.

Weingast, Barry R., and William Marshall. 1988. "The Industrial Organization of Congress." *Journal of Political Economy* 91:132–63.

Westlye, Mark C. 1991. *Senate Elections and Campaign Intensity.* Baltimore: Johns Hopkins University Press.

Wilson, Woodrow. [1885] 1973. *Congressional Government.* Reprint. Gloucester, MA: Peter Smith.

Wolfinger, Raymond E. 1971. "Filibusters: Majority Rule, Presidential Leadership, and Senate Norms." In *Readings on Congress*, ed. Raymond Wolfinger, 286–305. Englewood Cliffs, NJ: Prentice-Hall.

Wright, Gerald C. Jr. 1978. "Candidates' Policy Positions and Voting in U.S. Congressional Elections." *Legislative Studies Quarterly* 3:445–64.

Wright, Gerald C. Jr., and Michael B. Berkman. 1986. "Candidates and Policy in United States Senate Elections." *American Political Science Review* 80:567–88.

Young, Garry, and Vicky Wilkins. 2007. "Vote Switchers and Party Influence in the House." *Legislative Studies Quarterly* 32:59–78.

Contributors

JOHN ALDRICH is the Pfizer-Pratt University Professor of Political Science at Duke University. He specializes in American politics and behavior, formal theory, and methodology. He is the author of *Why Parties? The Origin and Transformation of Political Parties in America* (University of Chicago Press, 1995).

LAUREN COHEN BELL is an associate professor of political science at Randolph-Macon College. She teaches courses in American government, constitutional law, research methodology, and public policy. She is the author of *Warring Factions: Interest Groups, Money, and the New Politics of Senate Confirmation* (Ohio State University Press, 2002).

ERIN M. BRADBURY is a 2006 graduate of the College of William and Mary, where she majored in government. She is now a political fundraising consultant in Washington, D.C.

MICHAEL BRADY is a graduate student in political science at Duke University. His research interests include congressional politics, campaigns and elections, quantitative analysis, and American political institutions.

JAMIE L. CARSON is an assistant professor of political science at the University of Georgia. His primary research interests are in American politics and political institutions, with an emphasis on congressional politics and elections, separation of powers, and American political development.

MICHAEL H. CRESPIN is an assistant professor of political science at the University of Georgia. His research interests are in American politics and political institutions, with a particular focus on legislative politics and elections. He has published work on parties, procedure, and redistricting, both in the congressional and state legislative contexts.

RYAN A. DAVIDSON is a 2006 graduate of the College of William and Mary. A former government concentrator, he is now completing an M.A. in public policy at the University of North Carolina, Chapel Hill.

CHRIS DEN HARTOG is an assistant professor of political science at California Polytechnic State University. He specializes in American political institutions, Congress, the presidency, and public policy.

C. LAWRENCE EVANS is a professor of government at the College of William and Mary. He is a specialist in American national government. His books include *Congress under Fire: Reform Politics and the Republican Majority* (with Walter J. Oleszek; Houghton Mifflin, 1997) and *Leadership in Committee: A Comparative Analysis of Leadership Behavior in the U.S. Senate* (University of Michigan Press, 2001).

CHARLES J. FINOCCHIARO is an assistant professor of political science at the University of South Carolina. His research focuses on the role of parties and committees in legislative politics, the organization and development of American political institutions, and congressional elections.

LINDA L. FOWLER is a professor of government at Dartmouth College and holds the Frank J. Reagan Chair in Policy Studies. Her research interests include candidate recruitment, Congress and foreign policy, elections, and interest groups. She is the author of two books on political ambition and numerous articles on various topics in American politics. She is currently at work on a book, *Congress at the Water's Edge*.

SEAN GAILMARD is an assistant professor of political science at the University of California, Berkeley. His research focuses primarily on American political institutions—particularly the bureaucracy, Congress, and their interaction—and he specializes in game-theoretic and statistical modeling. In addition, he conducts research on individual choice in collective decision making.

MARC J. HETHERINGTON is an associate professor of political science at Vanderbilt University, specializing in American politics, political behavior, and party politics. He is the author of *Why Trust Matters: Declining Political Trust and the Demise of American Liberalism* (Princeton University Press, 2004).

JEFFERY A. JENKINS is an associate professor in the Woodrow Wilson Department of Politics and a senior scholar in the Miller Center of Public Affairs at the University of Virginia. His research interests include analysis of Congress and its institutions, political parties, and American political development.

GREGORY KOGER is an assistant professor of political science at the University of Miami. His research interests include the U.S. Congress, political institutions, institutional change, political parties, and elections.

R. BRIAN LAW is a graduate student in political science at the University of California, Los Angeles. He specializes in American politics.

SCOTT DE MARCHI is an associate professor of political science at Duke University. He specializes in the fields of computational political economy and other mathematical methods, individual decision making, the presidency, and public policy. He is the author of *Computational and Mathematical Modeling in the Social Sciences* (Cambridge University Press, 2005).

IAN MCDONALD is a graduate student in political science at Duke University.

NATHAN W. MONROE is an assistant professor of political science at the University of California, Merced. His research focuses on American political institutions, especially the U.S. Congress. He has published work on legislative term limits, conference committees, and party effects in the House and Senate.

BRENDAN NYHAN is a graduate student in political science at Duke University. His research interests include the presidency, Congress, elections, and political psychology.

BRUCE I. OPPENHEIMER is a professor of political science at Vanderbilt University. His research interests include legislative politics and political institutions. He is co-author (with Frances E. Lee) of *Sizing Up the Senate: The Unequal Consequences of Equal Representation* (University of Chicago Press, 1999).

KATHRYN PEARSON is an assistant professor of political science at the University of Minnesota, specializing in American politics. Her research focuses on the U.S. Congress, congressional elections, political parties, women and politics, and public opinion.

JASON M. ROBERTS is an assistant professor of political science at the University of North Carolina at Chapel Hill. He specializes in the U.S. Congress, electoral and political behavior, political history, and judicial nominations.

DAVID W. ROHDE is the Ernestine Friedl Professor of Political Science at Duke University. His areas of interest include legislative politics, campaigns and elections, positive political theory, and research methods. He is the author of *Parties and Leaders in the Postreform House* (University of Chicago Press, 1991).

MICHAEL TOFIAS is an assistant professor of political science at the University of Wisconsin–Milwaukee. He specializes in American political institutions, elections, and computational political economy.

Index

9/11, 134

ABC bill (Act for Better Child Care), 96–97
abortion roll calls, almost never the
    subject of whip counts, 83
Abourezk, Jamie, 203, 208
Abu Ghraib, 121
academic earmarks, 233
Adams, Brock, 76, 77
Adler, E. Scott, 43, 50n4, 126
AFL-CIO, 58, 63
agenda influence: agenda-setting theory
    of legislative influence, 144–45; higher
    costs for minority party than majority
    party, 149; of House majority-party
    leaders, 112–13, 145; of majority party,
    6, 143–44; Senate, 145, 146–47. *See also*
    negative agenda control
agenda-setting costs, 155; effect on
    majority parties, 144; for non-majority-
    party members, 145; in Senate, 145–47
Alaska, per capita pork, 239
Albert, Carl, 203
Aldrich, John, 5, 15, 74, 196n2, 200, 232
Alito, Samuel, 159, 172
American Conservative Union (ACU),
    58, 63, 66, 69n6, 170
American political parties, historical
    weakness, 200

Americans for Democratic Action
    (ADA), 25, 40, 58, 63, 69n6, 69n11
Ansolabehere, Stephen, 6, 25
anti-flag burning legislation, 84
appropriations bills, 233–34
Arctic National Wildlife Refuge
    (ANWR), 52, 53, 210, 211, 214, 217,
    228n14
Armstrong, William, 86
Arnold, R. Douglas, 28
assistant deputy whip, 76

Bagehot, Walter, 156
Bailey, Michael, 54
Balla, Steven J., 232, 233
Bargen, Andrew, 157n3
Bartlett, Dewey, 203
Barton, Joe, 218, 220
Bell, Lauren Cohen, 15
Bellmon, Henry, 203
Belson, Ben, 171
Bentsen, Lloyd, 96, 203
Berkman, Michael B., 26
Bingaman, Jeff, 95, 218, 220
"blue slip," 175n11
Bolling, Richard, 205
Bolling motion, voting on, 227n5
Boren, David, 97
Bradbury, Erin M., 16, 103

Brady, David W., 2, 6, 25, 30, 33, 54
Brambor, Thomas, 36
Brown, Janice Rogers, 171
Buchanan, James M., 231
Bullock, Charles S. III, 126
Bumpers, Dale, 142, 143
Burnham, Walter Dean, 24
Burns, James MacGregor, 199
Burr, Richard, 217
Bush, George H. W., 77, 81, 95, 99n24
Bush, George W., 14, 113, 121; energy
    legislation, 210, 226; and Jeffords, 9;
    judicial nominations, 17, 168, 169;
    pro-life Supreme Court nominees, 117;
    proposed 2003 tax cuts, 110; and Social
    Security privatization, 225; support
    for cloture reform, 170; Supreme
    Court nominees, 172; tax and foreign
    policy legislation, 224
Byrd, Robert C., 77, 81, 105, 112, 119, 148,
    161, 171, 239

CAFE (corporate average fuel economy),
    218
campaign-finance reform, 111
campaigns, party assistance on, 118
campaign spending, on Senate elections,
    26
Campbell, Andrea C., 15, 55, 75, 157n3,
    158n9
Canes-Wrone, Brandice, 25, 30, 33
Cannon, Joseph, 2
Cantwell, Maria, 52
Capps, Lois, 210
Carmines, Edward G., 41
Carson, Jamie L., 15, 25
cartel theory, 102, 184, 232, 242
Carter, Jimmy, 208, 209
Carter energy package, 201, 203–9, 227n2;
    effect of ideology on probability of
    voting yes on Bolling, House, 1978,
    206, 207; effect of ideology on voting
    yes on Metzenbaum, Senate, 1978,
    205; holding of legislation hostage by
    members acting as free agents, 207–8;

vote for Bolling as function of party
    and ideology, 205–6; vote for
    Metzenbaum as function of party,
    ideology, and constituency, 204–5
categorical grants-in-aid, 231
caucus tallies, 77
Chafee, Lincoln, 9–10, 171
Cheney, Dick, 8
Christian Coalition, 170
Citizens Against Government Waste
    (CAGW), 234–35
Clark, William, 36
Clausen, Aage, 83
Clinton, William Jefferson, 225
closed rules, 7
cloture rule, 88, 112, 175n3; catch-22
    for party leaders, 199; constraint
    on conditional party government,
    221–23; and energy-policy coalitions,
    2001–2005, 211–17; and move away
    from party median, 198, 210, 226;
    sixty-vote requirement to invoke, 119,
    157n3, 160, 196n1, 222; votes on mo-
    tions, 105
coalition building: on energy policy, 2001–
    2005, 211–17; on energy policy, 1970s,
    201; extremes-against-the-middle
    strategy, 201–9; idiosyncratic, 40
Coburn, Tom, 119
Cochran, Thad, 238
Cogan, John F., 25, 30, 33
Cold War, end of, 134
Collins, Susan, 171
Concurrent Budget Resolution for Fiscal
    Year 2006, 52
conditional party government, 19n3;
    effect on coalition building, 198; move
    toward since 1980s, 200; Senate as
    limiting force on, 199–200, 221–25, 226;
    theory of, 5, 18, 101, 102, 181, 196n2,
    200, 232
Condorcet-winning platforms, 40
conference-report votes: similarity
    of Senate and House in roll rates,
    186–87; similarity of Senate and House

minorities in negative agenda control on, 194

Congress: chamber-originated bills, 185; congressional campaign committees, 118; division of, 187; increasing partisanship and its consequences, 1–7, 101–3, 200; influences on voting decisions, 54; legislative conflict, 40–41; public criticism of since Iraq invasion, 139; rising party unity, 104

Congressional committees: distributive theories of, 231; and institutional power of Congress, 121–22; power and independence of leaders, 2; seniority ratio, 131. *See also* Senate committees

Congressional elections, 2000, and control of Senate by GOP, 8

Congressional Quarterly, 81

Congressional Roll Call, 31

Conrad, Kent, 115

constituents, effect on Senate voting decisions, 40, 56

"constitutional" option, 176n12

Cooper, Joseph, 2, 125

Corman, James, 208

Cox, Gary W., 4, 6, 12, 15, 55, 69n11, 74, 75, 157n3, 184, 232

CQ Weekly, 58, 103, 112, 114, 115, 221

Cranston, Alan, 76, 77, 80, 81, 98n3

Crespin, Michael H., 17, 234

Daschle, Thomas, 76, 115, 118, 169, 216

Davidson, Ryan A., 16, 103

Deering, Christopher J., 125, 129

defense issues, tendency to divide Democrats, 85

DeLay, Tom, 111, 121, 214

DeMint, Jim, 217

Democratic Congressional Campaign Committee (DCCC), 106, 118

Democratic Party: liberals less likely than moderates to defect from party position, 63; racial liberalism, 41, 200; role changes in the 1970s, 3–4; split by region on race issue, 45. *See also*

House Democrats; Senate Democratic Caucus; Senate Democrats

Democratic Senatorial Campaign Committee (DSCC), 106, 118

Department of Defense Appropriations Act of 2006, 52, 68n3

DeWine, Mike, 171

dilatory tactics, costs of, 146, 147

discharge petition, 145, 250n2

distributive (or gains-from-exchange) theories of politics, 230, 231–32, 250n10

divided government, and minority-party roll rates, 188

Dixon, Alan, 76, 85

Dole, Robert, 80, 96, 97, 203

Domenici, Pete, 208, 218, 220

Dukakis, Michael, 89

Durenberger, David, 96

DW-NOMINATE: combined models of by Congress, *47*; demographics-only models of by Congress, *46*; demographics-only models of by region and Congress, *48*; GOP coefficient by Congress for, *48*; models of 73rd–108th Senates, *44–45*; scores for House Democrats during 95th Congress, 227n1

earmark-request process, 250n9

earmarks, 229, 233, 235. *See also* pork, descriptive measures of; pork-barrel spending

Edwards, John, 217

electoral accountability, 23

energy legislation: Bush administration, 210, 226; mentions on evening news, 1974–2005, 219–20; 109th Congress, 201, 211–20, 226. *See also* Carter energy package; Murkowski amendment

Erikson, Robert S., 24, 25

Estrada, Miguel, 169

ethanol, 214, 216, 218, 219

Ethics in Government Act, 84

Evangelical organizations, 170

Evans, C. Lawrence, 16, 103, 142–43, 143

Family Research Council, 176n20
Federal Election Commission, 118
Fenno, Richard F., 10, 13, 54, 124, 236
Ferejohn, John A., 231
filibuster, 7–8, 16–17, 18; agenda-setting
 costs for majority party, 146; and
 blocking of judicial nominations, 159;
 defined, 175n1; as meaningful blocking
 instrument in modern Senate, 102,
 103, 105, 159, 185; minority obstruction
 on both substantive and procedural
 matters, 184; rise in, 112; threat of, 146;
 threats of reform as deterrence to,
 172–73
"filling the amendment tree," 158n9
final-passage vote, 7, 143, 196n4
Finocchiaro, Charles J., 17
Fiorina, Morris P., 231
flag-burning issue, 99n18
floor votes, party loyalty in, 103–5
Focus on the Family, 170
Ford, Wendell, 76, 81, 96, 98n3
Forgette, Richard, 55
Fortas, Abe, 175n2
fossil fuel alternatives, 202
fossil fuels, tax benefits for, 217
Fowler, Linda L., 16
Frist, Bill, 114; and Bush military-
 commissions bill, 113; and Bush 2003
 tax-cut bill, 110–11; and cloture vote
 on HR 6, 215, 217, 228n11; and "nuclear
 option," 119, 169–71, 173
FS-X issue, 84, 85
Fulbright, J. William, 139

Gailmard, Sean, 17, 55, 103, 194, 225
Gang of 14, 111, 171–74, 176n22, 176n23
Gerber, Alan, 26
germaneness rule, 8, 54
global warming, 218
Goff, Brian L., 40
Golder, Matt, 36
Goldwater, Barry, 41, 203
Graham, Bob, 76, 95
Graham, Lindsey, 113, 171

Greenaway, Ron, 77
Greene, Howard, 78, 80
Grier, Kevin B., 40
Griffin, John D., 38n7
Groseclose, Tim, 55, 75, 126, 140n6
Grosewart index, 124, 126, 127, 128, 130,
 138, 140n5, 141n11
"guardianship" model, 236
Gulf of Mexico offshore drilling, 217, 218

Han, Hahrie, 6
Hansen, Clifford, 203
Harkin, Tom, 76, 77
Hartog, Chris Den, 16, 75, 199
Hatch, Orrin, 96, 117, 169
Hatfield, Mark, 116–17, 117, 119, 228n17
Hawaii, receipt of pork, 238
Head Start program, reauthorization of,
 99n26
Heflin, Howell, 95
Helms, Jesse, 147
Hetherington, Marc J., 17, 183, 196
Hinckley, Barbara, 25
"hold," 182, 185
Hollings, Ernest, 96, 217
House of Representatives: consideration
 of oil-price decontrol and windfall-
 profits tax in 1975, 202–3; elections and
 electoral accountability, 24–25; increase
 in party unity votes since 1970s, 3–4, 74;
 majoritarian character, 4, 7; reforms of
 1970s, 13; under Republican rule, 5–7;
 seniority and committee chairmanships, 116, 224; whip process, 77
House Appropriations Committee, 117,
 236
House Democrats: decline in number
 representing energy-producing states
 and districts, 210–11; DW-NOMINATE
 scores during 95th Congress, 227n1
House Interstate and Foreign Commerce
 Committee, 202, 203
House majority-party leaders, 105; agenda
 control, 112–13, 145; centralized decision
 making and top-down control in 1990s,

53; disciplining of members, 101–2; losses, 1991–2002, 60, 62; more influence over committee assignments than Senate leaders, 13, 223–24; procedural powers, 74; Rules Committee dictation of outcomes, 6, 233

House minority party, negative agenda control, 191–95

House Republicans: increase in number representing energy-producing districts, 210–11; "Republicans-only" strategy, 119; Retain Our Majority Program (ROMP), 110; six-year term limits on committee chairs, 116

House Rules Committee, 6, 14, 112, 156, 233

House Ways and Means Committee, 202, 203

Humphrey, Hubert, 162

Hurley, Patricia, 53

ideological orientation: association of liberalism with leadership support on whip counts, 90–91; effect on vote for Carter energy package, 204–6, 207; effect on vote for cloture on HR 6, 214–16; effect on vote for cloture on Murkowski amendment, 2002, 212–13; extreme, 36, 37, 151; greater effect on party defections for minority-party members, 63; and poll position and the vote, 92, 93; and primary elections, 6–7

idiosyncratic coalitions, 40

Inouye, Daniel K., 171, 238

interest groups, 15; increase in, 123, 127; notification of members of Congress in advance of votes included on next ratings, 57; rewards for voting with, 57

interest-group scorecards, 57; effect on aggregate party success rates and individual members' decisions, 67; and congressional roll-call voting behaviors, 53, 56, 58–68; and party defection in the Senate, 1991–2002, 63, 64, 65, 66, 68

Iraq War, 121, 139

issue evolution, 41, 46, 49

Jacobson, Gary C., 25, 30, 31, 38n9

Jeffords, James, 8–9, 19n7, 69n7, 100, 111, 117, 157n3, 168, 172, 230

Jenkins, Jeffery A., 17, 55, 103, 194, 225

"Johnson rule," 122, 127

Johnston, Bennett, 96, 203, 208

Jones, Walter, 23

judicial appointments: blocking of by Senate Democrats, 168; Senate dispute over during Bush Administration, 17, 167–74; vulnerability to filibusters, 159

Kahn, Kim Fridkin, 27

Kassenbaum, Nancy, 225

Keating, Charles, 98n3

Kennedy, Edward, 95, 203, 225

Kenney, Patrick J., 27

Kenny, Lawrence W., 56, 57

key votes, 57; in 1978, 227n3; list, 81

Kiewiet, D. Roderick, 236

Kingdon, John W., 25, 54

Koger, Gregory, 16, 25, 157n3, 176n23, 183

Korean War, 134

Krehbiel, Keith, 4–5, 7, 8, 13, 40, 75, 101, 181, 196n3, 250n2

"label-defining" votes, 6

Landrieu, Mary, 171

Lapinski, John S., 126

Lautenberg, Frank, 95

Law, R. Brian, 16, 131, 133, 140n9

Lawrence, Eric D., 7, 63, 75

leadership PACs (political action committees), 2, 106, 109–10

League of Conservative Voters (LCV), 58, 65, 68

Leahy, Patrick, 76, 168

Lebo, Matthew, 25

Lee, Frances, 14

Legislative Reorganization Act of 1970, 122, 132, 138

legislative shirking, 40
Lieberman, Joseph, 11, 171
Limbaugh, Rush, 176n20
Lipinski, Daniel, 142–43
logrolling, 121, 231, 233
Long, Russell, 203
loss: defined as vote in which a majority of the majority party votes on the losing side, 68n1; majority-party, 52. *See also* House majority-party leaders losses; Senate majority party, losses
Lott, Trent, 80, 100, 101, 114, 238

Mack, Connie, 116
majority party: agenda control at virtually all stages of legislative process, 6; leadership PAC activity and status, 109; losses, 52; motions to table as means of killing unwanted amendments, 143; right of first recognition, 158n9; theory of advantage in dollar amount of earmarks in House, 232; treatment of votes on tabling motions as procedural votes, 155. *See also* House majority-party leaders; Senate majority party
Maltzman, Forrest, 7, 63, 75
Mann, Thomas E., 14, 25
Markey, Edward, 210
markup stages, 233, 234
Marshall, Bryan W., 148, 231, 236
Martinez, Mel, 217, 228n12
Matthews, Donald, 102
Mayhew, David, 23, 28, 156, 229, 231; *Congress: The Electoral Connection*, 2
McCain, John, 111, 113, 171, 229
McClure, James, 208
McConnell, Mitch, 80, 176n20
McCubbins, Mathew D., 74; on ADA scorecards, 69n11; cartel theory, 184, 232; on party effects in Senate, 4, 6, 12, 15, 55, 74, 75, 157n3, 236
McGlynn, Adam J., 25
McGovern, George, 203
Medicare Catastrophic Coverage Act of 1988, 86

Metzenbaum, Howard, 203, 204
midterm elections, 1994, 5
Miers, Harriet, 120n4
Mikulski, Barbara, 76
military expenditures, 134
minimal-winning-coalition arguments, 231
minimum wage bill, 86
minority coalitions, 182
minority-party leaders, 184–87; conventional wisdom on power of, 182; higher costs than majority-party members to place proposals on agenda, 154, 155; negative agenda control, 6, 103, 184–85, 187–95, 232; offering of nongermane amendments, 184. *See also* Senate minority party
minority-party roll rates: comparison of comparable legislative instruments across chambers, 186; decline when president and minority are of same party, 189; as measure of negative agenda control, 184–85; in Senate, by legislative vehicle, 45th through 106th Congresses (1877–2000), 188–90; in Senate and House, by legislative vehicle, 45th through 106th Congresses (1877–2000), 192–95; 45th through 106th Congresses (1877–2000), 185–86
Mississippi, share of pork, 238
Mitchell, George, 81, 96, 97, 115, 119
Mondale, Walter, 161
Monroe, Nathan W., 16, 75, 199, 234
Morton, Rebecca B., 56, 57
motions to table (MTTs), 14, 143; agenda-setting cost for minority party, 144; defined, 147; expectations about, 147–54; and higher cost of pure policy votes on amendments for minority-party senators than for majority-party senators, 147; by ideologically extreme senators, 151; by majority-party members, 151, 152, 154; by minority-party members, 151, 154; nondebatable and thus not subject to filibuster, 147, 156n1; number offered by minority-

party senators vs. majority senators, 154; offer and success rates, by type of motioner and party of amendment sponsor, 103rd and 104th Congresses, 153; probability of passage when offered by nonleaders, 152; procedural motion, 148; smaller electoral risks of vote on, 147–48; success rate by Senate majority party, 234; vs. amendment votes, 148

Moynihan, Daniel, 95

MTBE (methyl tertiary butyl ether) production, 214; liability provision, 210, 217; vote for cloture on HR 6 as a function of ideology and corn production, 215–16; vote for cloture on HR 6 as a function of party, ideology, and consistency, 214–15

Munger, Michael, 126

Murkowski, Frank, 221

Murkowski amendment: 2002 cloture vote on, 211–14; vote for as a function of party, ideology, and constituency, 2002, 211–12; vote for cloture as a function of ideology and energy production, 2002, 212–13

National Association of Manufacturers (NAM), 52

National Coalition to End Judicial Filibusters, 170

National Energy Act, 205

National Federation of Independent Business (NFIB), 57, 58, 60

National Republican Congressional Committee (NRCC), 106, 118

National Republican Senatorial Committee (NRSC), 106, 118

National Taxpayers Union, 117

negative agenda control, minority party, 6, 232; party "roll rates" as measure of, 184–85; in Senate, 17, 187–91; in Senate and House, 191–95

Nelson, Gaylord, 203

Newey-West standard errors, 188

Nickles, Don, 80

No Child Left Behind Act, 225

nongermane amendments, 184, 185, 194

"nuclear option," 167, 169–74, 176n23

Nunn, Sam, 97, 139

obstruction, 159, 175n1, 184

Oleszek, Walter J., 148, 194

O'Neill, Thomas P. "Tip," Jr., 118, 205, 206, 207, 227n5

open amendment process, 142

Oppenheimer, Bruce I., 17, 183, 196, 207

Ornstein, Norman J., 14

Owen, Priscilla, 171

parliamentary rulings, number of votes on by Congress, 1961–2000, 164

partisan theory of politics, 230, 232

party cartel theory, 101, 181

party discipline: in the House, 101–2; in the Senate, 16, 75, 100, 111–20

party effects: mechanisms of, 12–15; motivations for, 10–12; recruitment and, 13; in Senate, 7–15

party government, quest for, 199–201

party identification, and voting, link between, 2

partyless legislative models, 9

partyless majoritarian model, 7

party loyalty, 23; in floor votes, 103–5; fundraising loyalty, 105–10; increase in both chambers of Congress, 118–19; increase in House, 3–4, 74; and increasing homogeneity of party members' policy preferences, 105; in Senate as function of both member replacement and increased individual loyalty, 105

party unity: in Congress, 104; in House, 3–4, 74; in Senate, 31, 32, 33, 35, 37

party unity votes, 3–4, 74, 98n1, 148–49

Pearson, Kathryn, 16, 29, 75

People for the American Way, 168, 170

Planned Parenthood, 170

Poole, Keith, 6, 13, 40, 41, 42, 45

Pope, Jeremy C., 6

pork, descriptive measures of, 236–42; total pork dollars, 1995–2005, 236–38; total pork per capita, 1995–2005, 237, 238–39; total Senate pork dollars, 1995–2005, 238, 239–40; total Senate pork per capita, 1995–2005, 239, 240

pork-barrel spending: chamber differences in, 240–41; defined, 234; fiscal distribution of among states, by Senate subcommittee, 243–44, 245, 246, 247; hallmark of modern Congress, 229; majority party bias in, 17; Senate appropriations subcommittee differences in, 244–45, 248, 249; Senate delegation differences in, 241–42; spending on and number of projects, 1991–2005, 235

positive agenda power, 6, 196n2

prescription-drug benefit for senior citizens, 225

primary elections, and candidate ideology, 6–7

Prins, Brandon C., 148, 236

Proxmire, William, 203

Pryor, David, 95

Pryor, Mark, 171

public opinion, of salience of foreign and defense policy, 134

pure policy votes, 146, 147, 155

race, 41; Democratic Party split by region on issue of, 45; and Senate responsiveness to aggregate characteristics of constituencies, 47, 49

Rangel, Charles, 208

rational choice models, 39

Reagan presidency, 77, 200

recruitment, and party effects, 13

Reed, Thomas, 2

Reid, Harry, 115, 170, 171, 173, 174

"remote majoritarianism," 5

Republican Conference rules, 114

Republican Contract with America, 224

Republican Party: defection by moderates vs. conservatives, 63; racial conservatism, 41; transformation to more uniformly conservative party, 200

Republican Revolution, 13

"Republican Revolution," 5–7

Republican whip office, during 1980s, 77

Retain Our Majority Program (ROMP), 110

Reuss, Henry, 208

Rice difference scores, 163–64, 165; by Congress, 1961–2000, 165

Riegle, Donald, 203

Robb, Charles, 76

Roberts, Jason M., 15, 142

Roberts, John, 172

Rockefeller, Nelson, 162

Roe v. Wade, 117

Rohde, David W.: on committee preferences in Senate, 125, 127; conditional party government theory, 5, 18, 196n2, 200, 232; on motion to table as procedural motion, 148; on party effects in House, 3, 74

roll calls. See minority-party roll rates; Senate roll-call votes

roll calls near, 77

Rosenthal, Howard, 13, 40, 41, 45

rules. See Senate rules

Rybicki, Elizabeth, 125

S. Con. Res. 18, 52

S. Con. Res. 74, 52

Sala, Brian R., 55

Salazar, Ken, 171, 217

Santorum, Rick, 116

Sarbanes, Paul, 203

savings and loan roll call, 86

Schattschneider, E. E., 199

Schickler, Eric, 125, 139

Schiller, Wendy, 40, 158n9

Schlesinger, James, 208

Schmidt, Amy B., 56, 57

Schumer, Charles, 115

Senate, 28; absence of debate-limiting mechanisms, 54; absence of germaneness rule, 8, 54; absence of strict calendar system, 54; appeals of chair's decision, 160; barriers to conditional party government, 199–200, 221–25, 226; collective-action problems, 123; committee preferences, 125, 127; confirmations of executive nominees, 185; debate on resolutions, 160; disloyalty in, 110–11; effect of interest group scorecard intentions on voting, 53; effect of interest group scoring on party defection, 1991–2002, 63, 64, 65, 66, 68; filibuster (*See* filibuster); fundraising loyalty, 105–10; greater minority blocking power than in House, 196; increased individualism and partisanship, 30, 74, 102, 103, 119, 224; informal procedures, 182; legislative agenda as disciplinary tool, 111–13; legislative voting and electoral vote share, 1974–2004, *34–35*; limited influence of party leadership over selection of committee chairs, 223–24; limits of party power, 159; mutually assured destruction in, 2003–2005, 167; new interpretations on rules that advantage majority party, 174; open amendment procedures, 16, 155; opportunities to change actions taken in House, 229; party effects on, 7–15, 55–56; party unity scores, 31, *32*, 33, 35, 37; points of order, 160; reluctance to reform, 174; seniority and committee chairs, 116–17; sixty-vote requirement to invoke cloture, 102, 119, 157n3, 160, 196n1, 222; socialization in, 119–20; as a standing body, 162; treaty ratifications and presidential nominations, 28; voting behavior and consistency, 1933–2004, 39–50. *See also* motions to table (MTTs)

Senate Aeronautics and Science Committee, 141n10

Senate agenda influence: cost for minority party in attempting to get pure policy votes on amendments, 146; majority leader's right of first recognition, 146–47; majority party control of committee

chairs and committee majorities, 146; mix of pre-floor and floor tactics, 145

Senate Agriculture committee, 130

Senate appeals, outcomes of, 1961–2000, 166, 167

Senate Appropriations committee, 123, 126, 129, 230, 234, 236, 242

Senate Appropriations committee chair, and pork, 243

Senate Armed Services committee, 16, 113, 121, 124, 126, 127, 129, 133; prestige, 1949–2006, by Congress, 136–38; seniority ratio, by party, 132

Senate Banking committee, 129

Senate Commerce committee, 141n10

Senate committees: attractiveness, 126–32, 134; average number of committee assignments per senator, 123; burden committees, 127; chairmanships as avenue for party influence over members' behavior, 9; change in external environment, 122–26, 127; "constituency service" committees, 130; democratization of system, 122–23, 127, 130, 132; expansion of size of, 123; external vs. internal influences on prestige, 133–38; less independent power than in House, 13; "mixed" committees, changes in seniority ratio, 130; party caucuses as vehicles for expanding access, 127–28; policy committees, 129–30; seniority factors in award of committee requests, 128; subordination of to party leaders, 140n2; Super A committees, 113–14, 123, 126, 127, 129, 130, 131, 132, 139. *See also specific committees*

Senate Democratic caucus: automatic votes on committee chairs, 116; division into four groups for conducting nose counts, 76; "undecided" or "leaning" roll-call votes, 88

Senate Democrats: contributions to Senate candidates and party committees, 1988–2004, 108; effect of interest group scoring

Senate Democrats (*cont.*)
  decisions on, 63, 65, 67; losses on votes
  scored by LCV, 60; loss rate for majority-
  party, 60; selective blocking of appellate-
  court nominees, 168–69; whip counts, 73,
  81; whip system, 1989–1990, 76, 81
Senate elections, 25–27; influence of money
  on, 26; media coverage, 38n4; more
  competitive than House elections, 26,
  28, 38n1; Senators' contributions to party
  campaign, 106–10
Senate Energy and Natural Resources
  Committee, 218
Senate Finance committee, 96, 123, 126,
  129, 130, 218
Senate floor leaders, 102, 112
Senate Foreign Relations committee,
  16, 121, 124, 126, 127, 129, 133; prestige,
  1949–2006, by Congress, 136, 137;
  seniority ratio, by party, 132
Senate Intelligence committee, 140n3
Senate Judiciary committee, 117, 129–30, 168
Senate Labor and Human Resources
  committee, 95, 96
Senate majority leader: committee
  assignment power, 228n16; prevention
  of amendments from being offered, 14;
  right of first recognition, 112
Senate majority party: benefits from pork,
  229–30, 243, 249–50; committee assignments and chairmanships, 113–16;
  empowerment by procedural objections, 113, 160–61, 167; losses, 1991–2002,
  59, 60, 61; nearly always successful in
  use of motion to table, 234; negative
  agenda control, 15; party discipline,
  16, 75, 100, 111–20; rare restriction of
  obstruction, 174; theory of advantage
  in appropriations process, 233–34
Senate minority party: hindering of
  majority party, 55; negative agenda
  control, 17, 187–95; nongermane
  amendments, 194
Senate minority-party roll rates, 185;
  higher when filibuster pivot is member

of minority party, 195; lower than
  House minority-party roll rates on all
  comparable legislative instruments, 185,
  186; variations on S bills, conference-
  committee reports, and confirmation
  votes, 188, 189, 190
Senate national security committees:
  differences in size of budget authorizations and relevance to constituency
  concerns, 133; effects of democratization and changes in external environment on, 137–38; seniority ratio
  changes at different rates across time
  for Republicans and Democrats, 131;
  shifts in prestige of, 124; susceptibility
  to external pressures from executive,
  124, 125
Senate party leaders: control over committee assignments, leadership positions, and floor agenda, 55–56; home
  state receipt of pork, 243; limited ability and/or willingness to enforce party
  unity, 53, 55; low rate of losses, 67–68;
  manipulation of content of bills, 14;
  securing of preferred outcomes on
  roll-call votes, 53
Senate Post Office committee, 140n1
Senate-presidential control, divided, 188
Senate presiding officer: can be circum-
  vented, 163; willingness to intervene
  on behalf of reformers, 162
Senate Republicans: anti-filibuster
  telethon, 169; change in committee-
  assignment procedures, 11, 117, 140n2;
  contributions to Senate candidates
  and party committees, 1988–2004,
  107; and dispute over Bush judicial
  nominations, 167–74; effect of interest group scoring decisions on, 63;
  internal polling, 78; more success at
  preventing defections than Democrats,
  67; vote to change rules to cede more
  power to party leaders, 114–15
Senate roll-call votes, 23; and electoral
  accountability, 24; and interest-group

scorecards, 58–68; party influences on, 6; results by whip-count position, 1989, 83, 84, 85–94; theoretical electoral implications of, 27–30; "undecided" or "leaning" in Democratic caucus, 88

Senate Rule 20, 163

Senate Rule 22, 105

Senate rules: change by simple majority resolutions, 160; efforts to change, 8; "previous question" motion, 161; rule interpretation and parties, 1961–2000, 163–67; suspending of by majority vote, 162. *See also* cloture rule

Senate Rules committee, 54, 127, 129

Senate seniority ratio, 122, 128–29, 133, 138; and Grosewart index, 131–32; and variation in attractiveness of committees over time, 139

Senate Transportation subcommittee, distribution of greatest share of pork dollars, 244

Senate whip system, 16, 73–97; chief deputy whip, 76; and civil liberties, 84; deputy whips, 76, 81; impact on coalition-building process and legislative outcomes, 94–97; majority whip polls, and votes in the Senate, 1989, *91*; social welfare votes associated with, 83; tactical impact of, 97; whip-count data, 73, 74, *77*; whip-count data, 1989, 78, *82–83*, *84*, 86–88

sequential referral, 207

Service Employees International Union, 170

Shelby, Richard, 95, 97

Shepsle, Kenneth A., 231

"showdown vote," 28

Sierra Club, 170

Simpson, Alan, 78, 80

Simpson's paradox, 50n10

Sinclair, Barbara, 3–4, 6, 54, 74, 102, 228n18

Smith, Steven S., 7, 14, 63, 75, 129, 142, 184

Snowe, Olympia, 11, 110–11, 114, 171

Snyder, James M., 6, 25, 55, 75

socialization, in the Senate, 119–20

social welfare matters, highest level of partisan conflict on, 85

soft money, ban on, 106

Southern Democrats, 41, 49

Speaker of the House, loss of many formal powers in 1910, 2

Specter, Arlen, 105, 117, 119, 228n16, 228n17; Judiciary Committee chairmanship, 9, 11

Sprague, John, 126

Stevens, Ted, 68n3, 169, 228n14, 238

Stewart, Charles, III, 6, 25, 126, 140n6

Stimson, James A., 41

"strategic party government," 25

Stratmann, Thomas, 56

"strong-party theories," 181

Super A committees, 113–14, 123, 126, 127, 129, 130, 131, 132, 139

Tauzin, Billy, 214, 221

Theriault, Sean M., 13

Tullock, Gordon, 231

Ullman, Al, 202, 203

unanimous consent agreement (UCA), 112, 146

United States v. Ballin, 175n4

universalism, 231–32

Vander Wielen, Ryan J., 142

Van Houweling, Robert Parks, 13

variance-inflation factors, 38n11

Vietnam War, 134

Voinovich, George, 110–11

"vote the district," 29

Voteview Web site, 42

Waggonner, Joe, 208

Wallop, Malcolm, 203

Warner, John, 113, 121, 171

Weicker, Lowell, 203

Weingast, Barry R., 231

Whitehouse, Sheldon, 10
Wilkins, Vicky, 7
Wilson, Woodrow, 156, 199
windfall-profits tax, 202, 209
winning coalition size, by Congress, 1961–2000, 165–67
Wirth, Timothy, 76

Wolfinger, Raymond E., 25
Wright, Gerald C., 25, 26

Young, Don, 238
Young, Garry, 7

zone and tally sheets, 77, 79